Gift to the

Paul

and

Margo

Brown

Gift Book Fund

What

HERB

IS THAT?

What
HERB
IS THAT?

HOW TO GROW AND USE THE CULINARY HERBS

John & Rosemary Hemphill

STACKPOLE
BOOKS

Contents

Introduction 6

Herbs A-Z 8

CULTIVATION & USAGE *174*

Introduction

THIS BOOK CONTAINS our personal selection of the culinary herbs. We have concentrated on herbs which most people are able to grow and would like to have for everyday use in the kitchen, or for making perfumed gifts and beauty aids. Their medicinal use is discussed and a selection of simple remedies is provided.

In this expanded version of our book of herbs we have added some new information. In the A–Z list we have included the most popular and readily available salad herbs like rocket, lamb's lettuce and purslane. We have also looked at the uses of herbs in many different cuisines throughout the world, and we share with you such discoveries as pandanus leaf, which is so popular in Southeast Asia.

This book gives you the guidance to assist nature in providing a healthy environment in which your herbs can grow and flourish. Use the final chapters to help you make herbal gifts and select herbs for beauty and as medicine. Above all we hope you will enjoy time in the kitchen, with our own recipes and herbal teas.

Herbs A–Z

HERBS HAVE ALWAYS played an important part in human history. Since ancient times they have been used to flavor foods and for their range of medicinal qualities. In the pages that follow, the most common herbs have been listed and described, with information about their appearance, history and mythology, cultivation, harvesting, and uses in cooking, medicine, and cosmetics.

For ease of reference they are listed alphabetically by the botanical name. Many different species and common names may occur under an entry, and these can also be found in the index.

Yarrow

(*Achillea millefolium*)
   Compositae.
Perennial

PROPAGATION:
   *root division: Spring,
   Autumn (Fall); seed:
   Spring.*

POSITION:
   sunny.

SOIL:
   average, well drained.

HEIGHT:
   up to 2 feet (60 cm).

PART USED:
   stems, leaves, flowers.

Description

Yarrow is highly regarded for its many therapeutic qualities. The plant has thickly matted, tufted foliage growing from spreading, tenacious roots. Each leaf stalk has a myriad of finely cut, tiny leaflets neatly arranged in pairs along its length, the whole resembling a green feather. The flavor is faintly acid, yet pleasant. Leaves vary in length from 2 to 6 inches (5 to 15 cm) or more, depending on maturity and variety. Blooming from summer to autumn (fall) on erect stems about 2 feet (60 cm) tall, every flower is a composition of many diminutive florets closely packed together to form one flat and even bloom. Colors vary according to variety, and are mainly white, or rose pink tinged with white. There is also a golden flowering yarrow, and an especially ornamental, rare kind with double, creamy white blooms — it used to be called "the pearl."

History and mythology

Yarrow has a number of descriptive folk names in herb lore, indicating its ancient background and diverse uses. The botanical title *Achillea* comes from the Greek hero Achilles who, legend says, staunched his soldiers' battle wounds with this herb, while *millefolium* indicates its profusion of foliage. "Yarrow," as it is called today, derives from the Anglo-Saxon *gaerwe*. Its pungent leaves were once prepared as snuff, and this probably accounts for another curious name, "old man's pepper." Among yarrow's many traditional common names are "staunch-weed," "woundwort," and "knight's mil-foil," all evidence of yarrow's long-held reputation for staunching blood. It is still used in modern remedies for this purpose.

Cultivation

The quickest way to propagate yarrow is by root division in spring or autumn (fall). If you are doing this in autumn (fall), cut the stalks to ground level first. When there is no parent plant, seed may be sown in spring in prepared boxes. When deciding where yarrow is to grow, choose a sunny position. The type of soil is

not a problem as long as the ground is well drained; we have lost yarrow in damp conditions when excess water has remained for too long after heavy rain. Like tansy, yarrow is found growing happily in a wild state, and can become a nuisance if the vigorous roots become uncontrolled: dig out unwanted areas in this case. Yarrow stalks wither when cold weather comes, and should be cut back to their base. New growth will shoot in early spring.

Harvesting and processing

As the whole plant has a variety of medicinal properties, dried stems, leaves, and flowers are mixed together. Therefore it is customary to harvest in late summer when yarrow is in full bloom. Cut flowering, leafy stems in the morning after the dew has evaporated and hang in bunches in a shady, airy place, or spread out on a drying rack until completely moisture-free. Snip flowers off first, pull apart and put on one side; next, strip leaves from their stalks, crumble, and set aside also; then cut up the stems, and blend all parts into one mixture. Store in labeled containers. Some herbal remedies call for fresh leaves, which also have a fairly limited culinary use, but it is mainly the dried herb which is employed in medicine.

VARIOUS USES

Culinary

Yarrow's fresh young leaves are nutritious, and when a few are added to a salad they give a subtle tang. In some European countries, yarrow has been used instead of hops in brewing beer.

Yarrow has thickly matted, feather-like foliage and bears flowers of varying colors depending on species. It is widely known for its medicinal qualities.

YARROW

YARROW IS USED FOR DIVINATION IN CHINA, WHERE YARROW STALKS ARE THROWN TO INTERPRET THE BOOK OF CHANGES, THE "I CHING."

Golden yarrow

Medicinal

Yarrow has countless medicinal properties esteemed by all who are interested in nature's healing herbs. Yarrow tea, made from the whole plant as described in the harvesting section, has a powerful tonic effect on the system, and among other uses helps allay fevers, purifies the blood, lifts depression, is good for kidney disorders, and is said to prevent baldness when used as a wash. The green herb is sometimes made into an ointment for healing wounds; fresh leaves can also be infused and made into a wash for the same purpose. Yarrow can be used for menstrual problems, and in this case should be taken under supervision. It also has a reputation for "staunching" blood, and once again, should be expertly administered. It is always advised not to overdo drinking yarrow tea as various side effects can arise if taken too frequently. The effect is greater therapeutically when the need is there.

Cosmetic

A wash made from cooled yarrow tea helps to heal chapped hands. If you have a greasy skin, take a course of weak yarrow tea, drinking two cups a day: use the cooled tea also for bathing the face. One herbalist warns that extended use of yarrow tea may make the skin sensitive to light, so for cosmetic use, be especially watchful.

Companion planting

It has been noted that yarrow plants increase the aromatic quality of other herbs and vegetables, while helping them resist adverse conditions. Yarrow is also an excellent compost activator, altogether making it a good therapist for the garden.

Garlic

Description

Garlic grows into a tall, 3 feet (90 cm) high plant with long, flat leaves measuring approximately 1 inch (25 mm) across and 12 inches (30 cm) long. From the center of the plant a willowy, round flower stalk thrusts upward above the grayish leaves, the flower that appears being a compact collection of mauve-tinted white petals. These blossoms, either fresh or dried, are sometimes used in floral arrangements.

History and mythology

Garlic has been known for so many thousands of years that its origins are rather obscure. It is thought to have come first from south-eastern Siberia, from whence it spread to the Mediterranean countries where it became naturalized. It was known in antiquity, Homer having mentioned it several times. Other classic writers who recorded it were Pliny, Virgil, and Horace, and later, Chaucer and Shakespeare. Garlic was included in the diet of the ancient Egyptians, Romans, and Greeks and the knowledge of its excellent qualities circulated down through the centuries and into different countries.

(*Allium sativum*) Liliaceae. Perennial.
PROPAGATION: *segments of bulbs. Spring.*
POSITION: *sunny.*
SOIL: *well drained.*
HEIGHT: *3 feet (90 cm).*
PART USED: *bulb.*

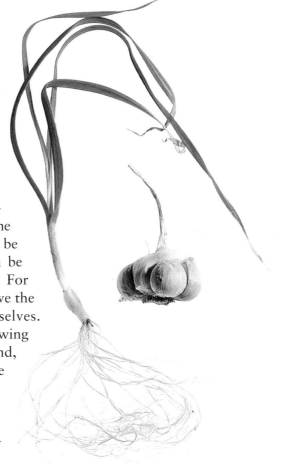

Cultivation

Mature garlic bulbs are made up of tightly clustered bulblets or cloves, each being sheathed in a pearly, papery skin. The whole bulb is "tissue-wrapped" by nature in the same type of covering, which must be removed so that the bulbs can be broken away from each other. For planting purposes, do not remove the skin from the cloves themselves. Spring is the best time for growing garlic. Separate the bulblets and, keeping them upright with the root end downward, press them into drills 2 inches (5 cm) deep into soil which has previously been dug deeply and thoroughly

Mature garlic bulbs are usually harvested six months after planting the cloves.

turned over — with the addition of well-decayed manure if the ground is poor. Keep the cloves 6 inches (15 cm) apart, cover them with soil, and water well. Soon the spear-like gray-green leaves appear, then come the flower stalks, each with a long, swelling bud at the end. As the stalks lengthen and the buds grow plumper, they eventually burst into flower.

Harvesting and processing

Harvesting of the bulbs usually takes place about six months after planting the cloves, when the flowers are fading and the leaves are yellowing and beginning to shrivel. Dig the bulbs, shake them free of dirt and plait several together with the remaining leaves. Hang the plaited garlic in a dry place where air is circulating. If the bulbs are exposed to a moist atmosphere they will mildew. When the bulbs have hardened, any remnants of foliage can be cut away and the knobs stored in a dry and airy container, such as an open-weave basket, until needed.

GARLIC

GARLIC HEIGHTENS
THE TASTE AND SAVOR
OF A DISH AND
AIDS THE DIGESTION
AS WELL.

VARIOUS USES

Culinary

Garlic is indispensable in many types of cooking. Not only does it impart its own unique aroma, thus heightening the taste and savor of the dish, but it aids the digestion as well. Before using the bulblets, or cloves, for eating, their transparent skin should be peeled away. There are many who feel that garlic is an acquired taste, and prefer only the merest whiff of the bulb's pungent scent. Therefore it is more acceptable for them to rub a salad bowl, a saucepan, or a casserole dish with a cut clove of garlic, rather than to use whole cloves in their food. Eventually, if, and when, one becomes addicted, the amount of garlic may be increased gradually until the ideal quantity for each person is reached. There are others who can never have enough garlic, and for them one of the most delicious foods is *aioli*, originating from provincial France. It is a thick, strong-tasting, golden mayonnaise made with eggs, olive oil, and crushed garlic, to be eaten with peeled, boiled potatoes and mopped up with bread, or served together with a bowl of shelled hard-boiled eggs, or to have as a sauce to accompany globe artichoke, avocados, asparagus, boiled fish, steamed chicken, or snails — the combinations are many and varied (see recipe page 248). In any case, garlic is accepted as a universal flavoring, whether in recognizable quantities or in discreet amounts. It is known in the dishes of the Mediterranean countries. Garlic is known as "toomah" in Morocco, where it is used to flavor many dishes. It goes with lamb, pork, veal, beef, tomatoes, eggplant, zucchini, in curries, in Chinese cooking, in salads, certain sauces, in mayonnaise, and in garlic bread. Commercially it is used to flavor salts, and it is available in dehydrated flakes, or as a powder.

Medicinal

Garlic has remarkable medicinal properties, and is known, because of its penetrating quality, to be a natural and powerful antiseptic. It contains the vitamins A, B, and C, as well as copper, sulfur, manganese, iron, and calcium, which make it valuable as a tonic for the cells and glands. People were bidden to eat it to cleanse the intestines, to help lower high blood pressure, to expel worms, to ward off colds, to ease chest congestion, and to alleviate rheumatism, while the raw juice was put on sterilized swabs during World War I and applied to wounds to prevent them turning septic. Garlic taken in capsule form is recommended when travelling overseas to help avoid infection. It is said to be beneficial to elderly people suffering from hardening of the arteries and general aging symptoms, while many people with sinus trouble and hay fever have been helped by taking garlic regularly.

Cosmetic

Garlic's contribution to cosmetic care is the work it does on the inside, as it has a remarkable effect on clearing the complexion. If the taking of garlic — either in capsule form or eating the raw cloves — is persevered with for a few days, a pimply skin will become quite clear and unblemished.

Companion planting

Garlic and roses benefit each other in the garden, garlic helping to repel aphids. But garlic near peas and beans will inhibit their growth. Pieces of garlic put amongst grain is an old European method of protecting it against weevils. A garden spray made from freshly crushed garlic cloves is a natural deterrent against many pests, and there are now garlic sprays already made up, which are available in specialty garden shops.

A bed of garlic in a botanical garden.

GARLIC

GARLIC WILL CLEANSE THE INTESTINES, HELP LOWER BLOOD PRESSURE, EXPEL WORMS, WARD OFF COLDS, EASE CHEST CONGESTION AND ALLEVIATE RHEUMATISM.

Chives

Chives, Onion:
(Allium schoenoprasum)
Liliaceae. Perennial.
Chives, Garlic:
(A. tuberosum)
Liliaceae. Perennial.

PROPAGATION:
seeds, division of bulbs.
Spring (Autumn – Fall –
in mild climates).

POSITION:
sunny, open.

SOIL:
fairly rich, well drained.

HEIGHT:
onion chives:
12 inches (30 cm);
garlic chives:
2 feet (60 cm).

PART USED:
leaves.

ABOVE: *Garlic chives*
LEFT: *Onion chives*
RIGHT: *Garlic chives*

Description

Onion chives, when young, resemble tufts of fine grass. As they mature the leaves become circular and hollow with a distinct taste of onion. The mauve flowers, which appear in summer, are made up of thick knots of cylindrical petals forming round heads like clover blossoms.

Garlic chives, or Chinese chives as they are sometimes called, look very much like onion chives when they are young, but as they mature the leaves become broad and flat, the color is a light green and the flavor is characteristic of garlic, but much milder. The flowers begin to bloom in summer, in white star-like clusters at the top of long, round stems which are strong and tough and not suitable for eating. In China they are known as "gau choy sum," "gau choy chow sin," and "gau choy fa" and as "kui chaai" in Thailand. "Yellow chives" are obtained by growing garlic chives without exposure to sunlight. They have a much milder, delicate onion flavor.

History and mythology

Chives belong to the same family as garlic, shallot and leek and are thought to be a native of Britain. They grow wild in rocky pastures in the temperate areas of Northern Europe. It is thought that they were known by the Ancients, as they grow wild in Greece and Italy. The old French name was *petit poureau* because of their rush-like appearance. Dr Nicholas Culpeper, in his *Complete Herbal*, says that chives are under the dominion of Mars, and are hot and dry in the fourth degree sending "very hurtful vapors to brain."

Cultivation

All chives can be raised easily from seed in spring, when planted in shallow drills in a box containing fine soil. Autumn (fall) sowing is also possible where the winters are mild. When seedlings

have passed the stage where they look like delicate grass, plant them out into the garden, or into 6 inch (15 cm) pots for the kitchen window sill. Chives form a small bulb, so when planting them, allow about 12 bulbs to a clump, keeping the clumps 12 inches (30 cm) apart. Both onion and garlic chives are attacked by aphids, which usually can be eliminated, first by watering the leaves, then applying Derris Dust liberally to the wet foliage. This should be carried out at least twice a week until the pests have gone. In winter, the tops of chives wither back, then in spring they begin to shoot again. This is the best time to divide the clumps, making sure they are no larger than 2 inches (5 cm) in diameter. It is very important not to let the bunch of chives get too large as the center will then die out, owing to lack of nourishment. Chives can also disappear if allowed to flower profusely, thereby exhausting the plants. So pick off flower buds as they appear. You will be rewarded with healthy plants if they are watered well and if a little decayed manure is dug into the soil occasionally. When gathering chives, do not cut the leaves with scissors, as this causes them to die back slightly leaving an unattractive brown edge. Always pick off the leaves at the base with your fingers.

Spectacular rows of large red chives.

Harvesting and processing

Drying chives in the normal way, either in bunches on a wire rack or in the oven, is not satisfactory as they lose their color and flavor. The chives that one sees in food stores in bottles are dried by the "freeze dry" method. Fresh chives, both onion- and garlic-flavored, may be chopped finely, mixed with a little water, and frozen in ice cube trays to be used when needed. Chive butter made by mashing chopped chives into softened butter, allowing to set in the refrigerator, then cutting into squares, may also be frozen in sealed polythene bags.

CHIVES

FRESH CHIVES, BOTH
ONION AND GARLIC
FLAVORED, MAY BE
CHOPPED FINELY, MIXED
WITH A LITTLE WATER,
AND FROZEN IN
ICE CUBE TRAYS.

Onion chives have attractive mauve flowers but these should be removed to ensure healthy plants.

The flowers of garlic chives are white and grow on tough stems which are not suitable for eating.

VARIOUS USES

Culinary

Onion chives are an excellent standby for giving a subtle flavor to food when onions themselves may be too strong and indigestible. This is because there is not as much sulfur in the composition of chives — in spite of what Dr Culpeper said. Garlic chives are used instead of garlic for the same reason. The classic blend of delicately flavored herbs known as "fines herbes" consists of onion chives, chervil, parsley, and tarragon. These herbs are finely chopped and mixed together in equal quantities making a deliciously savory yet mild blend, to flavor and garnish omelets, cooked chicken and fish, salads, steamed vegetables, soups, and mornays. In Southeast Asia, garlic chives are used in different ways: for instance, the leaves may be chopped into about 1½ inch (4 cm) lengths and added to noodles. Garlic chives are used in dim sum and soups in China, Japan, Malaysia, Thailand and Vietnam as well as being an ingredient in fried pork and prawn dishes. In Thailand, the leaves are made into a soup for new mothers to boost their milk supply. Garlic chives are a popular green herb in Iran, where they are known as "tareh". When the Chinese chive is allowed to flower, the vitamin A-rich flower is sometimes used as a garnish or stir-fried as a vegetable. The flavor of both onion and garlic chives is destroyed with long cooking, so if using them in hot food, add them during the last five to ten minutes. Finely chopped chives go into all kinds of salads, egg dishes, cream cheese, fish and poultry mornays, savoury sauces, and mayonnaise. Chopped chives make an attractive and tasty garnish.

Medicinal

Like the onion family, to which chives belong, they contain a pungent volatile oil with some sulfur present. Chives stimulate the appetite, have a tonic effect on the kidneys, and are said to help to lower high blood pressure.

Cosmetic

Chives, along with many other herbs, are a source of calcium, which helps strengthen the nails and teeth, always an important factor in achieving natural beauty.

Companion planting

Chives growing near the roots of apple trees which are infested with scab have helped reduce the scab. A chive tea made into a spray has been helpful in combating downy and powdery mildew on gooseberries and cucumbers. Chives also have a beneficial effect on carrots when grown near them. The carrots grow larger than usual. It has also been reported that chives are beneficial when cut up and mixed with the feed of very young turkeys. These findings only apply to onion chives.

Aloe Vera

Description

An aloe vera plant has thorn-edged leaves growing in a clump from the base, resembling a cactus, although it belongs to the lily family. The succulent, stiff leaf-blades grow from 12 inches (30 cm) to 2 feet (60 cm), and are pale green, sometimes lightly mottled. In spring, leafless, erect flower stalks thrust upward from the plant's centre, bearing at the tip a collection of tubular-shaped red or yellow flowers followed by seed capsules.

History and mythology

Many species of aloe are said to be native to south and east Africa, and have become naturalized over many centuries in other parts of the world where climates are temperate, including Spain, India, Asia, and the Caribbean islands. The type, aloe vera, is the most freely available and widely used variety today, and is also but known in folk medicine by such descriptive names as "first aid plant" and "medicinal plant," owing to the miraculous healing qualities of the thick, clear liquid stored in its leaves. Aloe vera, and others of the same medicinal family, have been recorded in different countries for thousands of years in historical documents describing their therapeutic and cosmetic qualities. The ancient Egyptians, Greeks and Romans, Arabians, Indians, and Chinese all knew of the qualities of this herb, and Cleopatra is said to have applied the gel to her body as one of her beauty requisites. The famous Egyptian papyrus "Ebus," dating from 1500 B.C., chronicles the wide medicinal use of aloe, and there are other reports by Greek writers of its countless applications, taken to alleviate both internal and external problems and ailments.

Cultivation

We have propagated aloe vera from large parent plants simply by breaking them up into pieces, allowing approximately two leaves with their roots, and putting into individual containers of potting mixture, and then watering — but only sparingly. The new plants establish very quickly and

(Aloe barbadenisis)
  Liliaceae.

Perennial.

PROPAGATION:
  shoots or leaves taken from main plant. Any time. Seed. Spring.

POSITION:
  sunny.

SOIL:
  well drained.

HEIGHT:
  to 2 feet (60 cm).

PART USED:
  fleshy leaves.

may be put into the ground shortly. If you have seed, sow in spring as described at the beginning of this book. By the way, aloe vera makes an excellent indoor plant. Whether inside or outside, it cannot tolerate overwatering, becoming transparent and pinkish. However, recovery is rapid when it is allowed to return to drier conditions: some watering is necessary.

Harvesting and processing

Aloe vera is not harvested like the other herbs in this book. Portions of leaf-blades can be cut, the thick juice squeezed out and applied immediately to an affected area. It is unsafe to bottle and store the raw substance for more than a day or so, even in the refrigerator. However, a weak solution for internal needs can be kept in the refrigerator for several days by placing some green peelings from a leaf in a jar of water, the liquid to be taken once or twice a week, then start again. When fresh from the plant, the juice is quite safe to use — unless you have an allergy to it, which has been known to happen. The liquid must be preserved and stabilized for keeping purposes, and an American chemical engineer, very impressed with fresh juice applied to his severe sunburn by friends, worked on this problem. He was successful, and now aloe vera liquid can be preserved for different purposes in many parts of the world.

ALOE VERA

FRESH OR PRESERVED
ALOE VERA JUICE
HAS GREAT HEALING
QUALITIES BOTH
INTERNALLY AND
EXTERNALLY.

VARIOUS USES

Culinary

The flavor of the sap running between the skin and pulp is bitter, and can be isolated from the gel. The latter is not palatable and appears to have no culinary value.

Medicinal

As described in the harvesting section, fresh or preserved aloe vera juice has great healing qualities both externally and internally. We

have used gel squeezed from a freshly picked leaf on a skin rash which disappeared within a few days. One day someone showed us the backs of her hands where skin cancers had been removed; she experimented by squeezing fresh aloe vera onto one marked hand to see what would happen. The skin on that hand was smooth and healthy with no discoloration or blemishes when we saw it; the other hand was covered with little blotches. Apart from healing skin scars, burns, and blemishes, relieving sunburn and other external afflictions, aloe vera is taken internally when prescribed, often in tablet form for digestive complaints. Some people take the fresh gel every day as a tonic, to aid kidney infections, as a mild laxative, and to assist arthritis and ulcers. If preparing the peel in water, follow the method described at the beginning of the harvesting section of this book.

ALOE VERA

ALOE VERA JUICE OR GEL IS ADDED TO MANY COSMETIC PRODUCTS FOR ITS HEALING, SMOOTHING, ANTI-WRINKLING EFFECT ON THE SKIN.

Cosmetic

Aloe vera juice or gel is added to many cosmetic lines for its healing, smoothing, anti-wrinkling effect on the skin. It is also beneficial for the hair and scalp. A very full and informative booklet on the wonders of aloe vera is the Aloe Vera Hand Book by Max B. Scousen. Our copy is from the Aloe Vera Research Institute, 5103 Sequoia, Cypress, CA. 90630. USA.

Companion planting

We have not experienced, or read of, any companion planting effects.

Lemon Verbena

(Aloysia triphylla,.
formerly *Lippia
citriodora*)
Verbenaceae.
Perennial.

PROPAGATION:
*hardwood cuttings: late
Winter; tip cuttings: late
Spring to early Summer;
seed: Spring.*

POSITION:
sheltered, sunny.

SOIL:
medium to light.

HEIGHT:
l0–l5 feet (3 m–4.5 m)

PART USED:
leaves, flowers.

Description

Lemon verbena is a small deciduous tree which can grow to 15 feet (4.5 m) in summer, when the pale lavender flowerets are clustered in scented plumes at the tips of leafy branches. In spring, summer, and autumn (fall) the tree is covered profusely with pointed leaves of light green, about 4 inches (10 cm) long, with a slightly sticky feel owing to their rich oil-bearing properties. Their perfume is strong and easily released, even by brushing past the foliage, when the air is immediately filled with a delicious lemony fragrance. As winter approaches, the leaves begin to turn yellow and fall, until by mid-winter the branches are quite bare.

History and mythology

Lemon verbena originated in South America and was introduced to England in 1784 where it soon became a garden favorite, as it has in different parts of Europe where the climate suits it We were once told that in Greece it is said that dried lemon verbena leaves in pillows will bring sweet dreams. The history of this tree does not go far back in European records, as it is such a comparative newcomer. There is another plant known as "verbena," the herb vervain (*Verbena officinalis*), which is prominent in old herbal lore: it was believed to have magical as well as therapeutic qualities, and was esteemed by Hippocrates, the Druids, the Romans, the Tudors, and Elizabethans, and on through the centuries to the present day. Vervain has modern uses in herbal medicine for relieving nervous disorders, and in mixtures for stubborn skin complaints.

Cultivation

Plant lemon verbena trees in a sheltered, sunny position where the soil is medium to light and well drained. In cold climates where winters are severe they are kept under cover. During hot summers mulch the roots with leaf mold or grass cuttings and water well; later, the roots will also need mulching to protect them from frost. In winter the tree is leafless. When it is about three years old it should be pruned, either in autumn (fall) or early winter, otherwise it will become straggly and sparse.

The deciduous lemon verbena tree bears clusters of pale flowers in summer.

If pruned regularly, the tree will reward you by growing thicker and taller every year. When propagating from hardwood cuttings in late winter, divide the wood into 6 inch (15 cm) pieces, trim off any side shoots, and press each piece into a deep pot of river sand, leaving one-third of the wood exposed at the top, and water well. When the cuttings have made strong roots, plant out. Tip cuttings are taken in late spring to early summer; trim the stems of foliage, allowing several leaves to remain at the top, then insert into the sand and continue in the same way as described for hardwood propagation. Seeds are sown in spring in prepared trays, as described in the section on growing from seeds on page 195 of this book.

Harvesting and processing

For harvesting the leaves, branches can be cut before midday at any time, particularly during the vigorous growing seasons of summer and early autumn (fall) — flowers on the boughs are an excellent addition, with the leaves, to potpourri. This will help to stop the tree from becoming too leggy. The leaves are dried quickly and easily by tying the cut branches together and hanging them in a shady, airy place. When ready, strip off all the foliage and store in covered containers.

LEMON VERBENA

TO DRY THE LEAVES QUICKLY AND EASILY, TIE CUT BRANCHES TOGETHER AND HANG IN A SHADY, AIRY PLACE.

VARIOUS USES

Culinary

Two or three fresh lemon verbena leaves placed on top of a rice pudding or baked custard before it goes into the oven, impart a delicate flavor. In the same manner, a few leaves put on the bottom

Lemon verbena trees

Lemon verberna flowers are an excellent addition to potpourri.

of a buttered cake tin before the mixture is spooned in, release their aromatic oils while the cake is baking; they can be peeled off when the cake has cooled. A traditional use for the leaves was to float them in finger bowls at banquets.

Medicinal

Fresh or dried, lemon verbena leaves make an excellent herbal tea for reducing fevers, to drink as a sedative, to help relieve indigestion, or as a cooling tea in very hot weather. A memorable and delightful clear, green lemon tea was once served to us in a Melbourne herb garden. Made with lemon verbena leaves, lemongrass, lemon balm, and lemon thyme, it was poured steaming hot from a strong glass teapot. Add one or two leaves to your pot of Indian tea for a refreshing flavor. Place some leafy tips or stalks in fruit drinks when the temperature soars.

Cosmetic

After a day's gardening or strenuous exercise, especially in hot weather, a bunch of fresh lemon verbena leaves in a steaming bath revives body and mind while subtly scenting the skin. Lemon verbena oil is now available and may be used instead if you do not have the leaves. The oil is also used in perfumery.

Companion planting

A strongly aromatic lemon verbena tree brings life and vitality to the garden, and when in flower is beloved by bees. We have never seen any disease on the 14 mature 18-year-old trees in our garden, or on pot plants grown for sale in our nursery. This sturdiness is a boon for gardeners.

Dill

Description

Dill is similar to fennel in appearance, although it is a smaller plant. It has plumes of dark green leaves and pale yellow flowerheads which form oval, flat fruit or seeds in abundance in late summer and autumn (fall).

History and mythology

Dill is native to the Mediterranean countries and to southern Russia. Once it was renowned for warding off evil spells:

> "Here holy Vervain, and here Dill,
> Gainst witchcraft much availing."

I once read that in America, dill and fennel seed were known as "meetin' seed," having been given to children to eat during long Sunday sermons.

(Anethum graveolens)
Umbelliferae.
Annual.

PROPAGATION:
seeds. Spring, Autumn (Fall).

POSITION:
sunny, sheltered.

SOIL:
light, well drained.

HEIGHT:
3 feet (90 cm).

PART USED:
seeds, leaves.

Cultivation

As dill seedlings are soft and delicate, they do not transplant easily, therefore sow in spring and autumn (fall) — where winters are not too severe — in a prepared bed, where they are to remain. The slender central stems are easily flattened by strong winds, so seedlings are best grown in a sheltered position and with as much sun as possible. If the soil is sour, lime it well before sowing the seeds in shallow drills 10 inches (25 cm) apart. Firm down the soil after covering and water well. During the summer, several sowings can be made for a continuous supply of leaves. If leaves are picked from the center, the setting of flowers will be delayed.

Harvesting and processing

The seeds ripen in autumn (fall) and can be collected as soon as the first few fall. Snip off the heads and spread them out on a tray in the sun for a few days. When they are completely dry, the seeds shake out easily from the heads. They should then be stored in airtight containers. If wishing to re-sow dill seed, it should be done within three years for good germinating results. When drying the

Dill seedlings are very fragile and do not transplant easily. They should not be planted in seed boxes but put straight into prepared beds, where they are to remain. Young plants need protection from the wind.

aromatic, anise-tasting foliage, to retain maximum flavor, start cutting the leafy stalks before the flowerheads appear. Then spread out the frond-like leaves on a wire rack in a shady, cool place. When dry, the leaves are rubbed away from their stalks and kept sealed until needed. For freezing, chop the fresh leaves finely, mix with a little water, and put into ice cube trays in the freezer. Sprays of fresh dill may be wrapped in foil, sealed, and kept in the deep freeze for some weeks.

VARIOUS USES

Culinary

DILL

WHEN DRYING THE AROMATIC, ANISE-TASTING FOLIAGE, START CUTTING THE LEAFY STALKS BEFORE THE FLOWERHEADS APPEAR.

Dill seed flavors and helps the digestion of steamed cabbage, coleslaw, sauerkraut, cucumbers, onions, various chutneys and pickles, pastries, breads, sauces, and cooked root vegetables.

The finely chopped leaves go with almost all foods, as their flavor is pleasing to most palates. Try mixing a little into cottage or cream cheese. Sprinkle some over omelets while cooking. Stir a spoonful into white sauce and into salad dressings. Use them lavishly in green salads, mix them through a potato salad, and sprinkle them over thinly sliced cucumber. Spread them quite thickly over lamb, veal, or chicken while roasting and add a little more to the gravy. Dill leaves are an excellent flavoring for fish, shellfish, rice, and egg dishes. Sprinkle them over cooked, buttered vegetables as a tasty garnish

and use them in the same way for soup. Dill soup is delicious. A few whole fronds of green dill make an attractive embellishment as a change from parsley.

Dill's fresh green leaves are much enjoyed in Middle Eastern and Mediterranean food. Its aniseed aroma gives flavor to meat, vegetable, and rice dishes, and it also goes into pickles. The Afghan name for dill is "shabit," in Armenian it is "samit," in Greek, "anitho," in Turkish, "dereotu", in Thai "pak chee lao", in India, "sua bhati," in Indonesia, "adas manis"adas manis". Fennel leaves are similar in taste and may be used instead. Fennel in Greek is "maratho," in Turkish, "rezene." The ferny green tops of dill are used in Thai, Vietnamese and Laotian cooking.

Medicinal

Dill's reputation as a soothing herb was well known to the ancient world, particularly to the early Norse peoples of Scandinavia. The name stems from the Norse word *dilla* meaning "to lull." The medicinal value of this plant lies in the seeds, which are rich in oils with beneficial digestive properties, thus helping the assimilation of food and dispelling flatulence. In cooking, both the seeds and leaves with their spicy flavor are used, although the foliage does not possess the same concentration of oil as the seeds.

Cosmetic

Dill is said to have properties which strengthen the fingernails. The Greeks and Romans used oil distilled from dill for essence and for perfume.

Companion planting

Cabbage plants are especially aided by dill growing nearby. Dill also helps corn, lettuce, and cucumber plants. When in flower, dill attracts honey bees to the garden. Dill, together with fennel and caraway as a feed supplement, helps increase the milk supply in cows and goats.

DILL

DILL'S REPUTATION AS A SOOTHING HERB WAS KNOWN TO THE ANCIENT WORLD. THE NAME STEMS FROM THE NORSE WORD *DILLA* MEANING "TO LULL".

The ferny green tops of dill are used in Thai, Vietnamese and Laotian cooking.

Angelica

(Angelica archangelica)
Umbelliferae.
Biennial.

PROPAGATION:
seeds. Spring (Autumn – fall – in temperate climates) within a week of collecting.

POSITION:
shady, sheltered. Soil: rich.

HEIGHT:
5–8 feet (1.5–2.4 m).

PART USED:
seeds, leaves, stalks, roots.

Description

Angelica has serrated, bright green leaves and branching, hollow stems with a celery-like texture. The round, whitish green flowerheads bloom in late spring in the second year of growth. When not allowed to flower at all by frequent cutting of the stems, the plant will continue to flourish for several seasons instead of for the customary two years. Angelica is completely permeated by a unique essence, giving it a delicately sweet and refreshing aroma.

History and mythology

The history of angelica goes far back into the legends and folklore of Northern Europe, and in particular the countries of Lapland, Iceland, and Russia. Because of its wonderfully benign qualities, both in the physical and spiritual realms, the plant held an important place in pagan rites, and later in Christian festivals. According to legend, during the Middle Ages, an angel appeared to a monk in a dream and revealed that angelica would cure the plague. This is why the herb was called angelica, the guardian angel.

Cultivation

When sowing angelica, it is very important to use only fresh seed, as the germinating period is very short. The seed can be sown in prepared boxes, or in the open ground. When seedlings are about 3 inches (8 cm) high, plant them out 3 feet (90 cm) apart in a moist and shady position. Rich soil and some shelter are essential for maximum growth. In poor ground, plants will become stunted and the leaves yellow.

Harvesting and processing

Harvest the seed just before it starts to fall, by snipping off and drying whole flowerheads. Sift out any dried husks and stalks, and store the seed in airtight containers for household use. But if required for sowing, plant the seed out within a week at the most. The stems can be cut and used at any time;

however, their full flavor and size are best just after flowering. The root is stored by digging, washing and keeping it in an airy, dry place until needed. The leaves may be cut from the stems and laid on sheets of clean paper or racks, in a shady, warm place until dry. When brittle, crumble them into airtight containers.

Delicately perfumed angelica enjoys a shaded spot in the garden and thrives in a rich soil. The flowers appear in the spring of the second year of growth.

VARIOUS USES

Culinary

A few young angelica leaves may be added to salads. The hollow stems and stalks can be crystallized and used for decorating sweets and cakes, and if you do not candy your own stems, they can be bought in many shops. The stems and stalks, either candied or fresh, give their sweet flavor and goodness to stewed fruits, especially acid fruit like rhubarb and plums, and to jams and jellies. The roots can be cooked and eaten like a vegetable.

Medicinal

Angelica was valued as a protection against all sorts of infections. It was used to aid digestion. One old remedy for flatulence directed that the stalks be slowly chewed until the condition was relieved, which was good advice, as it has been found that one of angelica's constituents is pectin, an enzyme which acts on digesting food. Another of the plant's components is a resin stimulating to the lungs and to the skin. In the cold countries where it was known best, angelica was

ANGELICA

MODERN-DAY HERBALISTS RECOMMEND ANGELICA TEA TO CALM THE NERVES, TO RELIEVE COLDS AND INFLUENZA...

The pink stems of the angelica can be crystallized and used for decorating sweets and cakes.

❧

Angelica grows to a height of 5–8 feet (1.5–2.4 m).

❧

prized for a sensation of warmth when it was eaten or taken as a tea. (A tea can be made from either the leaves, stems, seeds, or the dried root.) Modern-day herbalists still recommend angelica tea to calm the nerves, to relieve colds and influenza, and as a long-term preventive against winter illnesses. Many available herb tea blends contain angelica for its therapeutic properties and for its pleasant flavor. A number of the old herbalists regarded angelica as the most powerful of all medicinal plants, every part of it — roots, stems, leaves, and seeds — having health-giving properties. People with a tendency to diabetes are warned against it however, as it may increase sugar in the urine. The subtle aroma which suffuses the whole herb makes it an important ingredient in many luxury beverages, including vermouth and some liqueurs, such as Chartreuse. The earliest liqueurs were prepared in medieval monasteries, originally as medicines.

Cosmetic

Angelica seeds are used in the making of some perfumes. Dried angelica leaves go into a potpourri mixture and are an ingredient in sweet-smelling herb pillows. Use fresh or dried leaves (in a muslin bag) in a hot bath for relaxation and fragrance.

Companion planting

It has been noted that the common stinging nettle (*Urtica dioica*), when grown near certain plants, intensifies their essential oil content. In the case of angelica, this is increased by as much as 80 percent.

Chamomile

Description

There is a bewildering variety of chamomiles growing wild and in gardens, and superficially many of them look alike, with their finely cut fern-like leaves and miniature white and gold daisy-heads. (Some may be completely yellow.) But on closer inspection there are differences in appearance and foliage color and their uses are not all the same. The most usual kind found in gardens is the old self-sowing fever-few or febrifuge *(Tanacetum parthenium)*, which can have green or golden foliage; it is not used often today in herbal teas. I was told once that it was considered a cure for headaches and menstrual pain, although German chamomile is a better known aid for these problems. There is another pyrethrum daisy of the chamomile group with gray foliage and white flowers which is said to be the most effective for pyrethrum insect sprays, many of which are on the market now. Both English and German chamomiles are by far the most popular to grow. The English kind has fine, feathery leaves and a creeping, matting habit. In late summer it sends up stems of flowerheads which make a beautiful informal lawn if kept well watered in a low-rainfall area. The flowers are cut for herb tea, and then the mower, set fairly high, can be run over the plants. Some people have found that this does not make a successful lawn, and there is a hard-to-get variety known as the *Treneague* strain of chamomile which is the very best type for lawns. German chamomile grows quickly into a bushy little plant with fine foliage, and bears flowers profusely for quite some time. The fragrance of chamomile has been likened to fresh apples.

History and mythology

There seems to be some difference of opinion among herbal writers as to which is the "true" chamomile, and which has the most efficacy.

Chamomile, English:
(Anthemis nobilis)
Compositae.
Perennial.

Chamomile, German:
(Matricaria chamomilla).
Compositae.
Annual.

PROPAGATION:
seed for both types in Spring. Root division for English chamomile.

POSITION:
sunny to semi-shade in hot, dry areas.

SOIL:
light.

HEIGHT:
English chamomile: creeping ground cover until flowering, then 12 inches (30 cm).
German chamomile: 1 1/2–2 feet (45–60 cm).

PART USED:
flowers.

TOP LEFT: *German chamomile*
BELOW: *English chamomile*

*German chamomile grows
vertically into a small plant
and is seen here in a rockery
garden.*

An English chamomile lawn.

Maythen was the old Saxon name for English chamomile (which is also sometimes called Roman chamomile), and the Spaniards called it *manzanilla*, meaning "little apple." The ancient Egyptians prized it for its curative powers, as did the early Greeks and Romans. It has been used in folk medicine in Britain for centuries. It spreads in its natural state through Europe and the temperate regions of Asia. We saw it growing wild — or what looked very like it — in the ruined beauty of antique Ephesus in Turkey, and all along the roadsides leading to it. Chamomile was a favorite strewing herb on the floors of dwellings for its sweet fresh scent when trodden on and for its insect-repellent qualities.

Cultivation

Before planting English or German chamomile seeds in spring, or dividing roots of English chamomile at the same time, work the soil very well if it is heavy, add some sandy loam, dampen the ground, and put in the divided roots or seeds. As the seeds are very small, you may prefer to start them off in a prepared seed box. When large enough to handle, plant out the seedlings to about 6 inches (15 cm) apart, and keep them moist until well established. If wanting to make an area for a lawn, plant only English chamomile and keep it well watered in a dry climate. A fixed sprinkler is a good idea. As they begin to creep, a light top dressing, especially in hot weather, will help the plants to mat and spread. Your effort will be rewarded, especially if the plants are allowed to bloom. We recently saw a tiny chamomile lawn, enchanting with its scattering of starry flowers. The unexpected sight gave a magical lift to the spirits and it smelt most sweetly underfoot.

Harvesting and processing

Both English and German chamomile are grown for their flowers, and these should be harvested by midday if possible, before the sun has drawn the valuable volatile essences from the blossoms. Pick the opened heads carefully with scissors on a clear day, and spread them out on a wire sieve, or on sheets of paper, in a cool, airy place. When papery, put the fragrant heads in clean, dry screw-top jars.

VARIOUS USES

Culinary

A few whole chamomile flowers are an edible embellishment strewn over a tossed green salad. A pleasant and beneficial beverage to drink at lunchtime, or during the day at any time of the year, may be made with one or two quarts (liters) of half chamomile tea (sweetened with a little honey to taste) and half natural, sparkling mineral water. Pour into a (glass) jug with ice cubes, thin slices of lemon, and a few whole chamomile flowers floating on top.

Medicinal

Chamomile tea has been famous for centuries for its relaxing qualities and the calming of frayed nerves and soothing effect on the digestion. It is helpful to women suffering from menstrual pain and tension. Children also benefit from a mild infusion of this tea if they are restless and overtired. (Even Peter Rabbit was given a soothing cup of chamomile tea by his mother after a narrow escape from Mr. McGregor!). They usually prefer it sweetened with honey, or mixed with peppermint tea. It is a tea for everyone who is suffering from fevers or colds. It is an excellent tea for students studying hard, and for overtired businessmen. An infusion of the flowers, strained and poured into a hot bath, will reduce muscular weariness and fatigue. A well-tried folk remedy for a stye in the eye is to bathe it frequently with strained, cooled chamomile tea. We can vouch for its reliability, having tried this cure many times.

Cosmetic

An infusion of chamomile flowers, strained, cooled, and used as a hair rinse, has been used for centuries to lighten the hair. There are many shampoos, setting lotions, and conditioners on the market today containing chamomile, mainly to be used for fair or light brown hair. It benefits the hair at the same time as "blonding" it. Chamomile flowers in sleep pillows mixed with other slumber-inducing herbs (lavender, valerian, hops, roses, and lemon verbena) are effective, the warmth of the head releasing the various perfumes to induce relaxation which precedes sleep. Chamomile used in facial steams, or incorporated into cream, is soothing and strengthening to the tissues. It is also used in rejuvenating facial masks, beauty lotions, herbal soap, body lotions, lotions for sunburn, for tired eyes, and for aching feet.

Companion planting

Chamomile is an excellent addition to the compost heap, so put spent chamomile tea flowers there as well as any unwanted foliage or plants. When growing, small quantities of chamomile will intensify the oil content in peppermint plants, but if the chamomile increases too much, the peppermint oil will in turn decrease. Small clumps of chamomile growing near onions, cabbages and wheat plants will help them. Chamomile tea has been used to help combat plant diseases. On the farm, calves and other animals with hoof rot are helped by using chamomile in compresses.

Of the many different varieties, English chamomile is one of the most popular for growing in herb gardens. As can be seen from this potted specimen, it has a horizontal growth and delicate foliage.

CHAMOMILE

AN INFUSION OF CHAMOMILE FLOWERS, STRAINED, COOLED, AND USED AS A HAIR RINSE, HAS BEEN USED FOR CENTURIES TO LIGHTEN THE HAIR.

Chervil

(Anthriscus cerefolium)
    Umbelliferae.
Annual.

PROPAGATION:
    seeds. Spring, Autumn
    (Fall).

POSITION:
    semi-shade (winter sun
    if possible).

SOIL:
    average, moist.

HEIGHT:
    12 inches (30 cm).

PART USED:
    leaves.

Description

Chervil plants grow to 12 inches (30 cm) high and in appearance they resemble parsley, although the fern-like leaves are smaller and finer, the color is a brighter green, and the flavor has a mild taste of aniseed. The white flowers, which appear in early summer, grow in small, flat umbels, and the seeds which follow look rather like caraway seeds, except that they are a little longer and thinner. Chervil is native to Eastern Europe.

History and mythology

Chervil was taken to various countries by the colonizing Romans, who well knew its worth in food and in medicine. On the Continent, chervil soup has been traditional fare for Holy Thursday, as well as being a favored dish at other times. One authority mentions that chervil was once called *myrrhis* for its volatile oil which has a similar aroma to the resinous substance of *myrrh*.

Cultivation

Chervil is sometimes classed as a biennial, but it is best treated as an annual. The seeds can be sown in spring and autumn (fall) in a well-prepared garden bed. Never plant them in a seed box, as chervil seedlings are too fragile to transplant. Sow the seeds in shallow drills 12 inches (30 cm) apart, cover them with soil, and firm down with the back of a spade. When the seedlings are big enough to handle, thin them out, leaving 4 inches (10 cm) between plants. Keep chervil watered at all times. This herb is frost-tender and in cold areas it needs to grow in a sheltered position. It also dislikes hot, dry conditions, so try and protect the plants from the summer sun. A good idea is to grow chervil under a deciduous tree so that it is shaded in summer by the leafy boughs, yet is also warmed by the winter sun when the branches

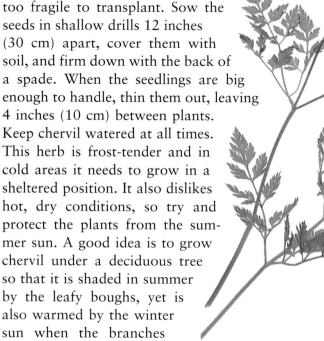

Densely clustered chervil makes an eye-catching splash of vivid green in a garden. It is also an ideal herb for growing in tubs. But the plants are delicate and dislike extreme heat or cold.

are bare. As the plants never grow large, chervil is ideal for cultivation in containers. Select a tub or pot 12 inches (30 cm) in diameter, fill it with a good, porous potting mixture and scatter the seeds over the surface. Press them gently down with a flat piece of board, and lightly sprinkle with water. Keep the pot moist, and when the seedlings are 2 inches (5 cm) high, thin them out to 3 inches (8 cm) between plants.

Harvesting and processing

Chervil can be picked at any time of the year. Break the stems off carefully, taking the outside leaves first, as with parsley, so that the new center leaves are allowed to grow. If you wish it to self-sow, which it will do readily, do not harvest all the plants when in flower: leave a third to go to seed. The foliage is dried by spreading the sprays out on a wire rack in a cool, airy place away from the light, which will fade the green color. When brittle, crumble the leaves from the stems and store in airtight containers. Fresh chervil leaves may be chopped finely, mixed with a little water, and frozen in ice cube trays to be used when needed. Chervil butter, made by pounding chopped chervil leaves into softened butter, then cutting into squares when cold, may also be frozen in sealed polythene bags.

> ### CHERVIL
> AS THE PLANTS NEVER GROW LARGE, CHERVIL IS IDEAL FOR CULTIVATION IN CONTAINERS.

VARIOUS USES

Culinary

Chervil is one of the four fragrant herbs which make up the delicate bouquet, "fines herbes," the others being chives, tarragon, and parsley in equal parts and all finely chopped. Chervil's soft leaves make

CHERVIL

DR NICHOLAS
CULPEPPER ADVISES
IN HIS *COMPLETE
HERBAL* THAT
"THE GARDEN CHERVIL
BEING EATEN DOTH
MODERATELY WARM
THE STOMACH...".

it indispensable for sprinkling over food when cut up finely, both as a garnish and a flavoring. Sometimes whole sprays may be used for garnishing. Chervil should never be cooked for more than 10 to 15 minutes, otherwise the fine flavor will be lost. Use this herb in chervil soup and in many types of sauces. Fold into scrambled eggs, omelets, creamed potatoes, and cream cheese. Sprinkle it liberally on salads and use it as a filling for sandwiches. Chervil goes with poultry and fish and is excellent sprinkled on cooked, crisp vegetables with a little melted butter and freshly ground pepper and salt.

Medicinal

Chervil has been traditionally valued as a blood purifier and for this reason it was widely eaten in the spring. It was known to help the kidneys and was taken to ease rheumatic conditions. Externally, a poultice of the leaves helped disperse swellings and bruises. Dr Nicholas Culpeper advises in his *Complete Herbal* that "The garden chervil being eaten, doth moderately warm the stomach . . ."

Cosmetic

Chervil's cosmetic value lies in its cleansing properties as a blood purifier, thus paving the way for a clear and healthy complexion.

Companion planting

Chervil and radishes help each other in companion planting, radishes growing near chervil having a hotter taste. It has been reported that a steeped tea made from equal parts of chamomile, chervil, and lemon balm, applied in a compress, is helpful in curing hoof rot in animals. Chervil is one of many aromatic herbs that aid vegetables when grown amongst them.

Chervil in flower.

French Tarragon

Description

French tarragon, with its unique, tart flavor and spicy aroma, is one of the most sought-after culinary herbs. The leaves are long and narrow and grow on either side of thin, wiry stalks which, together with the main stems, twist and fall in a tangled way, forming a thick, bushy plant 3 feet (90 cm) high. Small, tight, yellowish buds appear in late summer, which rarely open into full bloom, therefore they do not set seed. There is another variety which is grown from seed called Russian tarragon, a native of Siberia. At first glance it resembles French tarragon, but on closer inspection you can see that the foliage is bigger, with pronounced indentations here and there on the leaves. This species has very little flavor, although when French tarragon is hard to find, Russian tarragon, in greater quantities, can be used as a substitute in a recipe. Recently, we have come across another form of tarragon, which our relatives and friends in England insist on calling French tarragon. It is also known as "winter tarragon" and it has been given the botanical name of *Tagetes lucida*. It is a sturdier, neater looking plant than French tarragon, with firm, dark green leaves, and best of all, a strong, spicy aroma and flavor which is typical of true French tarragon. It has bright yellow flowers which set seed. If you cannot find French tarragon, winter tarragon is a substitute worth growing.

(Artemisia dracunculus)
  Compositeae.
  Perennial.

PROPAGATION:
  cuttings, root division.
  Late Spring cuttings,
  early Spring division.

POSITION:
  sunny

SOIL:
  light, well drained.

HEIGHT:
  3 feet (90 cm).

PART USED:
  leaves.

History and mythology

French tarragon is native to the Mediterranean countries, and has long been popular in Continental cookery. The name tarragon is adapted from the French word *estragon*, meaning "little dragon." There is a strange old legend about the origin of tarragon (unsubstantiated but quaint) that says the seed of flax put into a radish root, or a sea onion, and set in the ground, brought forth this herb! It was also recorded that it cured the bites and stings of reptiles, venomous insects, and mad dogs.

LEFT: *French tarragon*

Winter tarragon

Winter tarragon has yellow flowers which set seed.

Cultivation

To obtain a large quantity of new French tarragon plants, propagating by cuttings is advised. Take 6 inch (15 cm) tip cuttings in late spring when the new, soft leaves have become fairly firm. Insert the cuttings, which have had the lower leaves carefully removed, in a pot of coarse river sand, leaving approximately 2 inches (5 cm) of the cuttings above the sand. By mid-summer the roots should have become established enough for planting out. Allow 12 inches (30 cm) between plants. Propagating from root division will not yield as many plants, but is satisfactory for a limited number. The plant dies away to ground level in winter, (except in very warm climates), new shoots appearing early in the spring from a creeping root system. At this time, sever pieces of the main root 2 inches (5 cm) long, together with a new shoot, and plant 12 inches (30 cm) apart. Within about two months these root cuttings are roughly 1 1/2 feet (45 cm) high. Although this herb needs well-drained soil and a sunny position, it also needs to be kept watered, especially in dry weather. In severely cold climates, keep the roots covered in winter with grass clippings or straw.

Harvesting and processing

As tarragon withers away in winter and there are no fresh leaves to pick then, it is important to preserve them when they are in abundance. For drying, harvesting may be started in summer just as the flower buds appear, and continued from time to time until late autumn (fall) before the leaves begin to turn yellow. Hang the leafy stalks in bunches, or spread them out on wire racks for quicker drying, in a cool, airy place. When dry, strip the leaves from the stalks and store them in airtight containers away from the light. For freezing, strip the fresh leaves from their stalks, chop finely, mix with a little water, and put them into ice cube trays in the freezer. Sprays of tarragon may be wrapped in foil and frozen for some weeks. Finely chopped tarragon blended into softened butter, allowed to harden, then cut into squares and sealed in polythene bags or foil, may be frozen too.

VARIOUS USES

Culinary

French tarragon is one of the four essential ingredients in the "fines herbes" mixture (the others being chives, chervil, and parsley; each of these herbs having its own delicate and individual flavor and texture, which when put together in equal quantities make a delicious and subtle combination). It is interesting to note that of all the *Artemisia* group, tarragon is the only one which has culinary uses. The others, such as wormwood and southernwood, are much too bitter to eat, although they have their place among the medicinal

As French tarragon leaves are not available in the winter months, it is important that they are gathered and preserved while they are in abundance.

herbs. The warming, aromatic fragrance of tarragon complements fish and shellfish, the fresh leaves being especially useful for decorating and flavoring fish molds. It is an excellent herb to use with chicken, turkey, game, veal, liver, kidneys, egg dishes, and in chicken or fish soups. Tarragon can be added to a sour cream dressing, mayonnaise, a melted butter sauce, French dressing, tartare sauce, Bearnaise sauce, and to a green salad. Tarragon steeped in white vinegar gives it a particularly savory flavor.

Medicinal

This herb has long been respected as a source of "warmth forces." Culpeper says the leaves are "heating and drying" and John Evelyn says that it is "highly cordial and friend of the head, heart and liver." The leaves contain an exceptionally high quantity of warm, volatile oils, which is why it was advised to mix them with other herbs and with lettuce, that they may "temper the coldness" of a salad.

French tarragon grows into a thick, bushy plant.

Cosmetic

Tarragon is one of the few herbs that appear to have no contribution to make in the cosmetic field, although many herbal soaps today contain extracts and oils from nearly all the herbs, both culinary and scented. Oil of tarragon would be a fragrant addition to a beauty soap.

Companion planting

Tarragon is one of the aromatic herbs that are generally helpful to the other plants in the garden, and does not appear to hinder the formation of seed, or the growth, of any herbs or vegetables.

Mugwort, Southernwood & Wormwood

Mugwort: *(Artemisia vulgaris) Compositae.* Perennial.
Southernwood: *(A. abrotanum) Compositae.* Perennial.
Wormwood: *(A. absinthium) Compositae.* Perennial.

PROPAGATION:
seed, cuttings.

POSITION:
part sun to sunny.

SOIL:
light, well drained.

HEIGHT:
mugwort: 4 feet (1.2 m)
southernwood: 3 feet (90 cm)
wormwood: 4 feet (1.2 m)

PART USED:
southernwood: leaves; mugwort and wormwood: leaves, seed, roots.

RIGHT: *Wormwood*

Description

Mugwort, southernwood, and wormwood are all artemisias, with very bitter, inedible leaves, unlike another member of this family, French tarragon *(A. dracunculus)*, which is one of the most prized and sought after culinary herbs, and has a chapter to itself. *Mugwort* has ragged-looking, broad-cut leaves, dull green above, gray-white and downy underneath. The small, pale yellow flowers cluster on long stems in late summer and autumn (fall). The plant, like wormwood, grows tall, about 4 feet (1.2 m) high. *Southernwood* is a cottage-garden favorite. It has branching, feathery grayish green foliage with a piercing, lively aroma disliked by insects. The creamy-colored flowers are insignificant and rarely bloom; when flowers do appear it is in late summer to autumn (fall). When cut back early the plant becomes compact and bushy, growing to about 3 feet (90 cm). If not pruned it looks stunted and spindly. *Wormwood* has decorative, serrated silver-gray leaves, silky to touch, and grows to 4 feet (1.2 m). The tiny balls of lemon-green flowers are carried closely together vertically on long stalks in late summer and autumn (fall). The leaves have a very bitter taste and a warm yet acrid aroma. Another widely grown type is Russian wormwood, which has finely cut light green ferny foliage with a typically bitter taste and "dry" aroma. It too has small creamy flowers from late summer to autumn (fall) and grows to 4 feet (1.2 m). Some other wormwoods are sea wormwood *(A. maritima)*, Roman wormwood *(A. pontica)*, and dusty miller *(A. stelleriana)*.

History and mythology

The botanical name for the artemisia family comes from *Artemis*, the Greek name for Diana, the goddess with bow and arrow, who is said to have found this genus. *Mugwort* had a reputation in early times as being a witch's herb. In the Middle Ages it was used by crystal-gazers as its leaves habitually turned to the north, and were said to have a strong magnetic power. On a more everyday note, the leaves were also used to flavor and clarify beer. *Southernwood* was brought to England in the reign of Elizabeth I, and soon became popular in every garden. Sprigs went into fragrant country nosegays, thus earning its popular name of "lad's love." Another name for southernwood is "old man," probably because the bush has a hoary, whiskery appearance. *Wormwood* was one of the plants hung in the doorways to keep away evil spirits in the Middle Ages. Once it was said to prevent drunkenness, yet the leaves are an ingredient in the highly intoxicating French liqueur absinthe. The leaves go into vermouth too, which has many other herbs in it as well.

Cultivation

As *southernwood* rarely flowers, the seed, as far as we know, is unobtainable. When growing *mugwort* and *wormwood* from seed, sow in spring (and in autumn — fall — in temperate climates) in a prepared seed box: keep moist. Thin out the seedlings when large enough to handle and plant out. Propagating mugwort, southernwood and wormwood from cuttings is done in late spring, taking leafy tips 4 inches (10 cm) and snipping them just below a node. Insert cuttings into a pot of coarse river sand, leaving approximately 2 inches (5 cm) of the cuttings above the sand. Keep the cuttings watered, and by mid-summer the roots should have become established enough for planting out. A word of caution: mugwort can be invasive, and should be kept under control in the garden.

MUGWORT

MUGWORT HAD A REPUTATION IN EARLY TIMES AS A WITCH'S HERB. IN THE MIDDLE AGES IT WAS USED BY CRYSTAL-GAZERS AS ITS LEAVES HABITUALLY TURNED TO THE NORTH.

Mugwort.

Wormwood has silky, silvery leaves and grows to 4 feet (1.2 m). The leaves are inedible, with a bitter taste and acrid aroma.

Wormwood

Harvesting and processing

The best time to harvest mugwort, southernwood and wormwood for drying is in warm weather when the oil content in their leaves is most abundant. If needed, they can be picked and dried at other times of the year, as their aroma is always strong, although the etheric oils will not be as ample. Cut leafy branches on a dry day before noon, then hang in bunches in a shady, airy place. When dry, strip leaves from the stalks and seal in airtight containers.

VARIOUS USES

Culinary

Mugwort, southernwood and wormwood are grouped with rue and tansy as historically bitter herbs. Some were eaten on Easter Day as a reminder of the bitter herbs eaten at the Feast of the Passover. *Mugwort* has practically no place in the kitchen, although it can be an ingredient in stuffings for fatty fish, goose, duck, or pork; its therapeutic qualities are valuable in herbal medicine. There are no records in our research of *southernwood* having ever been used in food; however, we were once told an interesting cooking story about this herb. Often such aromatic plants growing wild in remote places have regional culinary uses, and a visiting couple recalled with delight a memorable meal they had enjoyed in a far-off European mountain area where villagers had roasted a tender lamb (or kid) on a smouldering bed of freshly gathered southernwood branches. The special aroma of southernwood smoke permeated the meat and surrounding air deliciously: the meal was a gourmet one, reminiscent of today's *nouvelle cuisine*. *Wormwood*, like its companions, has a lim-

MUGWORT

MUGWORT, SOUTHERN-
WOOD AND WORMWOOD
WERE EATEN ON EASTER
DAY AS A REMINDER OF
THE BITTER HERBS EATEN
AT THE FEAST OF THE
PASSOVER.

ited culinary use, except for counteracting the fat in certain meat and is sometimes put into a stuffing for goose.

Medicinal

An old belief was that if travelers carried a sprig of *mugwort*, they would never tire. The dried, flowering shoots, leaves, and roots are used in herbal medicine as decoctions, or teas, to assist women's problems, lack of appetite, and as an aid to digestion. The leaves may be used in tobacco. The whole of *southernwood* has medicinal properties; it has been used in tonics, antiseptics, expelling intestinal worms, and put into aromatic baths. *Wormwood's* leaves, flowers, and roots have many uses in herbal medicine. It too is an excellent tonic, an aid to digestion, and also expels worms. Wormwood is of course a necessary ingredient in the making of absinthe; it was also sometimes employed by brewers instead of hops. It is not wise to overuse these three herbs as they can have adverse effects. Take only when prescribed by an expert in the knowledge of herbal medicine.

A young mugwort plant. When mature, the gray-white color of the leaf's underside is more pronounced than in this young specimen.

SOUTHERN WOOD

THE LEAVES DRY WELL FOR POTPOURRI AND FOR PUTTING IN WARDROBES AND DRAWERS AS A MOTH REPELLENT.

Cosmetic

Mugwort does not have a cosmetic use. *Southernwood's* leaves can be made into an infusion as a wash to clean the skin, and it is also valuable, because of its antiseptic properties, to mix with chamomile and lemongrass for a facial steam where pimples and blackheads are present. *Wormwood* has some value in cosmetic therapy too: like southernwood, a leaf or two may be added with other herbs to a facial steam. It is also recommended to put a spray or two, with a few sprigs of fragrant lavender, into a cleansing bath.

Companion planting

Mugwort plants, or dried leaves, repel flies and moths. *Southernwood* growing in the garden is a protection against cabbage moth caterpillars. Planted near fruit trees, it wards off fruit tree moths. The leaves dry well for potpourri and for putting in wardrobes and drawers as a moth repellent, hence its French name of *garde robe*. *Wormwood*, fresh or dried, is also an excellent moth preventive. Sometimes when planted too near other plants in the garden it inhibits their growth, because of a substance excreted by the root. Anise, fennel, sage, and caraway are especially vulnerable. A clump of wormwood bushes growing in the garden makes a restful silver-gray picture as well as being a natural, living enemy to the dreaded cabbage moth caterpillar. When leaves are brewed into a strong tea and sprayed onto the ground, they will repel slugs and snails. The tea is said to rid domestic pets of fleas when rubbed into their coats.

Sweet Woodruff

Description

Sweet woodruff has dark green leaf whorls shaped like pointed stars; their stems are attached to a creeping root system which eventually forms a massed ground cover. In mid-spring to early summer, white, fragrant flowers appear in clusters rising above the foliage. This attractive herb is found growing in woods and on shady banks.

History and mythology

Woodruff is distributed throughout Europe where it is often seen carpeting woods; it is also found in Asia and North Africa. When introduced to America it became universally popular and now grows wild there too. It is especially esteemed in Germany where fresh sprigs are steeped in white wine for making a favorite beverage (which is also a digestive tonic) called *maibowle*, and is traditionally drunk on the first day of May. Woodruff was also highly regarded by the French, the old name for it being *muge-de-boys* (musk of the woods). Early English names for this herb were *wuderove* and *wood-rova*.

> *(Asperula odorata)*
> *Rubiaceae.*
> Perennial.
>
> PROPAGATION:
> *seed, root division.*
>
> POSITION:
> *shade.*
>
> SOIL:
> *moist, cool, loamy.*
>
> HEIGHT:
> *1 foot (30 cm).*
>
> PART USED:
> *leaves and flowers.*

Cultivation

Ripe woodruff seeds are sown in late summer to early autumn (fall) into moist, loamy soil in a shaded area. Otherwise, divide the roots after flowering has finished and select the same kind of soil and shade conditions as the seeds, placing the roots firmly into the ground about 1 foot (30 cm) apart. Woodruff grows to approximately 1 foot (30 cm) high and, as a shade lover, the leaves stay dark green unless they are exposed to sunlight which makes them paler. It is difficult to grow this herb successfully in climates where summers are humid. We saw woodruff carpeting the ground under shrubs in North America during a hot, but dry summer. Flourishing woodruff plants also do well in Hobart's Botanic Gardens where the cooler climate obviously suits it.

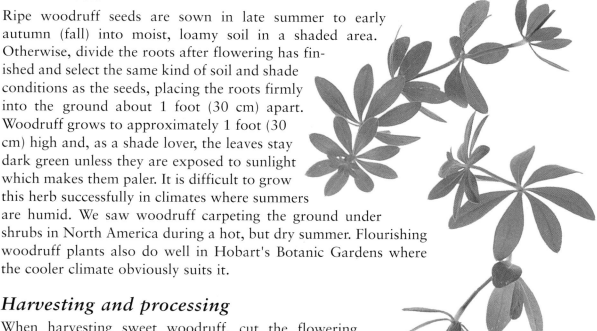

Harvesting and processing

When harvesting sweet woodruff, cut the flowering stalks almost to ground level, and dry them on airy racks in a shady place, or tie the stalks loosely together in bunches and hang them to dry. When leaves and flowers are crisp, rub from their stalks and put into

Sweet woodruff in flower.

airtight containers. Freshly gathered leaves do not have the unique aromas of the dried herb which has the special fragrance of freshly cut hay and lasts for many years. The green leaves were often pressed between the pages of books, where their star shape lies flat and thin, giving the paper a delicate scent — a practice still worth following. The dried herb was also mixed with roses, box, and lavender to perfume linen and to repel insects.

VARIOUS USES

Culinary

Sweet woodruff is not known as a culinary herb, although the tiny fragrant flowers make a delicious embellishment to a salad. However, woodruff is renowned for its addition to drinks, the most famous being the German *maibowle*, when newly picked leaves are steeped in white wine as a celebration drink on the first of May. The fresh or dried leaves and flowers make a delightful tea.

Medicinal

In the Middle Ages sweet woodruff was made into a decoction and taken as a diuretic. It was also given to relieve stomach pains, to assist digestion, and taken as a tonic. The fresh leaves were bruised and put onto cuts and wounds for their healing effect. As a tranquillizer, Culpeper recommends an infusion of 1 oz (28 g) of the dried herb to 20 fluid ounces (600 ml) of boiling water; 2 teaspoons to be taken three times a day.

Cosmetic

This is not an actual cosmetic herb, although useful in facial steam baths. Woodruff is an excellent addition to potpourri for its lingering subtle scent. The powdered leaves are used to enhance certain snuff blends, and beds were once stuffed with dried woodruff when warmth from the body would induce deliciously scented sleep. Garlands and bundles of flowering woodruff were hung in houses to cool and freshen hot summer air. At this time of year woodruff was gathered and strewn on the floors of houses and churches to impart its scent, and to effectively repel insects. A crystalline chemical constituent of woodruff, called coumarin, is used in perfumery for its characteristic aroma and its value as a fixative.

Companion planting

Sweet woodruff is excellent for underplanting in orchards, rose beds, shady borders, and in woodlands.

SWEET WOODRUFF

BEDS WERE STUFFED WITH DRIED WOODRUFF WHEN WARMTH FROM THE BODY WOULD INDUCE DELICIOUSLY SCENTED SLEEP.

Borage

Description

This herb has thick, soft stems and large leaves, both of which are covered in fine bristly hairs. The leaves when fully grown are approximately 9 inches (23 cm) long, and 6 inches (15 cm) wide. The flowers are star-shaped and a vivid sky blue, with an occasional pale pink bloom appearing amongst the blue. There is also a rare species with white flowers. The blooms are filled with nectar, making them an excellent source of food for bees.

History and mythology

Borage first came from the Middle East. Old chronicles say that Aleppo was its original home. Throughout the ages, wherever it was taken, this plant spread abundantly, adapting well to almost any soil and climate. The flowers, with their prominent black anthers and five-pointed petals of brilliant blue, were also favorite subjects in the needlework of past centuries, partly for their simple beauty and for their association with bravery.

Cultivation

Borage seed germinates so easily that it can be sown in all seasons in mild climates. In very cold areas, the best time for cultivating is in spring, when the oblong, black seeds can be sown into the open ground into shallow drills, 12 inches (30 cm) apart. Make sure that the ground has been well turned over first, so that the soil is reasonably fine. The position for growing the plants should be moist, with not too much sun. There should also be shelter from winds as the main stems, being soft, are easily broken. Borage is in bloom nearly all through the year, and is continually seeding itself, so that once planted, you should never be without it. It seems to do best when allowed to grow in thick clumps; the plants help to support each other and the massed effect of the misty buds and blue flowers is pleasing. If, on the other hand, borage begins to take over the garden, it is easily thinned out and the shallow roots dislodged — even when fully grown — by pulling out the stems by hand, remembering that the stalks are prickly.

Harvesting and processing

Borage leaves and flowers may be used fresh at any time of the year. Drying the leaves and flowers is possible, but the method must be

(Borago officinalis)
Boraginaceae.
Annual.

PROPAGATION:
seeds. All seasons in mild climates. Spring in cold climates..

POSITION:
semi-shade, sheltered.

SOIL:
average to moist.

HEIGHT:
3 feet (90 cm).

PART USED:
leaves, flowers.

The blue borage flowers are a most effective garnish when floated on the top of drinks or crystallized and used to decorate sweets and small iced cakes.

Borage has its origins in the Middle East, but over the centuries has been introduced into almost every kind of soil and climate. This white-flowered species is rarely seen.

quick to prevent spoilage. Take the flowers and leaves off the succulent stalks and place them on wire racks in a shady, airy place. When dry, store them in airtight containers. The flowers may be preserved by crystallizing and used for decorating cakes and trifles. Another method is to freeze them whole by carefully putting them one by one in an ice cube tray and gently covering them with water. When needed, a flowery ice block can be dropped into a glass of fruit juice or any other beverage.

VARIOUS USES

Culinary

The young leaves can be very finely chopped, almost minced, and mixed into green salads, or used as fillings, with a little salt and pepper, for sandwiches. Whole young leaves go into punches and wine cups, or they can be dipped in batter, fried, and eaten as a vegetable. Older leaves can be used for soup; these should be finely chopped too. Fresh or dried leaves make a health-giving tea. The blue flowers can be floated on top of all kinds of drinks and scattered over a green salad just before serving. When crystallized, they decorate cream-swirled sweets and iced cakes. The fresh or dried flowers make a tea.

Medicinal

The branching, leafy plants of borage are rich in potassium, calcium, mineral acids, and a very beneficial saline mucilage. It is often mixed with basil to make a delicious herb tea blend. Borage was recommended by Sir Francis Bacon as a heart tonic and by other authorities as a tonic for the adrenal glands and urinary tract. It was looked upon at one time as a herb to engender courage. Borage on its own is also beneficial to the circulation of the blood. Compresses made from the leaves help to relieve congested veins, especially in the legs when a person has been standing for a long time. Borage is related to another healing herb, comfrey.

Cosmetic

A facial steam for dry, sensitive skin may be made with borage leaves and flowers. Borage is also recommended as a tea to help cleanse the skin from the inside by helping to purify the system.

Companion planting

Borage and strawberries are helpful to one another. Because of the sprawling habit of the borage plants, it is advisable to put only a few among the strawberries and the rest outside the beds. Borage will bring bees to the garden.

Mustard Greens

Description

Mustard plants are upright with branching stalks bearing smooth, bright green, pointed leaves with notched edges. The small yellow flowers, bunched tightly together, appear from early summer until autumn (fall). The reddish brown to black seeds that follow are encased in erect-growing pods, each containing about 12 seeds. There is also a white mustard, *Brassica alba*; the leaves are not used as widely as those of *Brassica nigra*, also known as mizuna.

History and mythology

Mustard plants are widely distributed throughout Europe (except in northern areas) in northern Africa, parts of Asia, parts of India, and in North and South America. Ancient Greek physicians prescribed mustard seeds for various medicinal purposes, and the Romans are said to have eaten mustard leaves as a green vegetable. It was also an ingredient of soups and salads and helped to cleanse the system.

(Brassica nigra)
Cruciferae.
Annual.

PROPAGATION:
seeds in Spring, Summer, early Autumn (Fall), in cold climates. All year round in warm climates.

POSITION:
open, sunny.

HEIGHT:
about 3–6 feet (1–2 m).

PART USED:
leaves, seeds.

Cultivation

Mustard seeds are sown in spring in prepared loamy soil and firmed into shallow drills 1 foot (30 cm) apart in an open, sunny position. When grown as a seed crop for commerce the seed is broadcast over the field. Mustard germinates quickly and has green shoots within a week of sowing. Successive sowing is necessary for continual use of the leaves.

This is the same mustard which is often sown with cress in punnets for cutting. Children used to grow mustard and cress on wet blotting paper, but now there are more entertaining ways of doing this. Porous terracotta animals are available in different sizes and shapes with deep grooves incised into their bodies. Seeds are placed into the grooves of a dampened animal, which must be kept moist for the seeds to sprout and grow. Standing the animal in a shallow container of water ensures that shortly it will develop a green "coat" a couple of inches long when it is ready to cut. The process then begins all over again.

Mustard greens may also be pickled.

Harvesting and processing

For mustard greens, cut the plants when large enough and before they flower. Repeated sowings can be done throughout the growing period. For harvesting the seeds, wait for the pods to swell, then harvest and allow to dry out. Remove seeds, and if necessary dry them further before storing in clean, dry, covered containers.

VARIOUS USES

Culinary

Mustard leaves have a pleasing hot flavor, which makes a pleasant contrast to other salad greens. The leaves were once used on their own as a green vegetable and were put into spring soups. The strong flavor can overwhelm the palate, so for a piquant taste with wider appeal add a few leaves when cooking spinach, or to enliven puréed soups. The ripe seeds are collected for grinding to make mustard, and for marketing whole in jars for the spice cupboard.

Medicinal

It was widely accepted that mustard greens helped clear the blood in spring after a long winter's stodgy food. This was a time when wild herb soup was made from a mixture of specially selected young leaves and green shoots gathered from hedgerows and fields, including mustard leaves. Powdered mustard seeds were used in poultices to relieve chest congestion and rheumatism, and in hot water as a foot bath to appease the common cold.

Cosmetic

Mustard leaves or seeds are not known for their cosmetic use in Western countries.

Companion Planting

Mustard is often grown for its alkaline properties, which will counteract too much acid in the soil. The crop is also good for ground that has been damaged after too much mineral fertilizer, but continual mustard planting depletes the soil.

Box Tree

Description

The herb box is so classified because the woody parts, leaves, and roots have been used in different ways for millennia. All varieties are evergreen trees, but very slow-growing. If left unpruned, several varieties can grow to heights of between 6 and 23 feet (2–7 m). The hard center stem and branches of boxwood are copper-colored until, as the plant ages, they become overlaid with gray bark. The small, pungent, spicy leaves are oblong, smooth, and densely packed together on many branches. When small, it is hard to believe that this diminutive tree has the capacity to grow so tall (with the exception of dwarf box). There are variations in foliage color, depending on the variety. As box grows taller, it spreads branchlets which eventually touch those of its neighboring plants; this makes it a popular choice to plant as a hedge. Tiny clusters of pale yellow flowers open in mid-spring to early summer, becoming seed-bearing pods in autumn (fall). The root of box is "yellow and harder than the timber," according to John Gerard, the eminent 15th-century herbalist. Today, box is planted for its charm in garden compositions, although as a herb its usefulness in different ways is often overlooked or forgotten. Now that *Buxus* has become widely appreciated, both in private gardens and in municipal areas, available varieties have increased and there is often some confusion in their botanical nomenclature. A specialist boxwood nursery has grown over 40 kinds of box in the middle of a wood in Hampshire, England. A few of them are described in the June 1992 issue of the British magazine *The Garden*. They include an unusual weeping

Buxacea.
Perennial.

Box, English: (*Buxus sempervirens*).
Box, Dwarf Dutch: (*B. suffruticosa*).
Box, Japanese: (*B. microphylla japonica*).
Box, variegated – green and white: (*B. argentea*).
Box, variegated – green and gold: (*B. marginata*).

PROPAGATION:
cuttings, seed.

POSITION:
full sun to part shade.

SOIL:
well drained, limy or chalky.

HEIGHT:
English box, unpruned: 6–23 feet (2–7 m) approx.
Dwarf Dutch box: 1–3 feet (30 cm –1 m).
Japanese box, unpruned: 6 feet (2 m) or more.
Variegated box, both kinds:
the same habit as English box.

PART USED:
wood and leaves (occasionally the root).

The green and white variegated box tree.

A charmingly sculpted box tree hedge.

BOX TREE

ENGLISH BOX IS
USED EXTENSIVELY
FOR HEDGES AND
FOR ALL TYPES
OF TOPIARY.

box; a pale luscious-looking kind with new leaves the color of a golden delicious apple; and yet another that looks like a Lombardy poplar. However, the five kinds of box described in this chapter are easily identified by their markedly different foliage color.

English box, like all varieties of box, is evergreen as mentioned earlier. Looking like a miniature tree to begin with, it can reach a height of 6–23 feet (2–7 m) if unpruned. Once established, it becomes taller and broader more quickly. The woody stems are closely packed with small leaves that are smooth, dark green, and pointed. When the new young shoots appear in spring, it is completely covered in a mantle of fresh lime green. English box is used extensively for hedges and for all types of topiary.

Dwarf Dutch box is a miniature species, growing approximately 6–12 inches (15–30 cm) high, depending on the amount of clipping it has. Its leaves are a little larger than those of English box, oval, and greenish gold, while the new shoots are lemon-colored. This box is excellent for making Lilliputian hedges.

Japanese box grows 6 feet (2 m) or more in height. It has larger, rounder foliage than English box; it also has a dense habit and grows quite rapidly once established. This box is used extensively for topiary. Planted as a hedge, when the new pale yellow leaves are sprouting, gold-tinted Japanese box looks spectacular, especially in sunlight.

Variegated box (B. marginata) grows about 6–23 feet (2–7 m) high and has oval leaves edged with gold. It is ornamental, and can be used as a hedge or as an accent plant singly among green box. It is often trained into standards, made into pyramids or other topiary shapes that appeal. The golden leaf edges are an ornamental feature, while new shoots are entirely golden.

Variegated box (B. argentea) also grows approximately 6–23 feet (2–7 m) high and has green leaves outlined in silver, the new leaf shoots being entirely silver-white. This form of box looks equally as attractive as *B. marginata* and is often treated in a similar manner to *B.marginata*. A remembered delightful planting was an example of *B. argentea* used as a long, curving hedge about 3 feet (1 m) high around a rock garden; it inspired much admiration. An interesting specimen of topiary using two kinds of box is found in the Japanese Garden in San Francisco's Botanical Garden. In a replica of Japan's Mount Fuji, green English box was clipped into a broad sloping "mountain" at least 6 feet (1.75 m) high, and growing through the center, green and silver variegated box *B. argentea* made a striking contrast to the rest, being artfully trimmed at the top into a snowy peak with an uneven snowline just below.

BOX TREE

IN A REPLICA OF JAPAN'S MOUNT FUJI, GREEN ENGLISH BOX WAS CLIPPED INTO A BROAD SLOPING "MOUNTAIN" AT LEAST 6 FEET (1.75 M) HIGH.

History and mythology

Box is native to Europe, North Africa, and parts of Asia. Ancient civilizations domesticated box from the wild for their various needs, growing it around their dwellings. Later, box was clipped and shaped into neat hedges for marking boundaries in "physic" gardens, while it was also gathered for medicinal purposes. This accommodating small tree featured in landscape designs, was fashioned into a diversity of shapes — models of animals, birds, urns, pyramids, spirals, balls — topiary being the name given to the craft of clipping and training trees and shrubs into standards. A story is told that the aroma of box was disagreeable and "fox-like" to 17th-century gardeners, who turned against box for a time: but it was back in favour before long. The very hard, rigid timber was valued for using as printing blocks, engraving plates, weaver's shuttles, nutcrackers, and for making mathematical and musical instruments. In bygone days the roots of mature box were used by French cabinet-makers, being prized for its beautiful yellow color and extra hardness.

Box in a classic knot garden.

Cultivation

There are several ways of cultivating box plants oneself. The slowest method is to sow seed, but the resulting seedling does not always come true to the parent. A more successful and a quicker way is to choose the best specimens of the desired variety in spring or early autumn (fall), take cuttings with a leaf node, trim the cuttings, insert into a pot of river sand, and keep moist. Another method is to trim off firm cuttings, once again in spring or early autumn (fall), from established plants, then dip the pruned stems into cutting powder (optional) and put them straight into the ground at a minimum of 2 inches (5 cm) apart, where they remain green while making roots. An even easier method for the home gardener is to bury three-quarters of a well-grown box plant in soil, including leafy branches and trunk, for approximately six months. The covered parts will make

Miniature herb garden.

roots which can be cut off and planted. If buying potted box from a nursery, space them further apart. Box grows best in limy or chalky soil or planted in a well-drained position in full sun to part shade. It has been known to thrive in both these conditions.

Harvesting and processing

Although box timber is still sometimes used in the manufacture of chess pieces and turned boxes, it is not suggested that the home gardener should do this, unless the craft appeals, in which case the tree should be large enough to cut the wood into suitable sizes. If wishing to gather the glossy black seeds, collect them from spent flowerheads when ripe and sow in a prepared seed tray in spring or early autumn (fall).

VARIOUS USES

Culinary

Box is not a culinary herb.

Medicinal

Box was once a therapeutic herb, but nowadays does not have a wide medicinal use. Although some herbalists say that the bark and leaves are successful as a purgative, their use for this purpose should only be considered on the directions of a well-trained therapist. Extreme caution is advised. Animals have died from eating the leaves.

Cosmetic

Box is still employed today in treating the scalp for dandruff. Place 1 oz (30 g) of box wood shavings in a jar in enough cider vinegar to cover, then close the lid tightly for two weeks. Dampen some cotton wool in the mixture and rub thoroughly into all sections of the scalp. Dry the head then rinse in water. Massage the scalp but do not wash. This treatment should be carried out every 10 days, washing the hair in between. At one time the leaves and sawdust were prepared as a dye for turning hair auburn.

Companion planting

In companion planting some maintain that roses do not like the spreading woody roots of *Buxus*. The answer lies in chopping away any encroaching culprits, as box hedges around rose gardens are especially decorative. The vast *roseraie* within Salzburg's splendid Mirabelle Gardens is composed of low box mazes surrounding beds of flourishing roses; glittering pathways of crushed white marble define the maze's complex pattern and are a striking contrast to the green box hedges.

BOX TREE

ALTHOUGH BOX IS NOT A CULINARY HERB, IT HAS BEEN SUCH A CONSTANT FEATURE OF HERB GARDENS FOR CENTURIES THAT IT DESERVES MENTION.

Caraway

Description

Caraway plants grow to 60 cm (2 feet) high, their foliage is delicate, finely-cut and frond-like and their white, umbrella-like flowers bloom in summer. These flowers are followed by seeds, or fruit, which are brown and crescent-shaped and are marked with distinctive ridges. The roots are thick and tapering and are similar in appearance to a small parsnip.

History and mythology

Caraway is indigenous to all parts of Europe and is also claimed to be native to parts of Asia, India, and North Africa. Its qualities were recognized by the ancient Egyptians and the early Greeks and Romans. The herb was widely known in the Middle Ages and was popular in Shakespeare's day. Like aniseed, the fruit has been used for centuries in breads and cakes and with baked fruit, especially roast apples. Caraway-seed cake is as traditional in England as apple pie or gingerbread. The oil expressed from the seeds goes into the liqueur Kummel. Because caraway was said to prevent lovers from straying, it was once an essential ingredient in love potions. The seed, baked in dough, is given to pet pigeons to keep them, it is said, from wandering away.

Cultivation

Caraway seeds can be sown in spring and, where the climate is mild, in autumn (fall) as well. Choose a sunny, sheltered position in the garden and sow the seed in shallow drills, 8 inches (20 cm) apart. When the plants are about 3 inches (8 cm) high, thin them out to a distance of 6 inches (15 cm). As the seedlings do not transplant well, it is not advisable to start them in seed boxes.

Harvesting and processing

To harvest, when the seeds are about to drop cut off all the heads and, like anise seedheads, dry them on sheets of paper in a shady place, exposing them to the sun when possible to completely dry out any moisture. They are ready to store

(Carum carvi)
Umbelliferae.
Biennial.

PROPAGATION:
seeds. Spring (again in Autumn – Fall – in mild climates).

POSITION:
sheltered, sunny.

SOIL:
average, well drained.

HEIGHT:
2 feet (60 cm).

PART USED:
seeds, roots, fresh leaves sometimes.

For thousands of years the seeds, leaves, and roots of caraway have been used as a natural aid to the digestion and to ensure a clear complexion.

Although caraway is best known for its seeds, in summer it has attractive, umbrella-like blooms.

when the fruit falls away easily from the shriveled flowerheads if given a light shake. Sieve out any pieces of stalk and pack the seeds into airtight containers. If using the roots for culinary purposes, they should be pulled when young. If this is a favorite way to use your caraway, it is a good idea to make two sowings, one for the root crop and the other for the seeds.

VARIOUS USES

Culinary

The seeds go with boiled or baked onions during cooking and into potato dishes. Sprinkle them into the pot when steaming turnips, beetroot, parsnips, carrots, cabbage, and cauliflower. Blend them into cream cheese. Mix them into home-made breads, biscuits, and cakes. Shake a few seeds over apples, quinces, and pears when baking or stewing them. The roots, when boiled, are eaten like parsnips with a little melted butter or with white sauce. The young leaves go into spring soups and they give a spicy tang to green salads. They give added flavor to certain green vegetables such as spinach and zucchini.

Medicinal

Caraway's therapeutic and useful qualities as a medicine and in food were known as far back as Biblical times. The ancient Arabs called the seeds *Karawya*. The digestive properties of the fruit are identical to those of aniseed. However, the flavor is stronger and reminiscent of the zesty bite of orange or lemon peel. Caraway seeds, and the leaves and root also, are especially good for assisting the activity of the glands and increasing the action of the kidneys.

Cosmetic

As caraway is so good for the digestion, it is probably the reason that Dioscorides, the great Greek physician who lived in the first century A.D., prescribed it for "girls of pale face." Dr Nicholas Culpeper, another famous herbalist, also mentions its digestive and cleansing properties, which are conducive to a clear complexion.

Companion planting

Caraway and fennel dislike each other, and one hinders the growth of the other. It has been found that caraway grown in heavy soil loosens it and puts the ground in good condition. Caraway is helpful as a feed supplement for increased milk in cows.

Epazote

Epazote is a top favorite in Mexico where it is known as "the queen of herbs." Thought to be indigenous to that country, it is an annual plant with a unique, pungent scent slightly suggestive of musk, with fruity overtones. There is no substitute for it in Mexican food,  where it is essential in bean dishes. Some assert that when the herb is dried its flavor is stronger, but others disagree and prefer to use it fresh. The stems are reddish, the small leaves are bright green. Although it is seldom available commercially outside Mexico, except in India, it grows easily from seed and self-sows quickly. A tea is also made from this herb.

> (*Chenopodium ambrosioides*)
>
> PROPAGATION:
> *seed*
>
> POSITION:
> *part sun*
>
> SOIL:
> *average, moist*
>
> PART USED:
> *leaves*

Melokhia

Description

This plant was long grown as a source of inferior jute, but the younger stalks are also harvested for the oval leaves 1½–3 inches (4–8 cm) long , which have culinary uses. When cooked, melokhia has the gelatinous or mucilaginous quality of okra, and the flavor is likened to spinach. In Egypt, melokhia is widely regarded as a pot-herb.

History and mythology

Native to tropical regions, melokhia is thought to have been first used in Egypt as a fiber plant. From the times of the Pharaohs, the peasants found the young leaves made a pleasant pot-herb, discovering that its gelatinous properties and green color enhanced the appearance and flavor of vegetable, meat, and poultry soups. The plant was grown for its culinary use by the Jews of Aleppo and Syria; another name for it being "Jew's mallow." It is also used in India and Jamaica as a spinach substitute.

> (*Chorchorus olitorius*)
> Tiliaceae
>
> PROPAGATION:
> *seed*
>
> POSITION:
> *part sun*
>
> SOIL:
> *average, moist*
>
> PART USED:
> *leaves*

Melokhia.

MELOKHIA

A HERB KNOWN TO
THE PHARAOHS IN
EGYPT AND WHICH
SPREAD TO THE
MIDDLE EASTERN
COUNTRIES OF THE
MEDITERRANEAN.

Cultivation

Plants can be cultivated by sowing seed in a prepared box in early spring. When seedlings are big enough to handle, they should be planted out in prepared ground, well dug, raked, and watered. Leave 6 in (15 cm) between each seedling. Alternatively, seed can be sown directly into the prepared ground where the plants are to grow, then thinned out later to 6 in (15 cm) apart. A small application of manure is beneficial occasionally and it is vital to keep the plants watered in dry weather.

Harvesting and processing

Pick leaves during the spring in the growing season. For drying, place freshly picked, unblemished leaves flat on a wire rack in a cool, dark place where the air can circulate. When crisp-dry, store in airtight containers. Whole, washed leaves may be wrapped in foil sealed at the edges, and deep-frozen for some weeks. Leaves can also be chopped, mixed with a little water and put into ice-cube trays in the freezer. Microwave oven drying is a quick method. Pick the leaves, wash well and pat dry with a paper towel. Turn the oven to full power, and lay whole leaves on two layers of absorbent paper in an ovenproof dish. They should be dry in 4 minutes. Feel them, and if they are not crisp, leave them a little longer, making sure they do not discolor. If you are buying melokhia, look for the bunches of fresh, leafy stalks in city vegetable markets from late spring. Melokhia is available for about two months in its season. It can be stored in the refrigerator and used while fresh.

VARIOUS USES

Culinary

To prepare fresh melokhia, wash well and strip leaves from stalks. Drain, allow to dry, then chop finely with a sharp knife. About 1 lb (500 g) of fresh leaves are required for soup for 4 to 6 people, and should be added during the last 10–15 minutes of cooking. Or use a quarter of this amount of dried melokhia, rubbed to a powder and soaked with a little hot water before adding to the soup. The melokhia should remain suspended in the soup. Flavor with a mixture of chopped garlic fried in a little olive oil with some ground coriander, a little salt, and a pinch of chili powder. Melokhia can also be used as a green vegetable: prepare as for spinach and serve dressed with olive oil and lemon juice.

Medicinal

Melokhia's contribution to health is an important dietary one. It is an excellent source of magnesium, calcium, iron, vitamin C and vitamin A and it is a moderate source of phosphorus and protein.

Chicory

Description

Chicory is one of the taller herbs. The lower leaves are broad and long like spinach leaves, while the higher leaves are smaller and sparser and grow on many branching stalks. The large, daisy-like flowers are pale blue and grow in clusters of two or three along the stalks. They close about noon, except in dull weather when they stay fully open all day. The leaves have a very bitter taste and, for eating in any quantity, are much more palatable when they have been cultivated by forcing and blanching in the dark.

History and mythology

Chicory was known to the civilizations of the ancient world. Arabian physicians used it and we know the Romans valued it by the writings of Pliny and others. For many centuries it has been found growing wild in different parts of Europe and it is known by different names in different countries. The old English name for it was succory. It is also known on the Continent as witloof and Belgian endive. In England it was a favorite ingredient in love potions.

Cultivation

For growing in the garden, plant the seeds in spring in a prepared bed where they are to remain, in drills 1 inch (25 mm) deep and 12 inches (30 cm) apart. Keep the ground watered until the shoots appear, and watch for snails and caterpillars. For blanching, the number of roots required are dug out. This should be possible six months after planting, and takes place in the autumn (fall). The foliage is cut off and the roots are then stood upright, close together, in a deep box or pot, with a covering of light, sandy soil 6 inches (15 cm) above the top of the roots. They must be kept in a moist, dark place such as a glasshouse or warm shed. As they grow, the new young leaves become elongated and blanched. But if there is not enough darkness the foliage turns green and this results in excessive bitterness. As soon as the white leaves show above the soil the plants are ready for lifting. The root is then cut away, leaving sufficient at the base to hold the folded leaves together. The chicory now looks like an elongated lettuce heart of creamy-colored leaves, the outside ones measuring approxi-

---

(Cichorum intybus)
Compositae.
Perennial.

PROPAGATION:
seeds, Spring.

POSITION:
sunny.

SOIL:
average, well drained.

HEIGHT:
6 feet (1.80m).

PART USED:
leaves, roots (in coffee).

Chicory is a tall-growing herb with clusters of pale blue flowers along its stems. Its old English name was succory and it was used in love potions.

This young chicory plant is at the best stage for eating when the flavor is more delicate and subtle.

mately 6 inches (15 cm) long. It is important to use the chicory as soon as possible as it deteriorates quickly.

Harvesting and processing

Leaves for herb tea may be picked from their stalks and laid on wire racks until dry, then crumbled and stored in airtight containers. The procedure for drying, roasting, and grinding chicory roots is usually carried out by manufacturers with kiln-drying equipment. Large quantities of the plants are cultivated on the Continent for this, as ground chicory root sometimes forms an ingredient in or adulteration to coffee. It does not contain caffeine.

VARIOUS USES

Culinary

When chicory has been cultivated for blanching, it is classed as a vegetable and there are many different methods of cooking it. It may also be eaten raw in salads, the texture of the leaves being smooth and fine and the taste just a little on the bitter side. When left to grow wild in the garden, the new young leaves are best to use, as they are not as strong-tasting as the older ones. Tear up a few young leaves and add them to a green salad.

Medicinal

The leaves have excellent medicinal qualities, being helpful to the functions of the liver and gall. Chicory roots when roasted and ground can be made into a health-giving beverage which has been given to people suffering from bilious attacks and constipation. However, it is not supposed to be good for those who are anemic.

Cosmetic

As both leaves and roots of chicory are such an excellent liver tonic, any tendency to yellowness of skin and eyes should clear as bodily functions improve.

Companion planting

Chicory greens make an excellent fodder for some animals, including sheep, cows, and horses. A few leaves mixed with our son's horse's feed helped keep its general condition good.

Kaffir Lime Tree

Description

The lime leaves referred to here have no relationship to the linden or lime tree of Europe (*Tilia curopaca*). There are other varieties of citrus lime trees — Mexican lime, Tahitian lime, and West Indian lime — which are similar to kaffir lime, but these are different again in flavor. The kaffir lime is a typical evergreen citrus tree with dark green, smooth leaves that are long and flat, and are distinguished by their shape, having a marked indentation on each side of the leaf. The aromatic foliage is high in volatile oils, which give the leaves their unique flavor. The branches have long, sharp thorns, so be wary! In summer the white, fragrant flowers come into bloom, later followed by small green limes that are only moderately juicy.

History and mythology

All citrus trees are native to Southeast Asia, and it seems likely that they were first introduced to Europe in the Middle Ages by Moorish and Turkish invaders. In northern Europe, special heated glasshouses known as "orangeries" were built so that citrus trees could be protected from the colder climate.

Cultivation

As kaffir limes are grafted trees, buy them ready to plant from a nursery. Choose light, deep, well-drained soil in a sunny, frost-free position. Kaffir limes are tropical trees, and it is not advised to grow them in cold climates except under conservatory conditions. All citrus are surface-rooting trees, and need mulching to prevent quick evaporation of moisture from the soil, especially in dry weather. Keep weed-free and give the tree a good soaking in dry weather, rather than watering lightly. As citrus trees are gross feeders, an annual application of some good fertilizer is necessary in the spring. Be careful to cultivate near the surface so as not to injure or cut the fine, shallow roots. By fertilizing and cultivating regularly as the tree

(*Citrus lystrix*)
also called Daunlimau perut (Malaysia)

PROPAGATION:
buy from a reputable nursery, as grafted tree

POSITION:
sunny

SOIL:
light deep sandy loam, well drained

HEIGHT:
6–10 feet (2–3 m)

PART USED:
leaves, rind and juice of fruit

Dried lime leaves.

*Kaffir lime leaves are used
extensively in Asian cooking.*

KAFFIR LIME

THESE CITRUS
LEAVES ARE USED
EXTENSIVELY FOR
CHICKEN, SOUP,
AND FISH DISHES IN
THE COUNTRIES OF
SOUTHEAST ASIA
AND IN CHINA.

grows, the roots are encouraged downwards and are in a better condition to resist dry, hot weather. Prune away dead wood, being careful of the long thorns. Nurseries will advise on the best methods for guarding against scale and other citrus insect pests.

Harvesting and processing

If possible, harvest your own fresh lime leaves as needed. Apart from the "wet markets" of Asia, fresh lime leaves are not always available for purchase, but are becoming more frequently seen in greengrocer shops. Fresh lime leaves can be hung in bunches like bay leaves, and used in varying degrees of dryness.

VARIOUS USES

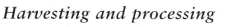

Culinary

Lime leaves are best used straight from the tree for maximum freshness and flavor. They are used extensively in Asian cooking, in sambals, with steamed fish, and the beef rendang (curry) of Indonesia. They add a nuance of freshness to chicken soup or fish dishes. In India, Sri Lanka, China and Southeast Asia, the leaves, and the juice and rind from the fruit, are all used in cooking. If kaffir lime leaves are not available, lemon leaves, or leaves from the West Indian and Tahitian lime may be substituted.

Horseradish

Description

Horseradish has large, dark green leaves resembling spinach, which under ideal conditions can grow up to 2 feet (60 cm) long. Being soft and fleshy, they are constantly attacked by leaf-eating pests, especially snails. The root system comprises a main or tap root about 12 inches (30 cm) long and 1/2 inch (12 mm) thick, with several smaller roots branching out from it at different angles. It is white and rather like a radish, but is more hairy and wrinkled.

History and mythology

Like all herbs, horseradish has been known and valued by various groups of the human race through the ages, while today it has a wide and faithful following in different countries. It is thought to have originated in Eastern Europe and has become part of the diet of many people. It was a favorite condiment with vinegar amongst the hard-working country folk in rustic Germany. Its reputation spread to England and France, where it became known as *moutarde des Allemands*. It is a member of the same family as mustard and cress and is rich in sulfur.

Cultivation

When planting, select the area required according to the number of plants you wish to grow, allowing 12 inches (30 cm) between plants each way. For instance, if wishing to grow four plants, the area needed will be 2 feet (60 cm) square. Measure out a plot of ground this size and dig a hole about 1 1/2 feet (45 cm) deep, spreading some well-decayed manure in the bottom before replacing the loose well-broken soil back in the hole. Do this in winter, about one month before planting. In early spring, after selecting four straight main roots 8 inches (20 cm) long, cut off any side roots and plant them in the prepared bed, making a hole 12 inches (30 cm) long and 1 inch (25 mm) wide for each root, and pour a little sand around the sides before covering with soil. Keep plants watered so that the roots do not become coarse.

Harvesting and processing

When the roots are cut for use, soil is scraped away from the side of the plant, and with a knife the small roots are then cut away from the main one, the small roots being the ones used. This can be done at any time. Every two years it is advisable to pull the whole plant out, keeping the long main roots for replanting. The side roots can be stored for some time in dry sand.

(Cochlearis armoracia)
Cruciferae.
Perennial.

PROPAGATION:
root cuttings. Spring.

POSITION:
shady.

SOIL:
rich, loose, moist.

HEIGHT:
3 feet (90 cm).

PART USED:
root.

Horseradish has dark green leaves which can grow to 2 feet (60 cm) long under good conditions. But it is the root of this herb which is most widely used in cooking.

HORSERADISH

WHEN TAKEN WITH RICH FOODS, HORSERADISH IS KNOWN TO AID DIGESTION. IT ALSO HAS ANTISEPTIC QUALITIES.

VARIOUS USES

Culinary

If you cannot grow your own horseradish, dried horseradish root which has been commercially prepared in the form of small grains or flakes is now available. These swell and reconstitute in liquid, giving a good texture. Powdered horseradish root is not recommended as it is weaker in flavor and has no texture. A little freshly grated or dried horseradish in spreads, dressings, and sauces gives an interesting tang. Horseradish sauce makes a tasty accompaniment to roast, broiled (grilled), or boiled beef, pork, fish, and poultry. Freshly grated apple mixes well with horseradish when making sauce, as does chopped mint. A little freshly grated or dried horseradish is excellent in a traditional bread sauce.

Medicinal

Anyone who enjoys the biting taste of grated horseradish will be interested to know that it also has a number of beneficial properties. It has long been known as a stimulant for many parts of the circulatory system, while having antiseptic qualities too. When taken with rich food it assists digestion, and when a little horseradish is grated into salads and taken regularly it will build up resistance to coughs and colds — and these are only some of its contributions to good health. Another therapeutic quality, when it is taken in a more concentrated form, is its ability to reduce catarrhal and bronchial complaints if one has succumbed to these ailments. (Once when suffering from a chest cold, I had a treatment of a horseradish and avocado rub, finished off under a hot lamp for 15 minutes. It was very effective.) Horseradish taken inwardly also relieves sinus pain and is said to help reduce blood pressure. An old recipe in a book of ours under the heading "To Relieve a Heavy Cold" says:
"Grate horseradish, and inhale the fumes that arise."

Cosmetic

Some beauty herbalists use horseradish root in conjunction with other herbs to relieve eczema. It is also used with yoghurt or milk to be dabbed on the skin to fade freckles. For an effective skin refresher, infuse some of the sliced root in milk and pat the milk on the skin.

Companion planting

Horseradish aids fruit trees in the orchard and helps prevent brown rot on apple trees. In the vegetable garden, horseradish, if kept restricted to the corners of the potato bed, will assist potatoes to be more healthy and resistant to disease.

All-Purpose Herb

Description

This herb is also known as "three-in-one herb, Cuban oregano, fruit salad herb." It is a type of coleus with a sprawling, dense-growing habit and has fleshy, juicy stalks and leaves which are easily broken. The whole plant gives off a warmly sweet fragrance. In summer it bears pale mauve flowers, rather like lavender heads.

Do not confuse this plant with other kinds of coleus, which should not be eaten. Another plant, *Plectranthus foetedus*, also looks very like this coleus: take note of the aroma, and if it is rank and unpleasant you have identified *Plectranthus foetedus*, which has flowers that also look like lavender-heads and are purple. It is attractive as a border plant but cannot be used like *Coleus amboinicus*.

History and mythology

This tropical herb is variously described as being native to Indonesia, Fiji, or the West Indian island of Cuba. The herb has become popular in temperate areas where cold weather will not kill it. Many people use this coleus in a wide variety of food preparations, from soups and stews to fruit salads.

Cultivation

Coleus must be the easiest herb of all to propagate: break off a stalk from the main plant with two or three leaves on it, and just put it straight into the ground. Water in dry weather. The cutting will make roots quickly, and providing it is in the right position, it will flourish. It needs warm, moist conditions, and can be placed in an area that catches the sun for half the day in summer, and for most of the day in winter.

VARIOUS USES

Culinary

When a juicy leaf of this coleus is broken, the fresh, sweet scent is very strong. A tablespoon of the chopped leaves, or more depending on taste, can be stirred into casseroles, soups and stews during the last half hour of cooking. This herb is often added to a fruit salad.

(Coleus amboinicus)
Perennial

PROPAGATION:
cuttings

POSITION:
sunny, frost-free

SOIL:
moist, well-drained

HEIGHT:
up to 2 feet (60 cm)

PART USED:
leaves

Coleus amboinicus

Coriander (Cilantro)

(Coriandrum sativum)
Umbelliferae.
Annual.

PROPAGATION:
seeds. Spring (again in Autumn — Fall — in temperate climates).

POSITION:
sunny, sheltered.

SOIL:
light, well drained.

HEIGHT:
*1¹/₂–2 feet
(45 cm–60 cm).*

PART USED:
leaves, seeds.

Description

Coriander has lacy, feathery foliage with a unique, strong aroma quite different from the other herbs it resembles so closely in appearance, such as anise, caraway, dill, and fennel, all of whose leaves have, in varying degrees of pungency, a warm, spicy anise-scent. A mixture of lemon peel and sage is one description of the flavor of fresh coriander leaves. The mauve-tinted white blossoms appear in summer in frothy profusion, followed by fruit, which, when green and unripened, have an even stronger scent than the foliage. In fact the name coriander is derived from the Greek *koris*, which means bug: the soft green seeds do smell exactly like an emerald-colored, odoriferous insect which infests citrus trees. When the small, oval coriander seeds have hardened and ripened to a pale fawn color, they are one of the most deliciously fragrant of all spices used in cooking. Fresh coriander is sometimes known as Chinese parsley.

History and mythology

Coriander grew first in Southern Europe, and centuries ago found its way to many other countries. The Romans introduced it to Britain; it also found its way to India, the Middle East, China, and Peru, to name some of the lands where it has become a favorite herb. The Egyptians made use of it in ancient days and for the Hebrews it was one of the bitter herbs used at the Feast of the Passover. In the Bible the seed is likened to manna, tasting "like wafers made with honey." (Exodus 16:31).

History records that it grew in the Hanging Gardens of Babylon. The Chinese believed that the seeds contained the power of immortality. The whole seed was once popular in confectionery and provided the centres of rainbow balls.

Coriander

Cultivation

Before planting the seed, choose a position which is both sunny and sheltered, as the young plants need protection from prevailing winds to prevent them from falling over. Work the soil until it is fine and crumbly, adding a little lime if the ground is acid. Incidentally, coriander seed remains fertile for five to seven years. Sow the seeds in spring (and again in autumn — fall — in temperate zones) directly into the ground in 1/2 inch (12 mm) deep drills, 12 inches (30 cm) apart. Cover and pack the soil down well, then keep moist until the seedlings appear. Water regularly in hot, dry weather, preferably in the late afternoon or evening so as not to scorch the plants. As they grow, they may need tying to thin bamboo or wooden stakes.

Harvesting and processing

Fresh coriander leaves may be picked at any time during the growing period. For drying, spread leaf sprays on sieves in a warm, airy place, and when crisp, crumble the leaves from the stalks and store in airtight containers. For freezing, the ice-cube method is not recommended, owing to the strong odor of the foliage. It is better to parcel up freshly washed sprays in foil, folding the edges firmly, and then put them into the freezer where they will keep for several weeks. To harvest the seeds, cut off all the heads when they are about to drop, and dry them, like ripe anise, on sheets of paper in a shady place, exposing them to the sun when possible. They are ready to store when the fruit falls away from the shriveled flowerheads if given a light shake. Sieve out any pieces of stalks, and pack the seeds into airtight containers.

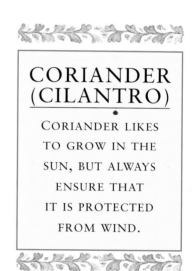

CORIANDER (CILANTRO)

•

CORIANDER LIKES TO GROW IN THE SUN, BUT ALWAYS ENSURE THAT IT IS PROTECTED FROM WIND.

VARIOUS USES

Culinary

You will find coriander leaves in Egyptian, Mediterranean, Oriental, and Indian cooking. We tasted it once in a French restau-

Coriander, also known as Chinese parsley, has delicate, feathery foliage and in summer it flowers profusely.

CORIANDER (CILANTRO)

THE UNIQUELY
AROMATIC GREEN
LEAVES OF THIS HERB
FEATURE IN THE
CUISINES OF MANY
COUNTRIES.

rant, employed discreetly in a simple chicken dish, giving it a hauntingly delicious flavor. The fresh leaves garnish curries, rice, and other ethnic dishes, and once you become used to the flavor, your palate will tell you when to add it for a piquant, individual touch. The seeds are used far more frequently, and when whole, contribute to other spices in a pickling blend. The ground seed flavors fish, poultry, and meat dishes. It is a useful spice in fruit cakes, gingerbread, biscuits, pastries, and bread. The ground seed is also excellent sprinkled over apples, pears, and peaches while baking. A pinch flavors eggplant (aubergine), zucchini, and bell peppers (capsicums). Ground coriander seed is a necessary ingredient when mixing a curry blend or a mixed spice blend.

Coriander's uniquely aromatic green leaves and the spicy mature seeds are used widely in the Middle East. The Afghan name is "gashneez," in Arabic it is "kazharah," in Cypriot, "koliandros," in Iranian, "geshniez," and in Turkish, "kisnis." Coriander is known in Morocco as "kosbor." The Berbers believe that coriander and parsley should always be used together. Coriander is also an ingredient in tagines (stews), chermoula (a marinade), and couscous.

Coriander leaves are known as cilantro in North and Central American cuisines. The distinctive flavor of the leaves makes them indispensable in much Mexican food and they are always used fresh. In Mexico coriander may be bought with its roots intact and stored in the refrigerator, standing in a jar of water and lightly covered.

Cilantro is used in Creole and Cajun cuisine, in the southern states of the USA. The distinctiveness of these cooking styles lies in the seasoning. For instance, coriander (cilantro) oil, is blended with garlic, salt, and pepper, and then rubbed into chicken breasts, or lamb chops, before grilling. Coriander oil also dresses a rocket (arugula) salad together with peppered goat cheese and roasted walnuts.

Traditional Louisiana gumbos may contain okra, seafood, meat, or vegetables, or any combination of these, with seasonings of chopped fresh herbs. Garlic, parsley, bay leaves, basil, thyme, fennel leaves, and cilantro are all recommended in different recipes, depending on the cook. Filé powder is another important ingredient, made of dried, ground sassafras bark, and thyme. It is used to thicken and flavor some gumbos and is always added after the pan is removed from the heat, otherwise the filé clots and becomes ropey.

Cilantro is important in South American dishes, such as cebiche, or ceviche. This seafood dish features peppers, red onion, lemons, limes, and fresh cilantro or other herbs. It is acknowledged that the best ceviches are found in Peru, Ecuador and Chile, followed by the rest of the Spanish-colonized countries of South America. To make a good ceviche the seafood and all the other ingredients must be absolutely fresh, including citrus juice, peppers, onions, and a choice of vegetables. Finely chopped cilantro is used in nearly all the recipes. In a mussel ceviche, cebiche choros, thyme, and Italian parsley are the herbs chosen. Often coriander and parsley are employed together. Dill can also be substituted for coriander in many ceviches.

Cilantro is used extensively throughout Asia, except in Japan. The leaves are frequently used for garnishing in India and China, but it is most popular as an ingredient in Thailand, where not only the leaf but the stems and roots are ground for use in curry pastes. There the plant is called "phak chee".

Medicinal

Hippocrates and other Greek physicians employed coriander in their medicines. The digestive action of the seed is particularly effective with carbohydrates and has been used traditionally, whole or ground, in breads and cakes. Coriander's use in cornbread, or polenta, goes back to the early Romans. Coriander water (like dill water) was used to ease windy colic. The ground seed, or fluid extract, was often incorporated into laxatives to help make them more palatable, and to prevent griping. Coriander seed, crushed and inhaled, will relieve dizziness. Because of this, it was once called "dizzycorn." It was among plants mentioned in the *Medical Papyrus of Thebes*, written in 1552 B.C. Coriander was also believed to be good for purifying the blood and was frequently prescribed for kidney stones and other urinary dysfunctions. European cultures recommend a tea infusion or a soup of coriander leaves and barley water as a tonic-stimulant for convalescents. Ancient Egyptians over 3000 years ago placed sprigs of fresh coriander in tombs to protect the souls on future journeys.

Companion planting

Coriander when grown near anise helps anise seeds to germinate and to grow into bigger, healthier plants. On the other hand, coriander has the opposite effect on fennel and will hinder germination of the seeds. It has been noted that coriander likes the company of chervil; they make good companion plants. Honey bees are attracted to coriander flowers.

CORIANDER (CILANTRO)

THE DIGESTIVE ACTION OF THE SEEDS IS EFFECTIVE WITH CARBOHYDRATES, HENCE THEIR TRADITIONAL USE IN BREAD AND CAKES.

Mitsuba

*Cryptotaenia
japonica*

PART USED:
leaves

Description

This low-growing plant has slim, sappy, dark green stems with three sharply serrated leaves on each. The herb grows in an upright, dense, spreading mound. It is related botanically to the parsley family, with a tasty, aromatic flavor, and is also known as "Japanese parsley," "Japanese trefoil" and "trefoil." Once considered exclusively an early spring herb, it is now grown commercially and is available all year round.

Uses

One of Japan's most widely used herbs, mitsuba is an ingredient in clear soups, tempura, and steamed egg dishes. The leaves and blanched leafstalks are eaten in salads, and may be used in sandwiches. Mitsuba is popular in Japan as a garnish: sometimes a few stems are tied into a knot close to the leaves, and the long ends trimmed off with a knife.

Mitsuba or "Japanese parsley."

Turmeric Leaves

Description

Closely related to ginger and galangal, turmeric is most familiar as a spice, which is made from the root. Native to Southeast Asia, it has strong, dark green pointed leaves growing from a lumpy, orange-fleshed rhizome which produces turmeric powder.

Cultivation

Perennial Turmeric is native to tropical areas, and will also grow in temperate zones in a warm, sunny position, favoring the same conditions as ginger. The soil must be well-drained, and the plant regularly watered and fertilized.

Uses

The root is dried and pulverized to make a brilliant yellow powder with a pungent aroma, one of the vital ingredients in most curries. The leaves — about the size of a large spinach leaf — are an important ingredient in Malay and Indonesian cooking, especially in rendang, the spicy, tasty meat dish particular to these regions. They are shredded finely and added to curries and other dishes. Shredded turmeric leaves can also be used as a garnish. Turmeric is known as "sa-nwin" in Burma, as "kunyit" in Indonesia and "kunyit basah" in Malaysia.

> (*Curcuma longa*)
> Zingiberaceae
>
> PART USED:
> *leaves, root*

Turmeric leaves.

Lemongrass

Cymbopogon citratus)
Gramineae.
Perennial.

PROPAGATION:
  *root division at any
  time, preferably Spring.*

POSITION:
  *sheltered, morning sun
  (does not like frosts).*

SOIL:
  rich, moist.

HEIGHT:
  3–4 feet (90 cm–1.2 m).

PART USED:
  *leaf tips, tender shoots,
  whole leaves.*

Description

Lemongrass grows in a bushy clump, increasing in size each year. The roughish, narrow leaves bend gracefully outward and have a slightly sticky texture. They are pale green and at certain times of the year are rust-colored at the tips. The foliage has a deliciously subtle lemon scent. We have not seen it flower during the many years that we have grown this herb. Lemongrass is a comparative newcomer to our herb gardens. It is a native of Asia, where it has been used for culinary and medicinal purposes for many years. This herb is relatively unknown in European cooking and herbal medicine, but its delicate flavor and health-giving properties are becoming more widely recognized.

Cultivation

In spring the old leaves should be cut down to where the new shoots are appearing, then divide the roots by digging well down into the ground with a spade, cutting cleanly through the main bush and taking as many clumps as you can without damaging the parent plant. Put the new shoots into prepared ground immediately, firm down the soil and water well. In mild areas the clump may be cut through and divided in the same way at any time of the year. The ground is prepared by turning over the soil on the chosen site and making several drills ready to take the new plants.

In temperate climates lemongrass will grow easily in the garden through all seasons; however, it does not like dry conditions, and flourishes best in a sheltered position. If your winters are cold and frosty, lift plants in mid-autumn (mid-fall), put into pots with a good soil mixture and keep indoors until spring, when they can go back into the garden. By the way, if the plant is becoming spindly and ungainly at any time, cut about 6 inches (15 cm) off the tops of the leaves. This will ensure that the plant regains its attractive bushy appearance.

Harvesting and processing

In autumn (fall), when the grassy clump is thick and green, cut the leaves back to within a couple of inches of the base. They may be dried by hanging them in bunches in a shady, airy place, or spreading them out on airy racks or on clean newspaper. As the leaves are full of etheric oils, they will dry quickly. When ready, cut them with scissors into short lengths and put into clean, dry, airtight containers. The swollen stem can be bruised and used whole or cut into slices.

VARIOUS USES

Culinary

Lemongrass is a popular ingredient in many Asian dishes. Lemongrass is called "akrai" in Thailand. The tips, the tender shoots, and the leaves are all used whole and then discarded before serving. Try snipping a few fresh pieces of leaf into a pot of tea for a refreshing, lemony flavor. In European cooking, a bunch of lemongrass leaves put in the water when steaming or simmering a chicken or fish, gives a delicate and delicious hint of lemon. The flavor of numerous other dishes can be enhanced by using the leaves in the same way.

Lemongrass is a relative newcomer to Western kitchens, although it has long been popular in Asian dishes.

Medicinal

Lemongrass taken as a tea, or in tablet form, has a tonic effect on the kidneys. The tea is beneficial during a fever, and either hot or iced, is very refreshing in hot weather. Lemongrass also has a wonderful effect on the skin, making its cosmetic use especially helpful for people of all ages.

Cosmetic

Lemongrass oil contains vitamin A and, used externally, improves the skin. When taken internally as a tea, or in tablet form, it helps to clear the complexion, giving it a fine texture and luminous glow. Teenagers with skin problems will benefit from a course of lemongrass tablets, or by drinking the tea. An extra bonus is that lemongrass taken in this way gives the eyes a bright, clear look. When a few drops of lemongrass oil are added to bathwater, the pores of the skin will open and absorb the essential elements from the oil.

Companion planting

A clump of lemongrass in the vegetable garden will have a good influence on plants in its vicinity, as all vegetables are improved in flavor by aromatic herbs growing nearby.

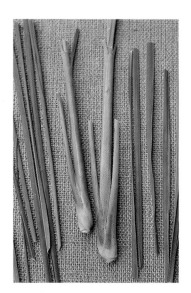

Lemongrass, showing the swollen bases of the shoots.

Rocket

Rocket, Salad: *(Eruca sativa)* Cruciferae.
Annual.
Rocket, Sweet: *(Hesperis matronalis)* Cruciferae.
Biennial.

PROPAGATION:
seeds; Spring or Autumn (Fall) for salad rocket; Spring for sweet rocket.

POSITION:
semi-shade hot climates; some sun cooler regions.

SOIL:
rich, moist.

HEIGHT:
salad: 3 feet (90 cm); sweet: 2–3 feet (60–90 cm).

PART USED:
salad: leaves; sweet: leaves sometimes, flowers for scent and for cutting.

Description

It is easy to confuse salad rocket, *Eruca sativa*, with sweet rocket, *Hesperis matronalis*; they are part of the same family and both are referred to as rocket, although each is grown for different reasons. Salad rocket becomes a branched plant bearing spear-shaped leaves that have an unusual mustard flavor with a distinctive musky undertone; Culpeper calls it rocket cress or garden cress. The small blooms open in mid- to late summer, according to climate, and are creamy yellow, or pale white with purple streaks. Salad rocket is often called arugula. Other names are ruchetta and roquette. Sweet rocket is a biennial and produces white, purple, or variegated scented flowers which can be single or double, the double kind being purple or white.

History and mythology

A native of the Mediterranean regions and Western Asia, salad rocket was cultivated by the Romans and is still widely used in Italy, France, and Egypt. Salad rocket is now considered an indespensable salad herb in many countries. In the past, references to salad rocket have been made by various herbalists. One writes that after the Great Fire of London 'young rockets were seen everywhere among the ruins." This was possibly wild rocket *(E. vesicaria)*.

Single or double-flowering rocket *(H. matronalis)*, also known as night-scented stock, is native to Southern Europe. It is valued for the blossom's exquisite evening perfume. The handsome double whites are greatly sought after. It is said that the species *H. tristis*, from Hungary, has the best perfume. Sweet rocket's scent is almost absent during the day. Once, when the language of flowers was well known to lovers because of chaperones and lack of private conversation, every bloom in a posy had a message. Sweet rocket meant deceit, since it gives out a beautiful evening perfume but is scentless during the day. Other names given to sweet rocket by the Ancients are dames violet and hesperis or vesper flower.

Cultivation

In spring or autumn (fall) sow seed of salad rocket into shallow drills where the plants are to grow. The soil should be rich and moist for rocket to produce big, healthy leaves. Keep the plant watered in dry weather. Rocket is often seen growing wild, but the cultivated herb has larger, milder tasting foliage.

Sweet rocket seeds can be sown in spring into shallow drills in boxes and planted out in semi-shade when big enough to handle. The soil should be rich and moist. If preferred, sow seed straight into drills in the prepared ground where the plants are to remain. Do not let plants dry out. It has been recommended that any young, green growths at the base of double-flowering stems can be removed and replanted to produce flowering plants the following year.

Harvesting and processing

When the leaves of the salad rocket are big enough, begin to pick them from the outside of the plant. Young leaves are particularly tender. Gather leaves repeatedly until the plant begins to flower. When the petals have fallen allow seeds to ripen and harvest them for resowing in spring or autumn (fall).

Sweet rocket is grown for its perfumed flowers. Harvest the seed in the same way as for salad rocket. Culpeper says if wishing to harvest for medicinal purposes, "the whole plant is collected when in flower, dried and powdered."

Salad rocket.

VARIOUS USES

Culinary

Leaves of salad rocket are excellent on their own with a light vinaigrette dressing. Both young and mature leaves can be mixed with other salad herbs like corn salad (lamb's lettuce), mustard cress, and French sorrel for a salad of interesting contrasts in flavors and textures. Greengrocers often keep a mixture of various kinds of lettuce and edible flowers with the addition of some or all of the herbs mentioned previously, calling this attractive assortment "mesclun." Sweet rocket's foliage may be used in salads before the plant flowers, although it has been described as being "very acrid in taste."

Recently, one chef has experimented with rocket leaves as a base for a pesto blend, instead of the classic basil leaves. He explains his preference by saying that rocket does not oxidize and darken like basil, and the rocket gives a spicy mustard flavor to the pesto. He recommends spreading this blend onto cold meats.

Medicinal

The fresh young leaves and stalks of salad rocket are a health food and are described as being a tonic and mild stimulant for the disgestive system. Sweet rocket leaves should be eaten before the plant flowers, otherwise their medicinal content is too high. The dried plant was administered in very small quantites in water for the prevention of scurvy.

Cosmetic

As yet neither salad or sweet rocket appears to have any contribution to make in the cosmetic field.

Companion planting

When in bloom, sweet rocket attracts honey bees and butterflies to the garden, even though the flower's perfume is not released until evening.

ROCKET

TRY USING THIS SALAD HERB AS A SUBSTITUTE FOR BASIL IN PESTO SAUCE, FOR A DISTINCTIVE MUSTARDY FLAVOR.

Florence Fennel

(Foeniculum vulgare
    dulce) Umbelliferae.
Annual.

PROPAGATION:
    seeds. Spring,
    Autumn (Fall).

POSITION:
    sunny.

SOIL:
    well drained, medium
    to light.

HEIGHT:
    3 feet (90 cm).

PART USED:
    swollen stem base,
    foliage, seeds.

Description

The fennel mentioned here must not be confused with the wild fennel (*F. vulgare*), which is a tall-growing perennial that does not produce the swollen stem base of the annual variety. Perennial fennel is usually found growing wild in low-lying places that are subject to flooding and also along roadside banks and ditches. It is often wrongly referred to as aniseed because of a similarity in flavor and appearance (see page 132 for a description of anise). Florence fennel is recommended for the home gardener because of its many uses in the kitchen: stem base, foliage, and seeds all being valuable in different ways. The foliage is feathery and light green, the bright yellow flower umbels bloom in summer and are followed in early autumn (fall) by seeds of pale green that dry to a light biscuit color.

History and mythology

Although fennel is a native of the Mediterranean lands, its origins are shrouded in mystical legends and the wondrous properties of the leaves, and especially the seeds, are found in the folklore of many countries. It was one of the good "magical" herbs, a sure defense against all evil. In Greek mythology, Prometheus concealed the fire of the sun in a hollow fennel stalk and brought it down to earth from heaven for the human race.

Cultivation

If growing Florence fennel for the swollen stems, sow the seed in late spring or early summer, straight into the ground, where plants are to remain, in rows of shallow drills that are 12 inches (30 cm) apart, the seedlings to be thinned out later to 8 inches (20 cm) apart. The seed bed should be well dug, then limed and manured if necessary. A rich soil will give best results. Autumn (fall) sowing can be done as well if the climate is not too severe, and the thickened stem base should be ready to use in early spring. For a sizeable base and a good foliage color, fennel requires plenty of water during dry periods. When the base has swollen to the size of a golf ball, cover it with earth, continually adding more to keep the bulb covered as it swells. Remove the flowerheads as they appear. After about 14 days, the swollen base or bulb will be large enough to use. Cut each one away from the roots, tie them together by the foliage and hang in a dry place until required. Florence fennel bulbs are seen hanging like this in greengrocer stores where they are usually referred to as finocchio. It is advisable to use the bulbs within 10 days after cutting, otherwise the fresh, crisp texture is lost.

Harvesting and processing

Drying of the foliage is not recommended. It is too sappy and by the time it has dried, most of the flavor has been lost. For freezing, chop the fresh leaves finely, mix with a little water and put into ice cube trays in the freezer. Sprigs of fresh fennel may be wrapped in foil, sealed, and kept in the deep freeze for some weeks. If wishing to dry the heads for the seeds, allow them to ripen in autumn (fall), then clip off the heads, sun-dry for a few days, and shake out all the seeds and store them in airtight containers.

VARIOUS USES

Culinary

Fennel seeds, whole or ground, help to digest starchy foods such as bread, pastries, biscuits, and pasta. They assist the assimilation of cabbage, Brussels sprouts, broccoli, cauliflower, and onions, as well as many root vegetables. Fennel leaves can be chopped and used sparingly to flavor and help digest potato salad, green salad, spaghetti sauce, and rice. Use with fish while cooking. In fact, the leaves are traditional with fish, and if baking a whole fish, branches of the foliage make a fragrant bed for it to rest on during cooking. The swollen base can be cut into thin rings and separated like an onion for salads; or the base can be cut in half and cooked as a vegetable and served with a plain white sauce, or a cheese sauce.

Medicinal

Fennel has always had a reputation for helping the eyesight (and some say second-sight also). Fennel seed tea is still used by many for bathing sore eyes. The tea also relieves flatulence and for hundreds of years has been recommended for those who wish to lose weight.

Cosmetic

Fennel seed has traditionally been used in home beauty preparations and is said to smooth lines away. Fennel seed made into a strong infusion (or tea) is blended with honey and buttermilk for a cleansing lotion. A mild infusion of fennel seed makes an excellent skin freshener. The same infusion refreshes tired eyes when pads of cotton wool which have been soaked in the liquid are placed on the eyelids for about five minutes. I have made a revitalizing face mask with a combination of a strong fennel seed infusion, honey, and yoghurt stirred together then spread on the face and neck. It should be left for 15 minutes, then gently rinsed off with cool water.

Companion planting

Fennel does not help caraway, tomatoes, kohlrabi, or dwarf beans. Fennel and coriander do not grow well together, coriander inhibiting the formation of fennel seed. Do not plant fennel and wormwood together either, as wormwood stunts the growth of fennel plants.

Florence fennel, here growing with garlic chives, is the type best recommended for use in the kitchen.

The bulb-like base of Florence fennel can be sliced and added to a salad or cooked as a vegetable.

FLORENCE FENNEL

FENNEL SEED TEA MAY BE USED TO BATHE SORE EYES. SOME SAY IT ALSO AIDS SECOND SIGHT!

Hyssop

(Hyssopus officinalis)
  Labiatae.
  Perennial.

PROPAGATION:
  *root division: Spring or
  Autumn (Fall); cuttings:
  late Spring to early
  Summer; seed: Spring.*

POSITION:
  sunny.

SOIL:
  light, well drained.

HEIGHT:
  2 feet (60 cm).

PART USED:
  *leaves, flowers. Stems
  sometimes.*

Description

In appearance, hyssop and winter savory plants look similar until they flower: both carry spires of small, lipped blooms in late summer and early autumn (fall). However, winter savory's flowers are white, hyssop's deep blue — except for scarcer pink or white varieties. The main resemblance between the two occurs when the plants are immature: like savory, hyssop draws back into itself in winter, looking squat, its narrow leaves dark green and unyielding. With the coming of spring, tender green shoots thrust upward on lengthening stalks in the same manner as savory and at this time the two herbs can easily be mistaken. However, there are differences when looked at closely: hyssop's foliage lacks savory's high gloss, and the scent and taste are unique to each plant. Hyssop's leaves have a curious musky aroma and a palate-tingling flavor of Angostura bitters, making it an interesting culinary herb when used judiciously. Plants are densely compact and grow to about 2 feet (60 cm), making it excellent for low hedge-work.

History and mythology

Hyssop is native to Southern Europe, and it was well known in the ancient world. Its early recorded name "azob," a holy herb, referred to its use for purification rites in temples. The conquering Romans are said to have introduced hyssop wherever they settled, valuing it as both a ceremonial and healing plant. Monastery gardens were planted with hyssop for holy and medicinal purposes — its bushy habit and sapphire flowers made it useful for the good monks to outline their cloistered, formal herb beds. Hyssop was also esteemed for its cosmetic properties, and was used for strewing on floors.

Cultivation

Hyssop can be propagated in several different ways: roots are divided in spring or autumn (fall); cuttings are taken in late spring to early summer when the leaves have firmed; or seed is sown in spring. When planting out, choose a sunny position and light well-drained soil. If growing hyssop as a low hedge, set seedlings 12 inches (30 cm) apart. In autumn (fall), prune stalks and stems back into the main plant, which will then assure its shape and vigor for the following spring.

Harvesting and processing

Dried hyssop flowers are used extensively in herbal medicine, and are harvested during peak blossoming time in late summer. The leaves, as well as flowers and stems, are also esteemed for the fine colorless oil distilled from them, which is used in the manufacture of some perfumes and liqueurs. Cut flowering stems in the morning and hang in bunches in a dry, shady place, or spread out on sheets of paper or on drying racks. When moisture-free, strip the flowers and some leaves from their stalks and store in airtight containers.

VARIOUS USES

Culinary

Hyssop has its place among culinary herbs for its unusual flavor which combines well with certain foods, and for its digestive action and other health-giving qualities. Add small quantities of finely chopped leaves with your usual seasoning herbs to stuffings for duck, pork, or goose to help cut their fattiness; for the same reason chop some leaves and stir into a rich gravy while it is thickening. Sprinkle a few crumbled leaves into soup during the last half-hour of cooking. When used sparingly, hyssop's distinctive aroma does not intrude and cause surprise; it intrigues. Whole, delightfully scented flowers, which are full of nectar and loved by bees, give color and wholesomeness to a green salad.

Medicinal

Hyssop has many medicinal applications, herbalists prescribing it, among other disorders, for chest complaints, as an appetite improver, for digestive and gastric problems, excretion of urine, expelling intestinal worms, as a sedative, and, combined with sage, a gargle for sore throats. Hyssop tea, made from the dried flowers and a few leaves, can be sipped during a heavy cold and for digestive upsets. Hyssop tea is made in the same way as other herb teas. An old country remedy for rheumatism was made from the fresh green tops brewed into a tea and taken several times a day. When hyssop flowers are blended with valerian root, chamomile flowers, a few peppermint leaves, and a pinch of lavender flowers, the mixture makes a powerful sedative tea on going to bed. A wash made from the leaves and applied to cuts and bruises is antiseptic and healing.

Cosmetic

The aromatic oil distilled from hyssop has been highly prized by perfumers. Because the leaves have antiseptic and healing qualities, they may be simmered and used as a facial steam for acne sufferers; a few drops of hyssop oil can replace the leaves if more convenient. A little hyssop oil added to a hot bath is cleansing, refreshing, and pleasingly scents the whole body.

Companion planting

Hyssop flowers are loved by bees; however they repel other insects, except for the cabbage butterfly, which it lures away from cabbages. Radishes will not thrive if hyssop is planted nearby. Hyssop planted near grapevines will increase the grape yield.

Hyssop's deep blue flowers appear in late summer and early autumn (fall). When dried, the flowers are used extensively in herbal medicines.

HYSSOP

THE FATTINESS OF CERTAIN MEATS MAY BE DIMINISHED BY USING CHOPPED HYSSOP LEAVES IN THE STUFFING.

Juniper

(Juniperus communis)
Cupressaceae.
Perennial.

PROPAGATION:
fresh seeds: Spring; tip
cuttings: late Spring in
mild climates, Autumn
(Fall) in cold climates.

POSITION:
sunny, or semi-shade.

SOIL:
average to alkaline.

HEIGHT:
10feet (3 m) or more.

PART USED:
ripe berries, leaves.

Description

The evergreen tree from which juniper berries are gathered is a neat conifer, described as a tall shrub or small tree, and is both useful and ornamental. The tiny blue-gray needle-leaves are tightly packed onto intricately woven thickets of tan branchlets densely covering the juniper from top to bottom. The miniature flowers — yellowish on the male, pale green on the female — are hard to see when they appear in early summer. These are followed by small, fleshy, green cones on the female tree only; they are known as berries, and contain three seeds each. When the berries ripen, they turn from green to bright navy blue flushed with a faint bloom, and are then ready to be picked and dried. While the berries are maturing, new cones are forming on the tree at the same time. There are other varieties of junipers, not so well known, including dwarf and prostrate forms. We once saw a golden, horizontal juniper growing vigorously in an earth-filled stone well, high above the Pacific Ocean. Noting the profusion of ripe berries, we thought, "surely not?" and dared to pick and taste — the flavor was identical to the common variety. Juniper trees are widely distributed throughout North Asia, Europe, North Africa, and North America.

Cultivation

Fresh, ripe seeds may be sown in prepared boxes in spring, and kept moist to enable germination. A quicker way of starting a tree is to propagate hardened tip cuttings in late spring in mild zones, or in autumn (fall) in cold climates. Put 4 inch (10 cm) cuttings into a pot of sand and keep lightly watered; roots will form quickly. When large enough to handle, plant out the seedlings or cuttings into well-drained soil in a sunny to semi-shaded position: they do best in limy alkaline or chalky ground. Junipers are reasonably fast growers, but once the green berries have appeared it will be about two to three years before they turn dark and are ripe enough to pick.

Harvesting and processing

When harvesting the fruit, put on stout gardening gloves and carefully, pruning shears ready, thrust your hand into the sharp protective foliage, and snip off the berries. Let them dry out a little by spreading them out on a shelf or airy rack, then put into airtight containers. They will go darker when dried.

VARIOUS USES

Culinary

Juniper berries have a sweetly sharp taste and a clean, resinous aroma reminiscent of pine forests; what is more, they give a unique flavor to certain foods. In France, juniper berries are included in many stews and casseroles; and in Germany, when a few are lightly crushed, they are a favorite addition to sauerkraut and coleslaw. These berries are the ideal complement to game dishes such as duck, grouse, quail, hare, rabbit, and venison. For a different and subtle aroma in a stuffing for chicken, duck, goose, or turkey, add 6 to 9 crushed juniper berries to the breadcrumbs and herbs. The back of a wooden spoon flattens them easily, thus allowing the release of their delicious (and helpful) essences during cooking. Small burning branches give the same piney scent to meat and fish when barbecuing them. The aromatic globes also provide flavoring and some medicinal properties to gin and some liqueurs.

The juniper tree is an ornamental conifer which grows to around 10 feet (3 m) high. Its needle-like leaves are tightly packed onto branchlets.

Medicinal

Besides having so many culinary uses, juniper berries are just as valuable in herbal, homeopathic, and veterinary medicines. It is the essential oil within the berry which has valuable constituents, including antiseptic properties, and is most effective just before the ripening and darkening of the fruit. (The leafy branchlets also contain much of the same substances.) The medicinal action relieves flatulence, helps release fluid retention in kidneys and bladder, and is helpful taken as a tea for menstrual problems. It is effective in alleviating gout, chest complaints, rheumatism, and arthritis; it stimulates blood circulation, is good against internal infections, and is a helpful tonic to increase the appetite. Herbal tablets consisting of juniper with celery seed make an excellent combination to tone up the kidneys and bladder and to lessen muscular aches and pains. It is strongly advised not to take juniper at all when the kidneys or bladder are inflamed, or during pregnancy. Externally, juniper oil broken down with olive oil is helpful in relieving aching joints and certain skin disorders. Some herbalists recommend juniper oil as an inhalant for bronchitis. The leafy branches also have antiseptic qualities and are a time-honored method of fumigation.

The berries have many culinary and medicinal uses.

Cosmetic

A facial steam prepared with a few drops of juniper oil, or the leafy twigs steeped in boiling water, is helpful in treating skin eruptions such as acne. Afterwards, dilute some pure olive oil with juniper oil, and gently smooth over the affected area.

Companion Planting

On the farm, it has been found that most animals, especially sheep, like to eat the berries, which help to prevent or alleviate dropsy.

Bay Tree

(Laurus nobilis)
Lauraceae.
Perennial.

PROPAGATION:
seeds, cuttings. Spring.

POSITION:
sunny, open.

SOIL:
good quality.

HEIGHT:
35 feet (11 m).

PART USED:
leaves.

Description

The bay is a very large, attractive tree, thickly covered with glossy, dark green leaves, which are narrow and approximately 4 inches (10 cm) long. When broken, they give off a warmly pungent aroma. Bay trees make excellent tub specimens, especially if grown as standards, when the lower branching stems are cut off and the tops are pruned into rounded shapes. In Europe and America they are often grown like this, either in gardens or on each side of a doorway, particularly in front of hotels and clubs. They look very elegant when treated in this way. The bay tree is native to the shores of the Mediterranean and among its popular names are "sweet bay," "bay laurel," "Roman laurel," "noble laurel," and "true laurel." There is another type of laurel, the cherry laurel (*Prunus laurocerasus*), which is poisonous and must not be confused with the bay tree. In spring, the white flower buds burst into waxy, cream blossoms with pronounced yellow stamens. When in flower, the tree is continually visited by swarms of bees. The flowers are followed by purple berries that go black and hard when dried.

History and mythology

When looking at this tree growing in our gardens, or when using the leaves in cooking, it is interesting to think about the old traditions and history associated with the bay. In early Greece and Rome, the greatest honor for those who were victorious on the battlefield, and in the sports arena, was to be crowned with a bay laurel wreath — as were outstanding men of letters too, hence the title of "poet laureate." The bay laurel was a part of pagan temple rites and ceremonies.

Cultivation

To propagate bay trees, cuttings are advised, as the seeds do not germinate readily. The seeds are about the size of a pea and are very hard, like a nut. It is necessary to sow them at least 1 inch (25 mm) below the soil's surface. Do not be disappointed if there is only about 5 percent germination. Cuttings

RIGHT: Bay leaves

are taken when the new spring leaves have hardened. Each cutting should be 6 inches (15 cm) long, and of new wood. Break the cutting away from the old wood, leaving a heel 1/4 inch (6 mm) long, which must be trimmed carefully with a sharp knife to eliminate any bark which overhangs the heel. Strip the bottom leaves off the cutting, leaving two-thirds of bare stalk to press into a pot of wet river sand, firming it in with the fingers. Keep cuttings watered at all times. By the end of spring they should have made roots and will be ready to plant out into containers holding potting mixture. It is always advisable to establish slow-growing plants such as bay trees in pots for at least a year, rather than put them straight into the garden. Bay trees are susceptible to white wax scale, which makes the foliage sooty and unattractive, and also causes poor leaf growth. This can be controlled by spraying with white oil in hot weather, or scrubbing the affected places with soapy water.

Harvesting and processing

The leaves can be used for cooking at any time during the year. If you wish to dry them, the best way is pick the leaves off the stalks, then spread them out on a wire rack, where they will dry quickly with a good, green color. An alternative is to hang leafy branches in bunches in a dark, airy place.

A formal garden of standard bay trees, surrounded by clipped box.

A potted bay tree is an attractive addition to any garden.

The bay tree, with its pleasing shape and dark, shiny leaves is often grown for ornamental purposes.

An avenue of bay trees gives a gracious air of Mediterranean elegance to a garden.

VARIOUS USES

Culinary

Bay leaves are indispensable in many different types of cooking. For instance, a bay leaf is an essential ingredient in a "bouquet garni," or savory herb posy, the other herbs being a spray each of parsley, marjoram, and thyme and a few peppercorns. These are tied together and dropped into casseroles, soups, or stews, and removed after cooking. Or, the dried herbs, including the bay, may be crushed and crumbled together to make a blend, which is then put straight into the pot and left to amalgamate into the stock during cooking. As a variation, when cooking an Italian-type casserole or soup, add oregano and a little garlic and leave out the marjoram and thyme.

For fish, replace the marjoram and thyme with dill. For lamb, replace the marjoram and thyme with rosemary. Bay leaves on their own flavor soups and casseroles; boiled, baked, or steamed fish; meat and poultry. A bay leaf gives a pungent aroma to marinades, and if a leaf is placed on top of a milk pudding as it goes into the oven, a subtle and unusual flavor is imparted.

Bay leaves are used widely in Middle Eastern and Mediterranean cooking in such dishes as meat stews, and in marinades for lamb and fish. In Arabic a bay leaf is called "warak al gar," in Turkish, "dafne yepregi," and in Greek, "thaphne." Bay leaves are known as "bai krawan" in Thailand.

Medicinal

There has been found in the bark of stem and root, volatile oil, starch, several acids, resins, and a red coloring substance. The bay had an important place in early medicine. Externally, an oil from the leaves and berries was applied to bruises and sprains. The oil was also dropped into the ears to relieve pain and was used to treat rheumatism, hysteria, and flatulence. The powdered berries were sometimes prescribed to improve the appetite and cure fevers.

Cosmetic

A facial steam bath containing herbs to clear the skin was popular with our grandmothers and has become so again today. For normal skins, a mixture of bay leaves, chamomile flowers, rosemary, and rose petals is recommended. Dried bay leaves go into potpourri blends and, with other soothing herbs, into sleep pillows for insomnia.

Companion planting

We have found that other plants will grow happily near pungent bay trees, except when the tree becomes too large and the roots rob the nearby soil of nourishment.

Lavender

Description

Among the various types of lavender, the most highly perfumed of plants, there are three basic kinds, known individually as English, French, and Italian lavender. There are many hybridized versions, some of them quite hardy and successful, like *L. allardii*, which is larger than most lavenders and has the long flower spikes and smooth leaves of English lavender, while the foliage has the indented edges of French lavender. There are several strains that have been developed from English lavender. Some are "Hidcote Giant," dwarf "Hidcote," and "Munstead." "Canary Islands" lavender (or "fern-leaf" lavender) looks quite different again with gray-green, finely cut foliage which has the same slightly eucalyptus scent as the purple blooms carried at the tips of very long stalks; the mature plant looks like a thick, leafy cushion with graceful stems curving upward from it. Flower colors available in English lavenders are beautiful and varied and may be snow white, dusty pink, shades of blue, and then going through the spectrum of mauves from pale lavender to deepest purple.

English lavender seems to be everyone's favorite. It is a bushy, small shrub growing 3 feet (90 cm) high, with silvery, smooth, pointed leaves and highly perfumed, tiny mauve flowers which grow at the end of long, spiky stems. When the bush starts blooming in summer it is a beautiful sight, especially if several plants are massed together as a hedge. This type of planting suits all the lavenders. English lavender is the most often used for making lavender articles and the highest concentration of essential oils is in the flowers.

French lavender is the hardiest, and in many ways the most rewarding of the varieties to grow. It can reach a height of 5 feet (1.5 metres). The bush blooms continuously for about nine months of the year, especially if mature flower stalks are cut back regularly to where two new shoots are

Labiatae.
Perennial.

Lavender, English:
(*Lavandula angustifolia*, or *L. spica*, or *L. officinalis*, or *L. Vera*).
Lavender, French:
(*L. dentata*).
Lavender, green:
(*L. viridis*).
Lavender, Italian or Spanish:
(*L. stoechas*).
Lavender cotton:
(*Santolina chamaecyparissus*).

PROPAGATION:
seeds, cuttings. Spring.

POSITION:
sunny.

SOIL:
well drained.

HEIGHT:
English lavender: 3 feet (90 cm);
French lavender: 5 feet (1.5 m);
Italian lavender: 2 feet (60 cm).

PART USED:
leaves, flowers.

LEFT: *French lavender*
CENTER: *English lavender*
RIGHT: *Italian lavender*

Lavender has long been a favorite with home gardeners. This English strain has white flowers.

French lavender is also very popular, although its fragrance is not as potent as English lavender.

beginning to branch. This helps to keep the bush a good shape while preventing it from having to feed flowers which are past their peak. These blooms can be dried for potpourri and sweet bags. Their perfume, although excellent, is not as potent as that of English lavender. The blooms are pale mauve and grow in a close head to the tip of a long, square stalk. If the location of the plant is particularly sunny, there will be a greater depth of color in the flowers. French lavender heads are very attractive bunched closely together for posies. The gray leaves are rough and serrated, densely covering the bush, giving it a thick, hazy look. Use them dried in mixtures for potpourri and sleep pillows.

Green lavender really has green blooms, fat heads of them with miniature white flowers starring each one, and two white "rabbit ear" petals on top. It must be a variation of Italian lavender because of the leaf and flower formation, although green lavender grows into a thicker, taller bush, about 3 feet (90 cm). Like Italian lavender, the fragrance is not strong. When two or three bushes are massed together, they are quite spectacular in a subtle way when in bloom, especially at dusk when the flowers emanate a magical, luminous glow. Propagate by taking cuttings in spring, and grow in the same position and soil as other lavenders.

Italian lavender is sometimes known as Spanish lavender, and occasionally, but wrongly, as French lavender. It is a scarcer variety than the others, but well worth cultivating. This type does not usually grow more than 2 feet (60 cm) high. Although similar to the other lavenders, it is also different enough to make a contrast in the garden. The gray leaves are tiny, smooth, and pointed and grow abundantly all over the bush. We have a curved hedge of 10 bushes growing together at the top of a low embankment, and from mid-winter through to early summer they are covered with deep purple flowers that look rather like smaller versions of French lavender flowers, except for a little top-knot of petal tufts at the end of each flower-head. Blossoms and leaves of Italian lavender are not as highly perfumed as other lavenders, but the blooms make attractive posies. It was sometimes known fondly as "sticadove."

The plant commonly known as "lavender cotton" does not belong to the *Lavandula* family, making it confusing for identification, so it seems a good idea to mention it here. We have seen two kinds. The first has fragrant foliage, resembling delicate gray coral, and round yellow flowers. It is a decorative addition to any garden; we saw long hedges of it lining the kitchen garden of a small chateau in France. In fact it was one of the herbs extensively used in outlining intricate knot gardens. The other type has bright green, needle-like foliage, very upright and bushy, and flat button-heads of lime to lemon blooms. This one is recommended for hedging too, and is scented. Lavender cotton (or cotton lavender) likes to grow in the same type of soil as the lavenders, light and well drained in a sunny position where it will reach a height of about 1½ feet (45 cm), sometimes more. It is successfully propagated by taking cuttings in spring. Prune lightly into shape when flowering has finished. Sprays of this herb were once laid in drawers to keep away moths, and oil for perfume from the plant is used industrially. The leaves and flowers of both kinds are excellent in potpourri, adding color and scent.

History and mythology

All the lavenders are native to the Mediterranean regions; the variety we call English lavender was not cultivated in England until about 1568. It was a favorite with the ancient Greeks, and one herbal writer of old says that it was known by the name of *Nardus*, from *Naarda*, a Syrian city near the river Euphrates, and that it was this herb which St. Mark referred to as "spikenard" in the Bible. Shakespeare refers to it, calling it "hot lavender" in *The Winter's Tale*.

Cultivation

The three basic types of lavender can be propagated from seed. If a hybrid lavender sets seed which is then planted, the new plants will probably revert back to the original type, so these must be increased by taking cuttings. If starting from seed, do this in spring by sowing into shallow drills in prepared seed boxes. Tip cuttings of any variety are taken when the soft, new leaves are firm enough not to wilt when they are put into a pot of sand. This is usually in late spring. When the seedlings are big enough, or when the cuttings have made roots, plant them out in a sunny, well-drained position. This is very important for lavender, as it will not grow sturdily nor flower well, if planted in a shady or damp place. When lavenders are in a position they like, the difference in the size of the bushes and the depth of color in the flowers is very marked.

Green lavender, with its lime green leaves, makes a pleasant contrast in the garden when grown with other lavenders.

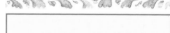

LAVENDER

THE FRAGRANCE OF LAVENDER OIL IS SAID TO HELP CREATE AN ATMOSPHERE OF TRANQUILITY, AND TO AID MEDITATION.

Pink lavender.

English lavender.

Harvesting and processing

The best time to pick and dry English lavender is before the last flowers on each stalk are fully opened. This is when their oil content is highest. Harvest the stalks on a dry day before the heat of the sun has drawn out the volatile essence, then tie them in bunches and hang in a shady, airy place to dry. When ready, strip the flowers from the stems and store them in airtight containers. When the plants have finished flowering, prune them hard, but not to ground level!

Leafy and flowering stalks of French lavender may be cut at any time for drying, providing there is no moisture in the air and harvesting is done before midday. Hang in bunches and dry like English lavender. Prune bushes quite severely when they finish flowering.

VARIOUS USES

Culinary

Lavender is not usually thought of as a culinary herb these days. Several centuries ago, many sweet-scented flowers were employed in the kitchen quite extensively, and there is a recipe by "W. M. Cook to Queen Henrietta Maria, 1655" for a conserve of lavender flowers, which consists of lavender petals finely chopped, then mixed with icing sugar and enough rosewater to make a thin paste to spread as a fragrant icing on plain cakes and biscuits. Lavender vinegar is made by infusing whole lavender stalks, with their flowers, in white vinegar for several weeks.

The Lavandula vera plant is known as "el khzama" in Morocco, where the dried flowers are an important ingredient in a herb and spice mixture known literally as "top of the shop." The piercing pungency of lavender is valued because it complements the delicious

Red lavender.

scent of the other herbs. In a similar way lavender is also used in a French provincial savory mixture with thyme, marjoram and rosemary. Dried rosebuds from the damask rose, "rous elword," are also an ingredient for a savory herb blend, and are also a separate ingredient in some Moroccan stews, especially those featuring rabbit. Orange blossoms from bitter orange trees are used in the same way.

Medicinal

The piercing, exquisite perfume of lavender flowers has a similar reviving effect as smelling salts when inhaled, for it is known that lavender calms the nerves and relaxes tensions. A bath at night impregnated with a few drops of lavender oil soothes and relaxes the peripheral nerves, while lavender flowers in a sedative tea mixture will help to bring on sleep. The leaves, as well as the flowers, have this wondrous effect. When you are stripping a quantity of dried lavender, notice how drowsy you become. Besides this, lavender was recognized as having a good effect on the digestion. Lavender essence has been widely used as a remedy for giddiness and faintness, nervous palpitations, and flatulence. It was administered by putting a few drops on sugar or in a little milk. Oil of lavender is still used by modern herbalists to rub into rheumatic joints to ease pain. It is also claimed that rubbing oil of lavender on burns assists with healing scar tissue.

Cosmetic

Lavender toilet water seems always to have been available. It is antiseptic for the skin, refreshing, and is especially recommended for an oily complexion and pimples. Fresh or dried lavender flowers or leaves tied in a muslin bag and infused in hot bathwater give the skin an all-over fragrance (use oil of lavender instead if you wish). Who does not respond to the wholesome smell of lavender-perfumed sheets and pillow cases? Lavender-perfumed notepaper and cards were once very much in vogue too. Lavender is indispensable in potpourri mixtures, in lavender-filled clothes hangers, in lavender bags, and for making lavender "bottles." Because of its soothing qualities, lavender is essential inside "sleep pillows." The warmth of the head releases the perfume and induces tranquil slumber. Not only the flowers are used, but the leaves as well. Never throw away the foliage: besides being perfumed. it provides valuable bulk when needed.

Companion planting

Lavender associates well with thyme in the garden. As an aromatic herb it has a good influence on vegetables growing nearby, helping to make healthier plants with more flavor. When in bloom, lavender attracts honey bees and butterflies It also helps repel moths and other undesirable insects in clothes cupboards and in carpets.

Italian lavender, also known as Spanish lavender, makes very attractive posies.

Perhaps the best known of the English lavenders is this sweet-scented strain with its mauve flowers.

Lovage

(Levisicum officinale)
Umbelliferae.
Perennial.

PROPAGATION:
  seeds. Spring.

POSITION:
  semi-shade.

SOIL:
  rich, moist.

HEIGHT:
  3–5 feet (90 cm–1.5 m).

PART USED:
  root, stems, leaves,
  seeds.

Description

In appearance, lovage bears a resemblance to angelica, although it does not grow as tall or as densely. The flowers are smaller and sulfur yellow, while angelica's great round heads are white to lime green. When young, lovage plants also look like a rather obscure herb called smallage, said to be the forerunner of our modern celery. Lovage's slim, hollow stems bear flat, serrated, dark green leaves in threes branching out from thicker, channeled stalks. The yellow flowers are followed by oblong brown seeds.

History and mythology

Lovage originated from the Mediterranean region and is one of the lesser known herbs today, yet it was formerly employed a great deal in medicine and cooking. In ancient times it grew wild in the mountainous districts of northern Greece and the south of France. It found its way to Britain many centuries ago and became one of the most cultivated of English herbs for use in herbal medicine for its root, stems, leaves, and seeds.

Cultivation

Like angelica, lovage likes rich, moist soil and a rather shady position to grow well. The seed can be sown in prepared boxes, or in the open ground in spring. When seedlings are about 3 inches (8 cm) high, plant them out to 1 1/2 feet (45 cm) apart. Keep them watered in dry weather.

Harvesting and processing

Harvest the seed just before it starts to fall by snipping off and drying whole flowerheads. Sift out any dried husks and stalks and store the seed in airtight containers. The stems can be cut and used at any time. If candying them like angelica stems, the flavor is best just after flowering. The root is stored by digging, washing, and keeping in an airy, dry place until needed. The leaves, for

making into a tea or for culinary use, may be cut from the stems and laid on sheets of clean paper or racks, in a shady, warm place until dry. When they are brittle, crumble them into airtight containers. Freezing for culinary use can be done by chopping the leaves finely and mixing them with a little water and putting them into ice cube trays. Whole leaf sprays may be stored for several weeks in the freezer when sealed in foil.

Lovage flourishes in a rich, moist soil and is best grown in a sheltered position. Today it is not one of the better known herbs, but in the past it was used extensively in both cooking and medicine. The leaves have a peppery tang which adds zest to soups, stews, salads, and sauces.

VARIOUS USES

Culinary

The flavor of the leaves resembles a combination of celery and parsley, but predominantly celery, with an extra peppery bite. They make an excellent, healthful addition to salads, soups, stews, and some sauces. For those on a condiment-free diet, use lovage for its spicy peppery taste. Chop the leaves finely for best results, as they are a little coarse. The hollow stalks and stems are often preserved as a confection in the same way as angelica.

Medicinal

The roots, stems, leaves, and seeds of lovage were used in herbal medicine for stomach disorders and feverish attacks. An infusion of the root was considered beneficial in many illnesses, including jaundice and urinary troubles. A decoction of the seeds was recommended as a gargle for infections of the mouth and throat, as a drink

An herbaceous border.

for pleurisy, and as a lotion for bathing sore eyes. The leaves eaten raw in a salad, or infused dry as a tea, are still recognized as being stimulating for the digestive organs and helpful in remedying gynecological disturbances. In special diets, the chopped leaves are an excellent substitute for pepper and other hot spices. Lovage was also regarded as an important pot herb in days gone by. In some regions where fresh vegetables are scarce, the roots are used for food and it is believed that chewing the stems will help prevent infection.

Cosmetic

Lovage is considered to be a deodorizing herb, both in solutions for the outside of the body, and as an inner cleanser for the system so as to acquire a clear skin outwardly. After a strenuous day, when one has perspired freely, try a lovage bath as an all-over body freshener. Make a strong tea with the leaves and add to a hot bath, or pick fresh leaves, bruise them and put them straight into the bathwater. This is a very old custom going back beyond the Middle Ages.

Companion planting

Lovage, as an aromatic herb, has a generally beneficial effect in the garden when sown in small patches, or as a border. Aromatic herbs have a particularly enlivening effect on the more stolid vegetable plants such as potatoes, swedes, and other root vegetables.

Horehound

Description

Along with other less familiar herbs, horehound has emerged a modern-day favorite with people interested in simple, natural remedies. The type described here is "white" horehound. "Black" horehound *(Ballota nigra,* also of the Labiatae family) is distinguished from white horehound by its taller growth, unpleasant smell, and purple flowers. White horehound is a bushy, rather sprawling herb growing to about 1½ feet (45 cm) or more. The small, soft leaves are oval, gray-green, finely "pinked" at the edges, and crinkled all over by countless veins. The underside of each leaf looks like oyster velvet, the semblance continuing down the woody stems and stalks completely covering them. The scent of horehound is both sharp and sweet and, when tasted, is very bitter. In summer the small, white whorls of flowers bloom at intervals in dense clusters encircling the stem.

History and mythology

The name of this herb is mostly associated with horehound beer, a popular non-alcoholic beverage. Horehound is native to parts of Europe, Asia, and North Africa. The Romans esteemed it highly. Some historical writers say it was one of the bitter herbs eaten by the Hebrews at the Feast of the Passover: the generic name is derived from *marrubium,* a bitter taste. Egyptian priests knew horehound and called it Seed of Horus or Bull's Blood. It was also an ingredient in antidotes for some types of poison. Its popularity in folk medicines made it a valuable part of one's belongings when traveling to new lands, and as merchandise for ancient trading vessels. These days horehound is widely spread in most parts of the world.

Cultivation

Horehound is a tough little plant and thrives in poor, dry soil in a sunny position. Propagation is by root division, or cuttings taken in spring; seed may be sown in spring and autumn (fall), and when large enough, planted out to 2 feet (60 cm) apart. In some countries, horehound has been declared a noxious weed, and the seed is banned for commercial use. If you wish to have a patch in your herb garden, ask if you can divide some roots from a plant if you see one growing, or if you come across it in the wild, pull up a few roots to take home with you.

(Marrubium vulgare)
Labiatae.
Perennial.

PROPAGATION:
  seeds: *Spring and Autumn (Fall); cuttings, root division: Spring.*

POSITION:
  sunny.

SOIL:
  average to poor, dry.

HEIGHT:
  1½ feet (45 cm) or more.

PART USED:
  leaves, flowers.

A popular ingredient in folk medicine, white horehound thrives in a sunny position. Slender stalks shoot again in spring from dormant roots.

Harvesting and processing

To dry horehound, pick stalks of flowers and leaves just as the plant begins to bloom, and before midday, and hang in bunches in an airy place. Air drying on racks is also satisfactory. When dry, crumble off the leaves and flowers, and break up the brittle stalks, which have value as well. Store in airtight containers.

VARIOUS USES

Culinary

Horehound candy, as well as horehound beer, have been well known in the past. The dried leaves have been used as a condiment, and horehound tea is a time-honored standby for several complaints. Horehound candy is made by boiling the leaves in water until the juice is extracted, strained off, and boiled again with sugar until thick, poured into an oiled flat container, and cut into squares when cold.

Medicinal

White horehound has been valued for centuries in treating colds and bronchitis; early herbals give detailed instructions for making syrups and infusions of horehound to take for coughs and "wheezing of the lungs." It is still considered effective as an expectorant, as well as having tonic and mildly laxative properties, and may be taken as a syrup, a tea, a gargle, or made into candy to take when suffering from a cold. A friend from Melbourne, Australia, goes to his horehound plant when he feels a cold beginning and simply chews some leaves as a successful antidote. Another use was told by a friend whose family has lived in our district for generations. As a child, he had suffered from a serious kidney complaint. An English settler who saw horehound growing wild on the side of a sunny dry bank, picked a bunch, and told his mother to boil the whole washed plant (minus roots) in a quart (1 L) of water and reduce to a pint (500 ml), then strain, and give a medicine glassfull every morning. She did this, gathering more horehound as needed, and he recovered within a month. The herb is a mild diuretic (increasing the flow of urine to flush the kidneys), and was highly successful in this case.

Cosmetic

Weak horehound tea can be patted onto affected areas for minor skin problems.

Companion planting

As an insect repellent, horehound steeped in milk and placed where flies are a pest has been found to lessen their activity.

HOREHOUND

EARLY HERBALS GIVE DETAILED INSTRUCTIONS FOR MAKING SYRUPS AND INFUSIONS TO TAKE FOR COUGHS AND "WHEEZING OF THE LUNGS".

Balm

Description

The strongly lemon-scented foliage of this herb gives it the popular name of "lemon balm.". The leaves are crinkly and shaped like mint leaves, although larger in size. The small, white flowers, which bloom in summer, grow in dusters along a thin, angular stem. The plant has a spreading habit, and the shallow roots are thick and matted.

History and mythology

Balm is native to the mountainous regions of Southern Europe and was used as one of the sacred herbs in the temple of Diana. Its botanical name of Melissa is Latin for "bee," as these insects are constant visitors to the nectar-laden blossoms when they are in flower. (How intricate is the world of nature, for when wax is poured into the honeyed flowers of the *Labiatae* family, which includes amongst its members thyme, sage, oregano, marjoram, mint, and rosemary as well as balm, the hardened shape that results is identical with the bee's proboscis, the organ it uses for extracting honey.) The name of balm has been abbreviated from the fragrant oil balsam, signifying the herb's aromatic sweetness. Bee-hives were traditionally rubbed with sweet-smelling herbs, especially balm leaves, to help keep the hive together and to attract homing bees. Honey was regarded as a necessary commodity for the household larders of bygone days, and there was much written about the art of bee-keeping, those who lived close to these industrious insects having a great respect for their wisdom. Herb gardens and bee-hives were traditionally linked together, and Thomas Hyll writes in 1579 that the hives should be placed near: ". . . the hearbe Baulme . . . ; and manye other sweete and wholesome floures."

Cultivation

The simplest way to propagate balm is by root division in spring, just as the new growth is starting. If you prefer to propagate by taking cuttings, wait for the new tips to grow to about 3 inches (8 cm) long, and when firm enough, take a 4 inch (10 cm) long tip, removing all the leaves except the top two. Press the cuttings deeply into a pot of river sand,

---

(Melissa officinalis)
Labiatae.
Perennial.

PROPAGATION:
 seeds, cuttings, root division. Spring (Autumn – Fall – in temperate zones).

POSITION:
 part sun.

SOIL:
 moist, rich.

HEIGHT:
 2½ feet (75 cm).

PART USED:
 leaves.

Balm of Gilead, mentioned in the Bible.

❧

BALM

BEEHIVES PLACED
NEAR HERB GARDENS
CONTAINING BALM
YIELD A HONEY PRIZED
SINCE AT LEAST THE
SIXTEENTH CENTURY.

Balm of Gilead in an open field.

❧

leaving one-third of each cutting exposed. Sow the seed in spring (or in autumn — fall — in temperate climates) into a prepared box, or in shallow drills straight into the ground, leaving a little space between plants. If seeds are sown fairly thickly, or seedlings are planted close together over an area of several square feet, a large clump will develop quickly. In certain areas the leaves of balm seedlings can get frostbitten: under these conditions, plant in a sheltered position where there will be some sun during the day. If the seedlings are grown in too wet and shady a place, fungus may give some trouble. Lastly, watch carefully for leaf-eating grubs and insects. If they occur, sprinkle the dampened foliage with one of the more natural insect repellent powders on the market.

Harvesting and processing

When drying balm for storing purposes, cut the stalks back almost to ground level just as the flowers begin to appear, and dry them on airy racks in a shady place. They may also be tied loosely together in bunches and hung to dry. Immediately the leaves are crisp and dry, rub them from their stalks and keep them in airtight containers. Fresh balm may be picked in sprays, washed, wrapped in foil, and put in the refrigerator where it will stay fresh for a week or two. For longer lasting results, fresh leaves may be chopped finely, put into ice cube trays with a little water, and frozen until needed.

VARIOUS USES

Culinary

Fresh or dried balm leaves go well in fruit or vegetable salads, milk puddings, and in certain soups. The fresh lemon fragrance of the herb enhances buttered, cooked vegetables. For a change, balm makes an excellent seasoning for chicken, fish, lamb, or pork. It is traditional to add fresh sprigs of balm to wine cups and fruit drinks.

The piquant lemon fragrance of balm makes it an interesting seasoning for chicken, fish, lamb, or pork. In the garden, balm foliage grows densely and has a spreading habit with shallow roots.

Chopped balm leaves may be added to stewed fruit. They are also delicious as a filling for sandwiches. Balm tea is particularly refreshing and reviving in the summer, even one leaf in the teapot with Indian tea will give a lift to both palate and spirits.

Medicinal

Balm leaves contain essences which were highly valued for their healing properties, and were used in treating many ailments such as melancholy, nervous headache, failing memory, neuralgia, and fevers. Balm tea is still taken today to help bring down high temperatures and to lessen the effects of exhaustion in hot weather. Together with sage, balm was said to contribute to longevity. It was also used to guard against senility. Balm has been widely used continuously for many years because of its tonic effect on the stomach. It assists in the digestion of food and is said to increase the appetite.

Cosmetic

Balm tea is used for outward as well as for inward purposes. It cleanses and perfumes the skin, and for this reason is used with other herbs in the bath water. An infusion for the bath should be made several times stronger than when balm is taken as a beverage. It is used as an infusion with verbena and other ingredients to make a natural cleansing cream. An infusion as a mouth wash sweetens the breath. The dried whole leaves of lemon balm make an excellent addition to a potpourri mixture and to a soothing blend for a sleep pillow.

Companion planting

It has been noted that balm plants in borders, together with certain other herbs, are helpful to all vegetables. Lemon balm in pastures is believed to increase the milk production in cows, and is also strengthening and soothing when given to them, together with marjoram, as a tea after calving.

BALM

BALM TEA IS A REFRESHING DRINK TO RELIEVE EXHAUSTION IN HOT WEATHER.

Mint

(Mentha) Labiatae.
Perennial.

Applemint:
(M. rotundifolia).
Catnip: *(Nepeta cataria)*
Labiatae.
Eau-de-Cologne Mint:
(M. piperita citrata).
Pennyroyal:
(M. pulegium).
Peppermint:
(M. piperita
officinalis).
Spearmint:
(M. spicata, or
M. crispa, or
M. viridis).

PROPAGATION:
cuttings, root division,
seed. Spring.

POSITION:
semi-shade to shade.

SOIL:
rich, moist.

HEIGHT:
1–3 feet (30–90 cm)
according to variety.

PART USED:
leaves.

RIGHT: Eau-de-Cologne mint

Description

The mints are a versatile family; there are quite a number with pronouncedly different flavors and scents, even though between them there is a strong outward resemblance, except for leaf color. We have listed six easily available varieties, although other more rare kinds include watermint, cornmint, Japanese peppermint, American wild mint, Egyptian mint, Corsican mint, woolly mint, European horse mint, liquorice mint, ginger mint, basil mint, lemon mint, and Asian mint (very hot). Mints hybridize with each other, which is one of the reasons for the wide diversity of types.

Applemint, as the name suggests, has a strong scent of apples. Growing approximately 12 inches (30 cm) high, it has oval, wrinkled, soft leaves and small white flowers which appear in autumn (fall). Sometimes this variety is called pineapple mint. Another variation is variegated applemint, also sometimes called golden applemint and variegated lemon balm. The reason for the different common names for the same plant comes about through mistaken identification, and after some time the incorrect name sticks.

Catnip, sometimes spelt *catnep,* and incorrectly called catmint, has mint-like, serrated gray-green leaves, rather limp, with a musky scent. The white flowers cluster on either side of long stems in summer and early autumn (fall). The bushy plant grows to about 3 feet (90 cm) high. Catnip has some medicinal qualities, but its main use is for the household cat: a constituent in this herb is highly attractive to most cats, giving them intense pleasure; they love to sniff the plant and roll in it. Toys like felt mice or an old sock filled with dried catnip are a favorite plaything for a special puss!

Eau-de-Cologne mint is yet another variety with several names. We have seen it listed both as bergamot mint and orange mint. This type has smooth, green leaves tinged with purple; they are oval in shape and grow up to 3 inches (8 cm) long and 1 inch (25 mm) across, with a strong, sharp perfume. The stems

LEFT: Variegated applemint

are square (as with all mints) and purple in color. The plants may reach a height of 3 feet (90 cm). In autumn (fall) eau-de-Cologne mint bears flowers typical of all mints, except that these are larger than most and a deep shade of mauve, making them a pretty addition to mixed posies.

Pennyroyal is another member of the mint family. It has small, shiny green leaves and a strong peppermint scent. It has a creeping habit and for most of the year never grows higher then 1 inch (25 mm) above the ground. For this reason it makes a good ground cover in a shady part of the garden. In spring the mauve flowers appear in a series of circlets along 12 inch (30 cm) high stems. When flowering has finished, plants can be cut down with the mower, thus making a lawn that needs no other attention, except for watering in dry weather.

Peppermint is a most useful plant as it is the herb that yields the true oil of peppermint. Growing to about 2 feet (60 cm) high, it has small, pointed, green leaves with a purple tint. The scent is so characteristically peppermint that it cannot be mistaken for any other mint.

Spearmint can have either elongated, smooth, bright green leaves, or oval-shaped, crinkly, dark green leaves, according to the variety. Both varieties have the same vital, typical mint scent. The smooth-leaved variety is often called English spearmint and is more difficult to grow than its coarser brother. The scent and flavor is clearer and stronger and the leaves have a finer texture, but it is susceptible to diseases and leaf-eating insects. Either of these mints is most suitable for culinary purposes, and can be grown in the garden in a moist position, or in a large tub under a dripping tap.

History and mythology

Mint's history goes back to Greek mythology and to Biblical times. The Romans introduced it to Britain and it was familiar to Chaucer and Shakespeare. One Greek historian wrote that: "the smell of Mint does stir up the minde and the taste to a greedy desire of meate." The Pharisees in the Bible were paid tithes of mint, anise, and cumin.

Cultivation

Mints are usually propagated by root division, as even the smallest piece will grow. However, if this is not possible, short stem cuttings taken after the new growth has hardened in late spring can be put

CATNIP

THIS HERB, SO NAMED BECAUSE IT IS ESPECIALLY DELIGHTFUL TO CATS, IS SOMETIMES CALLED 'CATMINT', BUT UNLIKE THE TRUE MINTS IT IS NOT A *MENTHA*. ITS BOTANICAL NAME IS *NEPETA CATARIA*.

Lemon mint

RIGHT: Basil mint

DRYING MINT

CUT THE LEAFY STEMS
JUST BEFORE THEY
COME INTO FLOWER,
AND HANG IN BUNCHES
IN A DRY PLACE WITH
GOOD AIR CIRCULATION.

Lemon mint in flower

straight into the ground, where roots will quickly form. They are best grown in rich, moist soil, in semi-shade, but will also grow in poor, sandy soil if the ground is fertilized from time to time. Cut the plants back to ground level in winter. If mint is attacked by rust, the plants must be dug out and burnt, starting again with new stock in a different part of the garden. Mint is not usually propagated by seed because it is small and difficult to harvest. If however, you grow mint from seed, sow in spring in prepared seed boxes, keep moist, and when the plants are large enough to handle, plant them out.

Harvesting and processing

Mints will dry satisfactorily by hanging the leafy stems, cut just before coming into full flower, in bunches in a dry, airy place. Make sure that when the crisp, dried leaves are stripped from their stalks they are kept in airtight containers, as this herb does not keep its full aroma and flavor if exposed to the air for long. For freezing, chop fresh leaves finely, mix them with a little water, and put them into ice cube trays in the freezer. Sprays of fresh mint may be wrapped in foil, sealed, and kept in the deep freeze for some weeks. Spearmint butter may also be frozen and is delicious with lamb. Chop the fresh leaves, pound them into softened butter, allow to set in the refrigerator, then cut into squares and seal into small polythene bags or other suitable containers. Small sprigs of peppermint or eau-de-Cologne mint may be individually frozen in ice cube trays in the summer, then dropped into cooling beverages on hot days.

VARIOUS USES

Culinary

Applemint can be mixed with spearmint for mint sauce. When frying bananas for chicken Maryland, roll them first in finely chopped applemint. Mix the chopped leaves into fruit salads and fruit jellies. Be adventurous and try new flavor combinations with this fresh-tasting herb.

Eau-de-Cologne mint has a flavor too powerful to use in any quantity, although one chopped leaf added to a mixture of other herbs gives a delicious tang. A bunch of this mint in a jug of water on a hot day seems to help cool the surrounding atmosphere.

Pennyroyal is not recommended for culinary use as it brings on abortions in cattle, and is said to do the same thing with human beings! If you are not at risk, we have found a few chopped leaves with new potatoes and butter very pleasant.

Spearmint, either fresh or dried, is the variety which gives mint sauce its flavor, as well as being used in mint jelly and mint julep. It is customary with green peas. Chopped mint goes with hot, buttered new potatoes, with tomatoes, in some egg dishes, in custards and ice cream. A few fresh leaves on buttered bread with cream cheese make delicious sandwiches.

Spearmint is a popular flavoring throughout the Middle East and Mediterranean, where it is used either fresh or dried. It gives its distinct aroma and taste to meat and vegetable dishes, to yogurt sauces, to soups and to salads. Its Afghan name is "nauna," in Arabic it is "na'na," in Armenian "ananoukh," in Greek "thiosmos," in Iranian "nano," in Turkish "nane."

In Morocco, where mint is known as "naa naa," spearmint is used to make mint tea, said to be the most popular beverage in Morocco. Mint tea is taken to restore energy, aid convalescence, and to help the digestive system. Other herbs and spices are sometimes included when the tea is ritually made, and the more exotic teas can contain precious saffron. Mint is also used in tagines (stews) and kefta (ground meat grilled on skewers or made into a meatball stew).

Several types of mint are used throughout India and Asia. Dried or fresh mint is used in the making of koftas and kebabs in India, as

PEPPERMINT TEA

TAKEN FROM THE END OF SUMMER AND THROUGH THE WINTER, PEPPERMINT TEA IS SAID TO HELP WARD OFF COLDS.

FAR LEFT: Pennyroyal
LEFT: Peppermint

A bed of peppermint has a very characteristic smell and from this herb peppermint oil is obtained.

RIGHT: Smooth-leaved spearmint

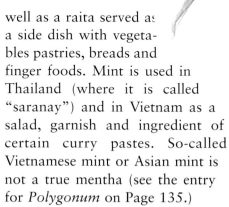

EAU-DE-COLOGNE MINT

THE DRIED LEAVES MAY BE ADDED TO POT-POURRI, AND FOR A REFRESHING SLEEP THEY MAY BE INCLUDED WHEN FILLING A HERBAL "SLEEP PILLOW".

Both varieties of spearmint are widely used in the kitchen, either fresh or dried. They give their taste to mint sauce, mint jello (jelly) and julep, and are a delicious accompaniment to green peas.

well as a raita served as a side dish with vegetables pastries, breads and finger foods. Mint is used in Thailand (where it is called "saranay") and in Vietnam as a salad, garnish and ingredient of certain curry pastes. So-called Vietnamese mint or Asian mint is not a true mentha (see the entry for *Polygonum* on Page 135.)

M. spicata is known as "hierba buena" or "yerba buena" in Mexico, meaning "good herb". It is the essential ingredient in a strengthening chicken broth for convalescents.

Medicinal

A tea made from fresh or dried peppermint leaves not only tastes pleasant, but if one is suffering from a heavy cold or indigestion, some relief comes soon after one or two cups. This beverage is also a soothing, relaxing drink, helping to promote sound, natural sleep, especially appreciated by students whose minds may be overactive through prolonged study. It is said that if peppermint tea is taken

regularly in autumn (fall) and then all through the winter, it helps build up a resistance to colds. As a routine, either start the day with a cup, or have it before going to bed at night. In summer, iced peppermint tea is refreshing, and a quantity can be made and kept in the refrigerator for one or two days.

Spearmint tea is revivifying too. A friend found that drinking spearmint tea while she was staying in Singapore for some time was most satisfying and refreshing. Peppermint and spearmint tea are becoming much more available now and are often sold in tea bags. They are also excellent when blended with other teas to make them more palatable. Children generally will like peppermint or spearmint tea.

ABOVE: Crinkle-leaved spearmint is one of two varieties, the other having elongated, smooth leaves.

LEFT: Crinkle-leaved spearmint

Cosmetic

Spearmint will help to prevent bad breath, and is incorporated into a number of herbal toothpastes for this reason. It also helps to whiten teeth and condition the gums. Spearmint has a beneficial effect on the head, and was used to wash children's heads when inclined to sores. Both spearmint and peppermint are excellent for conditioning oily hair. Oil of spearmint (mint) in the bath is stimulating and even floating a few sprigs of fresh mint in hot bathwater is effective. Spearmint has also been used for helping heal chapped hands. Dried eau-de-Cologne mint leaves make an excellent fragrant addition to potpourri and sleep pillows.

ABOVE: Curly mint in flower.

LEFT: Ginger mint in the Chelsea Physic Garden, England.

The unique scent of pepper-mint is unmistakable.

Companion planting

Peppermint in the vegetable garden aids cabbage plants. It has been found that the oil is greatly increased in peppermint plants if they are grown with stinging nettles. It has also been noted that production of the oil is retarded in peppermint plants if they are grown with chamomile, but that the chamomile itself will have a greater oil content.

Spearmint is an excellent insect repellent and will help to keep away black flea beetles, cabbage butterfly caterpillars, ants, fleas, and, to a certain extent, aphids. Spearmint is reported to repel various rodents. Indoors, dried mint leaves placed in drawers and cupboards keep away moths. Mint was valued as a strewing herb in houses, both for its perfume and insect-repellent qualities. All varieties have the reputation for preventing milk from curdling. Sprigs of mint placed in a room will overcome the smell of stale tobacco.

Pennyroyal when growing wild in pastures brings on abortions in cows. It is an excellent flea and mosquito repellent. It also repels ants. If sitting outside, or working in the garden, fresh pennyroyal rubbed on the skin is a protection against mosquitoes.

RIGHT: Pennyroyal has a matting, creeping habit and for this reason it makes an excellent groundcover.

FAR RIGHT: Eau-de-Cologne mint has smooth green leaves with a purple tinge and an attractive mauve flower.

Curry Tree

Description

The curry tree is evergreen, but can be deciduous in cold areas. It has a leaf which is small, shiny, and a neat mint-leaf shape, with a pungent, spicy fragrance. The clusters of tiny white flowers, which appear in summer, produce small, blue-black, edible fruits.

History and mythology

The curry tree is native to Sri Lanka and India, and is now found growing throughout tropical countries. In Malaysia it is called "daun kari pla," in India it is known as "kitha neem," and in Thailand, "bai kari."

Cultivation

Cuttings and seed are very slow to grow, so it is more satisfactory to propagate from suckers or runners which spread from the parent root base, and will do well in a large container in a sunny position. A well-drained, moist soil rich in organic matter will ensure a healthy tree: planting in a raised bed for maximum drainage is advised by specialist nursery growers. The tree can be pruned in spring. Although it is a tropical plant, the curry tree will survive in temperate climates if well protected from frost.

Harvesting and processing

Unlike most herbs, which are more pungent when dried, dry curry leaves have less flavor, and are a poor substitute for the fresh leaves. If drying the leaves, however, strip them from the main stem and spread out in an airy, warm place, or dry in a microwave oven. Store in airtight containers.

(Merraya koenigii)
Rutaceae

PROPAGATION:
from runners or seeds

POSITION:
full to part sun

SOIL:
light to medium, moist

HEIGHT:
average 13 feet (4 m)

PART USED:
leaves, edible fruit

The curry tree.

VARIOUS USES

Culinary

Fresh curry leaves are used in Asia in a similar ways to bay leaves in Western cooking. Frequently sold dried, the whole leaves can be added to curries and soups, or they can be ground and included in curry pastes. A curry flavor is also obtained by adding leaves of the curry plant (*Helichrysum italicum* syn *H. angustifolium*) sparingly to dishes.

The curry plant is not related to the curry tree, but its leaves also have a curry flavor.

Bergamot

(Monarda didyma)
Labiatae.
Perennial.

PROPAGATION:
seeds, root division,
Spring.

POSITION:
shady, morning sun.

SOIL:
rich, moist.

HEIGHT:
4 feet (1.2 m).

PART USED:
leaves, flowers.

Description

The flowers of bergamot, in size, color and form, are amongst the showiest of all herb blossoms. There are several different shades varying from pink and mauve to a rich red, which is the popular Cambridge Scarlet. Bergamot's slightly hairy leaves are oval — approximately 3 inches (8 cm) long and are attached in pairs to square stems. The pompom-type flowers start blooming on 3 feet (90 cm) tall stalks in early summer. If the plants are in the right position, where the roots are shaded and there is morning sun for several hours, flowers will bloom right through to the midde of autumn (fall). The whole plant is fragrantly scented and the tubular flower petals are full of nectar, making them a magnet for bees. For this reason, bergamot is often called "bee balm." Honey-eating birds are also attracted to the blossoms. Like mint, which is a member of the same family, bergamot has a matted, spreading root system and does not start shooting upward until spring.

History and mythology

Bergamot is native to North America and received its botanical name from the 16th-century Spanish physician, Nicholas Monardez, who first discovered and described it. The leaves, which contain the essential oil thymol, were widely used in an infusion by the Oswego Indians. The herb soon became known to the early American settlers, who called it Oswego Tea, a name which is still popular today. Oil of bergamot, a fragrant essence, does not come from this plant, but from a citrus tree, the bergamot orange (Citrus bergamia). The aromas are similar.

Cultivation

A dressing of well-decayed humus may be applied in spring when the plant begins to shoot upward. Grass cuttings should be sprinkled over the roots during the hottest part of summer. Bergamot may be grown in clumps as background plants in herb gardens, or in decorative clusters in standard garden beds, the lovely, plush red pincushion blooms making splashes of vivid color. Ours grows in a faraway bed set in a green sward surrounded by a glade of leafy trees. When in bloom, the scarlet flashes draw one from a distance to investigate and admire. A flower is always picked and the honeysuckle-petals tasted for their sweetness. If necessary, lightly tie the slender and rather brittle stems to garden stakes.

Propagation by root division can be done throughout the year. However, the best time is in early spring, when new growth is beginning. The seeds, which are very small, can be sown in a prepared box in spring and planted out when big enough to handle, leaving 6 inches (15 cm) between plants. The fact that bergamot likes to grow in a shady position, where the roots can be kept cool and moist, also encourages snails, so be prepared for this by laying a suitable bait nearby, especially when the soft leaves are young. After the plants have finished flowering, cut stalks back to ground level.

Harvesting and processing

For drying, harvest both foliage and flowers in late summer when the plant is in full bloom and dry them as quickly as possible. Do this by picking the leaves and blooms from the stems and spreading them out on a wire rack in a shady place. When they are dry, store them in airtight containers. Fresh bergamot leaves may be chopped finely, mixed with a little water, and frozen in ice cube trays to be used when needed. The flowers may be frozen whole by carefully putting them one by one in an ice cube tray, then gently covering them with water.

VARIOUS USES

Culinary

Bergamot leaves go into salads, teas, and cooling summer beverages. Their savory yet fruity aroma enhances such widely differing foods as vegetables and sweet jellies. They combine well with pork and veal. Fresh or dried, they may be used instead of mint leaves for a change. The flowers can be gently torn apart and added to a tossed green salad.

Medicinal

A herb tea made from bergamot leaves was taken by the Indians and early Americans as a remedy for sore throats, colds, and chest complaints.

Cosmetic

Fresh or dried bergamot in a hot bath is revitalizing and perfumes the water. An essential oil is made from this plant, both for incense and as a bath oil. The dried flowers and leaves make a fragrant addition to potpourri.

Companion planting

Bergamot's attraction for bees makes it an excellent plant to grow near the vegetable garden and in the orchard.

The Cambridge Scarlet is the best known of the red bergamots and is the type most often used in cooking.

Bergamot can vary in hue from mauve through pink to deep red and is very striking when grown in garden beds. Fresh or dried, this herb is a pleasant addition to a warm bath as it not only has a revitalizing effect but also perfumes the water.

Banana

(Musa paradisiaca)
Perennial

PROPAGATION:
suckers from main plant

POSITION:
sunny, sheltered, frost-free

SOIL:
rich, moist

HEIGHT:
1–25 feet (1–7 m) high (according to species)

PART USED:
stems, leaves, flowers, fruit

Description

There are many varieties of banana plants. They can grow from 1–25 feet high, according to variety. They have straight trunks, and the green stems carry very large green leaves. The huge pendant flowers are spectacular and vary in size, color and shape depending on the species, as does the fruit that follows. Banana fruit hangs in dense clusters or "hands." and each banana is called a "finger."

History and mythology

The banana family is native to tropical regions throughout the world, where the hot climate ensures ripening of the fruit. Banana plants are said to have originated in the region from India to New Guinea, then to have been introduced into Africa by the Arabs, and taken later into America and other colonies by the Spanish and Portuguese. Banana leaves are used as a herb in many countries where the plant grows.

Cultivation

Banana plants must grow in rich soil in a sheltered sunny position. Plenty of water is needed, and a damp part of the garden is ideal for them. Once the tree has flowered and fruited it will not do so again, so it is neccessary to cut the trunk away to allow new suckers from the parent plant to grow.

Harvesting and processing

Banana leaves may be used at any time for wrapping various foods before cooking. The leaf stems are also employed by peeling away the outward fiber until the pale green, or white, porous middle portion is revealed. The flowers also have their uses and are picked fresh, or are pickled. Harvest the fruit in clusters, usually at their peak in autumn.

VARIOUS USES

Culinary

Banana leaves are used for their aroma when wrapping food such as rice and fish, before steaming; the leaves are first soaked in boiling water to make them pliable.

The peeled stems may be cut into pieces and added to salads for taste and texture, or may be steamed with vegetables. The Burmese

The broad leaf of the banana tree is perfect for wrapping foods.

BANANA LEAVES

THE LEAVES OF THE
BANANA PLANT ARE
USED IN MANY
TRADITIONAL CUISINES
TO WRAP FOOD BEFORE
IT IS STEAMED,
IMMERSED OR BAKED.

Banana fruit and the flower, which has a delicate flavor that makes it an interesting accompaniment to piquant dishes.

put the prepared, chopped stems into a special curried soup which thus gains an additional, subtle aroma. In some Southeast Asian countries it is a custom to serve curries on a banana leaf instead of a plate.

Banana leaves are used in Mexican cuisine to wrap tamales, dishes of fish, or chicken. The tamale is also made in South America: it begins as a dough surrounding a seasoned filling of vegetables, or meat, fish, or poultry. Banana leaves are preferred to wrap tamales because of their excellent taste. The prepared leaves are passed through an open flame to bring out the natural oils and flavor, or they can be dipped in boiling water for a milder taste. The tamales are then wrapped and steamed, or slowly simmered.

Packaged banana leaves are available in Latin American and Oriental markets.

Medicinal

Though banana leaves are valued for their aromatic flavor, it is the fruit which is richest in nutrients, containing sugars, fiber and protein.

Sweet Cicely

(*Myrrhis odorata*)
Umbelliferae.
Perennial.

PROPAGATION:
*seeds, Spring; root
division, Spring and
Autumn (Fall).*

POSITION:
*part shade in warm
climates; tolerates full
sun in cool regions.*

SOIL:
*medium rich, well
drained.*

HEIGHT:
2–5 feet (60–150 cm).

PART USED:
*green leaves, fresh seeds,
roots.*

Description

A European native, sweet cicely is one of the tall, stately herbs, reaching a height of 2–5 feet (60–150 cm) when grown in the right position, and is so ornamental when in flower that it is often included in a herbaceous border. It has been said that if "lavender is the queen of herbs, sweet cicely is surely the princess." The large, ferny leaves have a silky texture and are covered in a soft down, verdant green on top but paler underneath. The foliage has a sweet, warm, anise taste and grows from thick, hollow, and branching stems. In spring white umbels of frothy flowers cover the plant and attract honey bees. The seeds are long and dark brown.

History and mythology

Dioscorides, the Greek, wrote a great deal about herbs, describing them in detail. He first used the name "Seseli," and this is how cicely is pronounced. The strong scent of the foliage, traditionally smelling of myrrh, is responsible for its botanical name, *Myrrhis*, meaning perfume, and *odorata* for fragrance. The common prefix, sweet, refers to the plant's delicious aroma. Old-fashioned names for it are fern-leaved chervil or giant sweet chervil, although it is a much bigger plant in every way than the real chervil. Once, the oil-rich, ripe seeds were gathered for crushing to a powder as a polish for furniture and oaken floors. Culpeper writes of its "pleasantness in salads" and that "it is so harmless you cannot use it amiss".

Cultivation

Sweet cicely does not like humid areas and will thrive in conditions that are mainly cool. Where climate and soil suit, especially in mountain regions, sweet cicely may spread and become rampant. Choose a well-drained place in semi-shade for the plants, and if the soil is poor, add a little compost. Sow seeds in spring into shallow drills in a box containing fine soil, or sow where the plants are to remain. When large enough, plant out the seedlings. For root division, cut the taproot into sections and replant. This should be done in spring or autumn (fall). Water in dry weather.

Harvesting and processing

The sweet leaves are preferred fresh in salads, but they may be harvested and dried on a flat surface in a shady, cool place for use as a digestive tea. When the flowers have dropped, collect the aromatic, green seed for chopping and using in salads. The ripe seed can be collected for sowing again. You may wish to use ripe seeds like our

grandmothers did as a fragrant furniture polish, in which case you should grind the seed to a powder in a blender.

VARIOUS USES

Culinary

Most parts of sweet cicely are edible. The leaves, green seeds, and hollow stems are chopped and used in all kinds of salads. The roots when cut up and boiled were once a popular vegetable, especially for elderly people. The hollow stems may be candied like angelica. The finely chopped leaves are excellent to use when cooking sharp fruit like rhubarb to counteract acidity. Use them as a natural sweetening agent in cooling summer drinks.

Medicinal

Sweet cicely's fragrant leaves are very useful as a sugar substitute for diabetics and are recommended for this purpose. Chop the leaves and green seeds and add them to salads. Steam the leaves like a vegetable and use in soups. In the past, both the leaves and root have been used to alleviate coughs and flatulence. Fresh or dried leaves infused as a tea are taken to strengthen the digestion and the cooked roots have been said to assist the system. The roots were once an ingredient in an ointment for healing wounds and, in earlier times, were preserved and candied and reckoned a good preservative in time of plague.

The leaves of sweet cicely are edible.

Cosmetic

As the leaves contain a weak antiseptic, you may like to add a few when preparing a facial steam to give it a pleasing scent as well as helping to cleanse skin eruptions.

Companion planting

The nectar-laden blossoms will bring honey bees to the garden.

Myrtle

(*Myrtus communis*)
Myrtaceae.
Perennial

PROPAGATION:
*cuttings, late Spring,
early Summer.
Seeds Spring.*

POSITION:
sunny

SOIL:
*well-drained, medium
rich*

HEIGHT:
3–10 feet (1–3 m)

PART USED:
leaves, flowers, berries

Description

Myrtle is a compact, evergreen shrub usually growing to 10 feet (3 m) high, but sometimes taller. The small, oval leaves are pointed, glossy and sweetly scented. The plant bears perfumed blooms in mid-to late summer: each tiny five-petalled white flower is almost hidden by prominent gold stamens; the tightly folded white buds burst into flower in a day. This plant should not be confused with the crepe myrtle (*Lagerstroemea indica*).

History and mythology

The myrtle was assigned to Aphrodite (Venus) the goddess of love, so not surprisingly has a reputation for being an aphrodisiac. It is mentioned in the Old Testament, and in Greek and Roman manuscripts. It has a double symbolic link with the idea of love, being connected with both fidelity and immorality. Myrtle as a symbol of the first quality is included in an Israeli bride's wedding bouquet.

Cultivation

Myrtle grows wild in its native Mediterranean regions and in western Asia. It is propagated by taking woody cuttings in summer. Divide the wood into 5–7 inch (12–15 cm) pieces, trim off any side shoots, and press each piece into a deep pot of river sand, leaving one-third of the wood exposed at the top. Water well. When the cuttings have made strong roots, plant out. If wishing to grow from tip cuttings, take them in late spring to early summer; trim the stem of foliage, allowing several leaves to remain at the top, then insert into river sand and continue in the same way as for hardwood propagation. Seeds are sown in spring in prepared trays, as described in the section on growing from seeds on page 195. When plants are large enough and have a good root system, put in the ground as either single specimens, or as a hedge. Myrtle needs a well-drained, medium-rich soil in a sunny position. Nourish with fertilizer from time to time and water in dry weather. Myrtle can be clipped to make an evergreen dense hedge, looking most attractive when covered with its white, perfumed flowers. The blossoms are followed in late summer by berries which turn blue when ripe.

Harvesting and processing

The fragrant fresh leaves are picked for culinary use. The fresh flowers may be gathered for culinary use also. When the petals have

Myrtle berries were used by the Greeks and Romans to freshen breath.

dropped, the fruit begins to form, and gradually turns blue. Pick the berries when they appear and air-dry on a gauze rack or on sheets of paper in a warm, dark place. When completely dry, store in an airtight jar. Grind in a pepper-mill, or crush in a mortar and pestle just before using.

VARIOUS USES

Culinary

Myrtle leaves are used in their native Mediterranean countries to flavor roasted meats and game birds. The cooked meat is wrapped in the leaves, or the cooked birds are stuffed with leaves for five to ten minutes before serving. Where myrtle grows wild, or branch trimmings are collected after pruning, they can be burnt in a barbecue to give fragrance to meat while cooking. A few of the gently resinous flowers can be strewn over green salads or fruit salads, or used as a garnish for desserts. The dried fruit when ground makes a peppery seasoning with an interesting aroma.

Medicinal

A decoction is made from the leaves by some herbalists, for application to external bruises.

Cosmetic

Myrtle has been valued since before Biblical times. Dried, powdered leaves made a dusting powder for babies in the Orient. The Greeks and Romans chewed myrtle berries to freshen the breath.

Cupid, the Roman God of love, son of Venus. Myrtle has always had a symbolic link with love, and has the reputation of being an aphrodisiac.

Cress

Cress, Water:
(Nasturtium officinale) Cruciferae.
Perennial.
Cress, Land: *(Lepidium sativatum) Cruciferae.*
Annual.

PROPAGATION:
seeds. Spring, Autumn (Fall).

POSITION:
semi-shade.

SOIL:
loamy for all cresses. Water cress in watery conditions.

HEIGHT:
water cress: 1½ feet (45 cm); land cress: 6 inches (15 cm).

PART USED:
leaves.

Description

Cress is native to Europe and parts of Asia. We have mentioned several types of cresses, because it is often believed that the only one that grows is water cress, and then only in a stream. However, it can be grown successfully in soil, as long as it is kept damp and shady. All cresses have a peppery flavor.

Water cress has a creeping habit, the stalks are sappy and hollow, the small leaves are almost round, and the tiny flowers are white.

Land cress has three types, all of which can be grown in the garden or on sprouting trays, and which we can recommend. Their popular names are curled cress, American upland cress, and French cress. They are all annuals. Curled cress, when growing, looks like a fleshy-leaved parsley. The leaves are light green and the flavor is hot and sharp. American upland cress has jaggedly cut green leaves which grow from the center of the plant in thick, round layers. The flavor of this cress is typically hot. French cress differs again in appearance. The leaves are pale green with a ruffled edge and their texture is fine. This cress grows in small clumps.

Arabis caucasuca is a cress belonging to the same *Cruciferae* family as the other cresses described here. It is similar to watercress in appearance and flavor, the leaves being larger and closer together on the stem. This herb is used fresh and green in Iran, Iraq, and the Gulf States as a salad herb. In Arabic its name is "barbeen," in Iranian, "shahat."

History and mythology

Water cress is described in an early AngloSaxon herbal as being one of nine sacred herbs included in a chant sung by magicians to repel evil, especially the "loathed flying venom". The song is thought originally to have been a heathen lay of great antiquity. The name for water cress was "stime".

Cultivation

Water cress needs water as well as soil for growing. The water must not be stagnant, so if there is no running stream nearby, try a shallow trough for water cress. Start by sowing seeds in a prepared box in spring or autumn (fall). When the seedlings are big enough, transfer them to the trough, which is half filled with loamy soil. Place the trough under a tap in semi-shade, and as the seedlings grow, gradually fill the trough with water, tipping it away carefully about once a week and refilling with water. The more cress is cut, the

TOP: *American upland cress.*
BOTTOM: *Water cress.*

more it will branch. In summer, close cutting will prevent flowering.

The land cresses are all cultivated in the same way. Sow the seed in shallow furrows straight into the garden in prepared soil, cover, and water well. As germination is rapid, the plants are ready for picking within a short time. Curled cress can be sown repeatedly throughout the year. Where winters are severe, do not sow once the frost starts. Water the plants in dry weather and if the soil is poor, dig in a little fertilizer from time to time. The best position is in semi-shade, although plants will grow in full sun if they are kept watered. There are commercial packages now on the market containing seeds and trays, which are excellent for growing cress indoors. When grown without soil, the cress is ready for cutting before it matures into a fully grown plant. The type of cress used is the choice of the manufacturer and is usually accompanied by mustard, its traditional companion.

Harvesting and processing

Cress is a difficult herb to dry for culinary use as its main contribution to a dish is its fresh flavor and appearance. For herb teas, water cress leaves may be dried on an airy rack, and when crisp, crumbled into airtight containers. Cress may be chopped finely, mixed with a little water and deep frozen in ice cube trays for use in flavoring soups and stews when added at the end of cooking time. Sprigs of cress may be wrapped in foil, sealed, and kept in the deep freeze for some weeks.

VARIOUS USES

Culinary

Cress leaves are invaluable in salads. They are excellent for garnishing. Cress sandwiches are delicious. Cress soup has an unusual and excellent flavor as well as being healthful. If you have enough cress, use it instead of spinach in a quiche.

Watercress is cultivated in southern China where it is known as "yeung choy". It is used in salads in Thailand, Laos and Vietnam. It is used as a garnish in Japan, and is known in India as "chamsur".

Medicinal

All cresses are rich in vitamins and minerals and contain sulfur, iron, iodine, and phosphorous. They are a natural blood purifier and are said to clear the complexion and brighten the eyes. Cress soup or "pottage" according to Dr Culpeper was: "A good remedy to cleanse the blood in the spring, and helps head-aches . . ."

Cosmetic

As mentioned, cresses abound in vitamins and trace elements which are essential for maintaining a healthy body. If taken regularly in the form of tea, soup, or raw in salads, they clear the complexion, bring a sparkle to the eyes, and help to prevent hair from falling out.

American upland cress has serrated leaves and small yellow flowers. The flavor is distinctively hot.

Water cress grows naturally in flowing water, but it can also be successfully raised in a trough if kept in semi-shade and regularly given plenty of water.

Lotus

Nelumbo nuciferum
Nelumbonaceae also
known as *bua luang*
(Thailand) *leen ngau*
(China) *nadru* (India)
renkon (Japan)

PROPAGATION:
rhizome division

POSITION:
open expanses of water

HEIGHT:
*3–4¹/2 feet (1–1.5 m)
above water surface*

PART USED:
*roots, leaves, petals,
seeds*

Lotus seeds.

ॐ

The lotus flower is a Buddhist
symbol.

ॐ

History and Mythology

The lotus flower has long been associated with the cultures of China, India, and Egypt. It is one of the important flowers of Chinese culture, bringing mental associations of cool summer mornings, where red-and-white tipped blossoms stretch for half a mile, their perfume sweetly scenting the air. The Sung scholar Chou wrote an essay explaining why he loved the lotus, pointing out that the lotus, like the gentleman, might grow out of dirty water but was not contaminated by it. The lotus flower is seen as a symbol of Buddhism, and is frequently found in the Hindu and Moghul architecture of India. Lotus flowers and leaves can be seen in paintings and carvings of ancient Egypt, although the lotus no longer grows there in modern times. Puréed and sweetened lotus seeds are used in Chinese "moon cakes" eaten during the festival in the middle of autumn (fall).

Description

This aquatic herb grows to 3–4¹/2 feet (1.5 m) high, with a long, bulbous series of rhizomes. The round, bluish-green leaves, up to 2 feet (60 cm) in diameter, have a waxy upper surface. Tight, pear-shaped buds open to reveal beautiful petals of pink, white or yellow. The flowers stand above the surface of the water, and are 3–5 inches (8–12 cm) in diameter.

VARIOUS USES

Culinary

In China, every part of the lotus flower is utilized. A cooling drink is made from the root, food is wrapped in the broad green leaves for steaming, the flowers are enjoyed for their fragrance, and the seed eaten raw, fresh from the pod, or dried and sugared. The Thais eat the young leaves with a coconut milk and fermented soybean sauce. The petals are eaten either raw or cooked with nam prik (shrimp sauce), and the seeds are used in both sweet and savory dishes such as sweet lotus seeds in syrup, which is served with coconut milk and rice.

Lotus root is a popular vegetable in Japan and Thailand, and the seeds are an ingredient in Chinese "eight treasure" dishes. The bitter core of the seed is removed before cooking.

Medicinal

The leaf and flower stems are used as a treatment for diarrhea in Southeast Asia, and the stamens are diuretic. Lotus seeds are used as a restorative tonic.

Some waterlilies of the Nymphaea genus are also edible. These nymphaeae are in Claude Monet's garden at Giverny, France.

Lotus root powder, used in Eastern spice mixtures.

Basil

Description

There are different types of basil plants with varying scents, flavors, and leaf coloration. Just a few are mentioned here. One kind has foliage with a distinct aroma of camphor, which is interesting, but does not encourage one to eat it. Another type we have grown has reddish stalks and coarse, shiny, green leaves which have a typical basil aroma and could be used for flavoring soups. But the leaves are too tough to be palatable when eaten raw. There is also an ornamental, colorful variety of sweet basil, with rich, purple leaves and pale pink flowers. It is an attractive garden plant and is highly perfumed. However, the actual taste is rank and is not recommended for cooking purposes. The old favorites, sweet basil and bush basil are still the best varieties to grow for the kitchen. The tender foliage of both these basils is bright green, with a spicy, clove-like aroma. Sweet basil leaves have a stronger perfume than the leaves of bush basil, which are also much smaller. Both varieties have small, white, lipped flowers in the autumn (fall).

With a similar growing habit to other basils, hairy basil (*Ocimum canum sims*) has slender oval-shaped leaves with some deep serrations on the edges. The flower spikes are white. It is used in the cuisine of Thailand where it is called "maeng lak."

History and mythology

Basil originated in India, where it was regarded as a sacred herb. It was also known in ancient Egypt, Greece, and Rome and there are many different legends concerning it. The unique and pronounced fragrance it releases into the surrounding atmosphere must have caused much speculation as to the plant's attributes among the wise ancients, who were close to the elemental world. Basil's botanical name of *basilicum* has kingly associations. One early writer said that the smell was so excellent, that it was "fit for a king's house." On the other hand, some say that the

In this traditional-style garden, sweet basil makes an attractive border around flagstones and a sundial.

BASIL

NEVER GIVE BASIL
AS A GIFT TO
A LOVED ONE,
SINCE SYMBOLICALLY
IT IS TAKEN
TO MEAN "HATRED."

name was derived from *basilisk*, a mythical serpent-like creature that could kill with a look, and for many years the plant was linked with poison and "venomous beasts." At the same time an application of the herb was prescribed to draw out the poison from stings and bites.

Cultivation

As basil must have warm conditions, early spring sowing is not advised. For best results, sow the seed at the end of spring, or at the beginning of summer. Both basils are susceptible to cold weather and are very frost-tender too. A cold change will kill the plants, even though there may be no frost. Sow the seed directly into the ground in shallow drills. If the soil is sour, lime it well two weeks before planting, making sure that the bed is well broken up and as fine as possible. If the soil is heavy, a small quantity of river sand will help to make the ground more suitable, both for sowing and drainage. When sweet basil is 3 inches (8 cm) high, thin out to 12 inches (30 cm) between plants. For bush basil, a distance of 6 inches (15cm) between seedlings is sufficient. As the plants grow, it is important to pinch out the centres to ensure a spreading, bushy habit. Bush basil is a very suitable plant for growing in pots, as it is so compact. A 7 inch (18 cm) pot is an excellent size for this. Fill the container with potting soil, and sow three to four seeds in it. Water them well and keep them moist to ensure germination and satisfactory growth. When the seedlings are 3 inches (8 cm) high, choose the sturdiest looking one to leave in the pot, then prick out the rest, which may be planted into other containers or into the open ground. Remember that basil (or any other herb) will not grow as a houseplant; a sunny terrace, or a

Many Hindu homes have a pot of holy basil growing by the front door.

Sweet basil is a popular culinary herb and is included in a number of dishes, including pasta.

Bush basil has a spicy, clove-like aroma.

window sill where there is sunshine and fresh air, is the ideal position. Hairy basil is happiest in tropical conditions, so it must grow in a sunny position, sheltered from cold winds.

Harvesting and processing

It is necessary to harvest basil in the early autumn (fall) before the cold weather turns the leaves limp and yellow. (In hot climates, basil grows throughout the year, and under these conditions, the seeds will often self-sow). For fullest flavor, cut long, leafy stalks for drying just before the plant comes into flower, spreading them out in a shady place on wire mesh to encourage quick drying. Do not hang them in bunches, as the soft foliage will then dry too slowly and may possibly spoil. Oven drying is not satisfactory, as the leaves, which bruise easily, are liable to scorch. Fresh basil leaves may be chopped finely, mixed with a little water and frozen in ice cube trays to be used when needed. Basil, together with pine nuts, garlic, oil, and Parmesan cheese may be made into *pesto* (a Mediterranean sauce) and frozen. Basil butter (chopped basil leaves pounded into butter then cut into squares when cold) may also be satisfactorily frozen in sealed polythene bags.

VARIOUS USES

Culinary

Basil's mouth-watering aroma makes it a versatile herb to use in many different types of food. It has a special affinity with tomatoes, and tomato-based dishes and is excellent with eggplant, zucchini, marrow, squash, and spinach. Added during the last half hour of cooking, it gives zest to pea soup and lentil soup. It is delicious with cream cheese in sandwiches, gives a lift to green salads and sliced cucumbers and is excellent in all pasta dishes. As mentioned above, it is the main ingredient in *pesto*, for which there are varying recipes (one of which is given on page 249), but all contain basil, which is essential to its character. Basil also goes well with poultry, veal, liver, kidneys, fish, and shellfish and makes a savory vinegar when the leaves are steeped in it for a few weeks.

Sweet basil is an important ingredient in Thai, Laotian, and Vietnamese cooking. In Thailand, sweet basil is known as "bai horapa" and is used in curries, and salads. The leaves are eaten raw with vermicelli, chopped and served as a garnish on fish curries, or included in clear vegetable soup. The seeds are sometimes used as an aid to slimming, as they swell when mixed with liquid.

In Indonesia and Thailand the seeds of sweet basil are soaked in water until they become thick and gelatinous, and are then included in cooling, sweet drinks. There is no distinctive basil flavor in the seeds, but they are believed to aid the digestion.

Note that the herb referred to as Japanese basil is in fact shiso (see page 127), and is not related to European basil.

Cinnamon basil.

The leaves of bush basil are smaller than those of sweet basil and its fragrance is less strong .

Medicinal

Basil's old connection with poison has been interpreted by one modern herbalist as an antidote to much that is not wholesome in today's food. Basil has long been a herbal remedy for diseases of the brain, heart, lungs, and kidneys and bladder. It is often mixed with borage to make a healthful, palatable, tonic tea to revive lowered vitality. The dried leaves have been made into snuff as a remedy for headaches and colds.

Lemon-scented basil, which also has a warm aniseed aroma and a pretty mauve-pink flower, is the "Tulasi" or "Holy Basil" of India. Many a Hindu home has a pot of this basil growing by the front door. We are told by a Hindu friend that besides being used in various foods, it has a medicinal value as well. An infusion of lemon basil leaves is taken to alleviate the symptoms of diabetes.

The leaves of hairy basil are considered beneficial to nursing mothers, as well as having carminative and anti-asthmatic properties. The seeds have been credited with the contradictory qualities of being both laxative and a cure for dysentry!

Cosmetic

Basil leaves have been preserved by an old method which directs that alternate layers of fresh leaves, coarse sea salt, and vegetable oil be put in a preserving jar and sealed. Later the aromatic mixture is strained and the resulting fragrant oil used as a toning body rub. An infusion of basil in wine is sometimes used on the skin to close enlarged pores.

Camphor basil.

Companion planting

Basil plants help to enliven and stimulate vegetables growing in the garden, especially tomatoes. After close observation by an eminent gardener of our acquaintance, it was noted that basil also helped to repel white fly, which is troublesome to tomatoes. It is said that basil and rue do not grow well near each other.

Marjoram & Oregano

Marjoram:
  *(Origanum majorana)
  Labiatae.
  Perennial.*
Oregano: *(O. vulgare)
  Labiatae.
  Perennial.*

PROPAGATION:
  seeds, cuttings. Spring.

POSITION:
  sunny.

SOIL:
  average, well drained.

HEIGHT:
  *marjoram: 1½ feet
  (45 cm);
  oregano: 2 feet (60 cm).*

PART USED:
  leaves.

Description

These two herbs are so closely related, and their cultivation is so similar, that it is not necessary to classify them in separate sections. However, in appearance they are slightly different. Marjoram leaves are small, soft, and gray-green, while oregano leaves are light green and are much firmer. Their growing habit is also different. Marjoram is a compact, upright, shrubby plant while oregano has a dense, spreading habit. The flowers of both these herbs are small and white and form tight clusters at the tips of their stems. The herb we know as oregano is a wild form of marjoram. It is more robust, coarser in texture and stronger in flavor than its gentler cousin, the sweet marjoram of our herb gardens. There are variations of both oregano and marjoram, which are all easy to identify as their scent and leaf texture are characteristic of each strain. Oregano is always more piercing in scent, although the leaves of other forms may vary in size and the flowers in color. The marjoram described here has white, tufted flowers on long stems. There is another quite common kind known as knotted marjoram with tiny, white flowers bursting out from tight green "knots." The aromas are the same.

History and mythology

Botanically, these herbs are all *origanums.* Scholars tell us they first grew in the Mediterranean regions and were also widely distributed in parts of Asia and North Africa. Marjoram was one of the strewing herbs once used to give houses a pleasant, clean smell and it was a favorite in

RIGHT: Marjoram

sweet bags for the linen cupboard. John Gerard, the 16th-century herbalist, mentions it as "marvellous sweet" and "aromaticall." Another old herbalist says that to smell marjoram frequently keeps a person in good health.

Cultivation

To propagate these plants by cuttings, take new shoots about 3 inches (8 cm) long in late spring, when the young leaves have firmed enough not to wilt when placed in a pot of coarse river sand. When well rooted, they can be planted out in pots, or put straight into the ground, leaving at least 12 inches (30 cm) between them. When growing from seeds, sow them in a prepared seed box in spring and plant them out when the seedlings are 3 inches (8 cm) high. Both have a tendency to become woody as they get older, so to delay this as long as possible, it is advisable to cut out the old wood at the end of winter before the new spring growth appears. After approximately four years, the plants often become so woody that it is best to replace them.

MARJORAM, OREGANO

CUT THE OLD WOODY GROWTH FROM BOTH THESE PLANTS AT THE END OF WINTER, TO PROMOTE NEW SPRING GROWTH.

Harvesting and processing

Both marjoram and oregano should be harvested just before the plants are in full flower in the summer or early autumn (fall). Cut the long stems, together with any flowerheads, and hang them in bunches in a cool, airy place. The leaves tend to fall as they dry, so it is a good idea to enclose the bunches in mosquito net or muslin. When the leaves and flowers are crisp-dry they are very easily stripped by running the thumb and forefinger down the stems. When stored in airtight containers they will stay fresh for many months, and for pungency and flavor they will be almost equal to, and sometimes better than, the fresh leaves. For freezing, chop fresh leaves finely, mix them with a little water, and put them into ice cube trays in the freezer. Sprays of fresh marjoram or oregano may be wrapped in foil, sealed and kept in the deep freeze for some weeks. Marjoram or oregano butter may also be frozen. Chop the fresh leaves, pound them into softened butter, allow it to set in the refrigerator, then cut it into squares and seal into small polythene bags or other suitable containers.

A healthy bed of oregano.

MARJORAM, OREGANO

BOTH HERBS WILL
KEEP THEIR PUNGENT
FLAVOR FOR MANY
MONTHS IN AIRTIGHT
JARS IF THOROUGHLY
DRIED BEFOREHAND.

VARIOUS USES

Culinary

The Greeks call wild marjoram or oregano *rigani*, and in Greece, as in Italy, it is the very pungent dried flower tops which are mainly used in cooking. Marjoram, of course, is a classic ingredient in traditional mixed herbs, together with thyme and sage. Marjoram's subtle aroma makes it an ideal addition to many herb mixtures as it helps give "body" and depth without being too dominant. On its own, it goes with poultry, fish, egg dishes, vegetable dishes, and sauces. Put it into salads, scones, dumplings, and clear soups.

Oregano's pungency is even stronger when dried and this herb is a popular ingredient in the tasty regional dishes of many countries. It is used in pasta and rice dishes, in pizzas, moussaka, avocado dip, tomato dishes, meat loaf, rissoles, sauces, and dressings, and with zucchini, sweet peppers (capsicums), and eggplant. It is often sprinkled on beef, lamb, and pork before cooking.

Oregano is one of the most widely used herbs in its native country, Greece, where it goes into many dishes. It is known there as "rigani." In Morocco marjoram, "mrdeddouche," is an ingredient in kofta (meatballs), and berbbouche or boubbouche, a snail dish. This herb is valued for the teas that can be used to promote sleep, to ease depression, and to promote perspiration.

At least two different kinds of plants are known as Mexican oregano: they are *Poliomentha longiflora* and *Lippia graveolens*. Neither is a true oregano, although *P. longiflora* belongs to the *Labiatae* family. Mexican oregano is essential in pozole, a pork and hominy stew.

This marjoram plant is just coming into flower. When the blooms appear, they are in tight clusters. The flowerheads together with the leaves are used in cooking.

Oregano is closely related to marjoram, but has a coarser texture and a stronger flavor.

Medicinal

Greek physicians used marjoram or oregano extensively, both internally and externally. The cosmic warmth it has accumulated from the sun helps put right bad colds, cramps, and digestive disorders. Hot fomentations of the dried leaves and tops applied in bags is helpful to painful swellings, rheumatism, and colic. An infusion of the leaves taken as a tea relieves nervous headaches, induces sleep, stimulates excretion, and is recommended as a spring tea.

Cosmetic

Marjoram, like sage, will help darken hair for brunettes, and for this purpose may be made into lotions or rubs for the head, or for a beard. Marjoram sprigs tied into a bath bag are refreshing. Dried marjoram leaves are a fragrant addition to a sleep pillow blend and to a potpourri mixture.

Companion planting

Marjoram and oregano, by their fragrant presence in the garden, are a good influence on other plants and when they are in flower they are a strong attraction to honey bees. It is said that marjoram has been fed to cows to prevent abortion. After calving, marjoram mixed with balm and made into a tea is given to cows to soothe and strengthen them. Marjoram's content of essential oil increases if stinging nettle is growing nearby as a companion plant.

OREGANO

THIS HERB IS STILL ONE OF THE MOST WIDELY USED IN ITS COUNTRY OF ORIGIN, GREECE, WHERE IT IS KNOWN AS "RIGANI."

Pandan Leaf

(Pandanus amaryllifolius)
Perennial

POSITION:
part sun

SOIL:
medium, moist

HEIGHT:
to 26 feet (8 m)

PART USED:
leaves, male flower

Description

These leaves are from the fragrant screwpine tree, called "toei hom" in Thailand. The screwpine tree has stiff branches supported on stilt-like masses of aerial roots. The sharp-edged leaves are spirally arranged, and the small, decorative and fragrant white flowers are followed by large fruit heads 8 inches (20 cm) in diameter, looking rather like green pineapples. Besides *Pandanus amaryllifolius* there are other varieties; variegated screwpine (*P. veitchii*), and the walking stick palm, or kewra, (*P. odoratissimus*).

History and mythology

Pandans are found in Madagascar, and throughout Southeast Asia, the Pacific Islands and tropical Australia. In older times, the tough, fibrous leaves were used for house thatching, and were woven into sails, clothing, floor mats, and baskets. The grass skirts worn by Pacific Island women were often made of split, bleached pandan leaves.

Cultivation

Grow the screwpine tree in warm, damp areas in part sun. The soil should be medium quality, and moist.

Harvesting and processing

The long flat leaves are collected and either crushed or boiled to extract the flavor and color. The leaves are air-dried and finely chopped for use in curries. Dried pandan leaf is sold in some shops as

In Malaysia and Indonesia, the flavor of pandan is as popular as vanilla in Western countries.

"rampé" (Sri Lanka), and as "daun pandan" (Malaysia and Indonesia). Store in a cool, dark place to retain color and flavor.

VARIOUS USES

Culinary

The flavor of pandan in Malaysia and Indonesia is as popular as vanilla is in Western countries. It is used to make the grass-green pandan cake, a favorite Asian sponge, usually topped with a green jelly-like icing, and may flavor rice and curries. Strips of pandan leaves are woven into artistic baskets for serving glutinous rice or savories. The male flower cluster of the pandan has a strong perfume that is used sparingly in Indian sweets, and may be bought as an essence or concentrate. On festive occasions, essences of rose and pandan are used to flavor the delicious spicy rice dish, biryani.

Medicinal

The whole plant is diuretic. The roots are anti-diabetic, and leaves can be used for treating skin diseases.

Cosmetic

An ingredient in perfume.

The fragrant screwpine tree is supported on stilt-like masses of aerial roots.

Shiso

Description

Shiso or "shiso-no-ha" is a leafy plant much used in Japan (hence the inaccurate name, "Japanese basil"), where two main types, green "ao-jiso," and red "aka-jiso," have different uses in cooking. The leaves are almost round, but with a sharply pointed end which creates a heart shape, and crisply cut serrations around the edges.

History and mythology

The plant is a native of Burma, China, and the northern regions of India, particularly the Himalayan mountains, but it has been cultivated in Japan for centuries and is now rarely used in its countries of origin.

(*Perilla*)
Perennial

PROPAGATION:
root division, cuttings. Spring

POSITION:
semi-shade

SOIL:
medium-rich, moist

PART USED:
leaves

Umeboshi, or pickled plums. Shiso is used to process this Japanese delicacy.

Cultivation

Like members of the mint family, shiso likes to grow in semi-shade in medium-rich moist soil. Propagate the plant by root division, or take cuttings in spring.

Harvesting and processing

Pick the spearmint-flavoured leaves and use them fresh. The foliage may be dried in several different ways. Cut the leafy stalks and hang them in a warm airy place until dry; spread them on airy racks until crisp; or dry in a microwave oven, (page 193). Store the leaves in airtight containers.

VARIOUS USES

Culinary

Occasionally fresh shiso leaves are available in highly specialized Japanese food shops, but you are more likely to find the salted and pickled varieties.

Use the fresh leaves, either whole or chopped, for garnishing. The leaves are battered and fried as a vegetable in tempura and are used in sushi. The attractive seed pod stems, when in flower, are also used by themselves as a garnish. The red leaves of aka-jiso, available only in midsummer in Japan, are employed in the processing of "umeboshi", the pickled sour plum so popular in Japan. They are also pickled in their own right, and are served as an accompaniment to rice. The red color of the leaves has earned the herb the additional name "beefsteak plant."

SHISO

COOKS OUTSIDE JAPAN ARE MORE LIKELY TO FIND THE SALTED AND PICKLED VARIETIES OF SHISO THAN THE FRESH LEAVES.

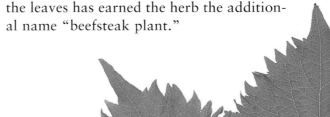

Parsley

Description

Curled parsley, as the name suggests, has tightly curled leaves of bright green. Some kinds may be more crinkled and tightly curled than others, for instance the triple-curled and moss-curled varieties. *P. crispum* is the variety of curled parsley that people usually refer to as parsley, and is the most widely used.

Italian parsley, which is not so familiar, has leaves which are not curled, but are deeply cut and serrated like the tops of celery or lovage, the flavor being regarded by many as stronger than curled parsley. However, curled parsley is preferred for garnishing because of its more decorative leaves. There is another variety called Hamburg parsley which has a long white root like a parsnip and is mainly grown for these roots which can be cooked and eaten as a vegetable.

History and mythology

It is widely believed that parsley originated in Sardinia, although an early writer says that parsley has the "curious botanic history that no one can tell what is its native country. Probably the plant has been so altered by cultivation as to have lost all likeness to its original self." It occurs in mythology, and was believed to have sprung from the blood of a Greek hero, Arche-morous, the forerunner of death. The Greeks crowned the winners at the Isthmian games with parsley chaplets and warriors fed their chariot horses with the leaves. Grecian gardens were often bordered with parsley.

Cultivation

To propagate parsley, sow seed in spring and also in autumn (fall) in temperate climates, in finely dug soil, in drills 12 inches (30 cm) apart,

---

Parsley, Curled:
(Petroselinum crispum)
Umbelliferae.
Biennial.
Parsley, Italian:
(P. crispum neapolitanum)
Umbelliferae.
Biennial.

PROPAGATION:
seeds. Spring (again in Autumn (Fall) in temperate climates).

POSITION:
sunny.

SOIL:
average, well drained.

HEIGHT:
curled parsley: 10 inches (25 cm); Italian parsley: 1 1/2 feet (45 cm).

PART USED:
leaves, root (sometimes).

LEFT: *Curled parsley*
RIGHT: *Italian parsley*

Although parsley is mainly thought of as an eating herb, it is most decorative when growing in the garden.

Parsley is such a versatile herb that no kitchen garden is complete without it. Lack of space is no problem as it can be grown successfully in tubs.

where the plants are to grow, thinning out later to approximately 3 inches (8 cm) between plants. Curled parsley is the most difficult type to grow, the seeds sometimes taking two weeks to germinate, during which time the bed *must never* be allowed to dry out, or the seeds will cease germinating. If this has occurred, further watering is of no use, the seeds must be resown, and more care taken. Covering them with up to 1/2 inch (12 mm) of soil will help retain moisture in the ground for a longer period. Italian parsley is much easier to grow. Three to four days after sowing, the seeds will usually germinate, provided that they are very lightly covered with soil to not more than 1/4 inch (6 mm) in depth, and kept moist. As parsley is a biennial, to keep it from going to seed during the first year, cut the long flower stalks as they appear. However, the second year's growth is never as good. We prefer to sow seed each year to ensure strong and healthy plants.

Harvesting and processing

Parsley can be cut for drying at any time. It will keep its green color and flavor if dried quickly in a warm oven preheated to 250°F (120°C). After turning the oven off, spread out the parsley heads, which have been snipped from the stalks, on a large tray or baking dish, and leave in the oven for 15 minutes, turning several times until crisp-dry. Store them in airtight containers away from the light. For freezing, chop fresh leaves finely, mix with a little water, and put them into ice cube trays in the freezer. Sprays of fresh parsley may be wrapped in foil and frozen. Parsley butter freezes well too.

VARIOUS USES

Culinary

Parsley's taste could be described as fresh and crisp and perhaps a little earthy. It is also unassertive which makes it complementary to other herbs in mixtures. For instance it is one of four in a "fines herbes" blend, the others being chervil, chives, and tarragon. A spray of parsley, together with a bay leaf and a spray each of thyme and marjoram, comprises a bouquet garni. Parsley leaves, whether freshly chopped or dried, go into sauces, omelets, scrambled eggs, mashed potatoes, mornays, salads, soups, pasta dishes, and vegetable dishes and with poultry and fish. The fresh curly sprays are used for garnishing and when crisp-fried make a delicious accompaniment for fish. Nourishing parsley jelly is made from the fresh leaves. Parsley tea is made from either the fresh or dried leaves.

The Italian flat-leaf parsley is the kind most used in Middle Eastern and Mediterranean food. It is preferred because it has more flavor, and the prolific large clumps go further than the smaller clumps of curled parsley. Finely chopped stalks are used as well as the leaves. Parsley is the main ingredient in a healthy and delicious salad, tabouleh, which also includes fresh mint with the other ingredients. The Arabic name for parsley is "bakdounis," in Armenian it is "azadkeg," in Greek "maidano," in Iranian "jafari," and in Turkish "maydanoz." In Morocco is is called "manouss" and in Egypt "bakdounis."

Italian flat-leaf parsley is also the most widely used type of parsley in Morocco, and is most frequently combined with coriander. Parsley goes into a typically Moroccan main dish called tagine, a type of stew also prepared in Algeria and Tunisia. Parsley is an ingredient in chermoula, a marinade of herbs, oil, spices and lemon juice. The chermoula is used with meat or fish. *P. crispum neapolitanum* is known as "perejil" in Mexico, where it is a popular herb.

Medicinal

All parts of the plant, roots, stems, leaves, and seeds, are useful and beneficial. The roots were once boiled and eaten as a vegetable, particularly the large Hamburg variety. The stalks of Italian parsley have been blanched and eaten like celery. The foliage of all varieties is rich in iron and in vitamins including A, B, and C, and the culinary value is well known. An oil called apiol, which is extracted from the seeds, has medicinal properties. Although nowadays the seeds are not normally used for culinary

A stone trough (above) or this unusual Apostle jar (below) look most attractive when used as a container for parsley grown by itself or with other herbs.

PARSLEY

ARGUABLY THE BEST
KNOWN AND MOST
WIDELY USED HERB IN
THE WORLD, PARSLEY
ALSO FEATURES AS A
VEGETABLE IN SOME
TRADITIONAL DISHES.

purposes, there is a story that the ninth-century Emperor, Charlemagne, after having tasted a cheese flavored with parsley seeds, ordered two cases of these cheeses to be sent to him yearly. Parsley tea made from leaves or root assists kidneys, digestion, and circulation.

Cosmetic

Parsley has been included in rubbing lotions for the scalp and hair before shampooing, and to make dark hair shiny. Parsley is also used in herbal lotions for closing large pores and as a freshener for the skin and to reduce puffiness around the eyes.

Companion planting

Parsley is helpful to roses in the garden, a low border of curly parsley plants being attractive and beneficial at the same time. Parsley also aids tomatoes. Honey bees are attracted to parsley when it is in bloom.

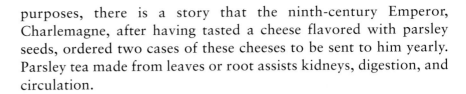

(Pimpinella anisum)
Umbelliferae.
Annual.

PROPAGATION:
   seed. Spring (and again
   in Autumn – Fall –
   in temperate climates).

POSITION:
   sheltered, sunny.

SOIL:
   light, well drained.

HEIGHT:
   1¹/2–2 feet
   (45cm–60cm).

PART USED:
   seeds, foliage sometimes.

Description

Anise has feathery leaves and flat, white flowerheads which bloom in late summer. Aromatic, small brown seeds or fruit follow with a strong licorice taste, most of them having a distinguishing fine hair at one end. The seed is the most useful part of the plant.

History and mythology

Anise is native to the Middle East and was known in ancient Egypt. Its usefulness as a fragrant and health-giving herb spread to Greece and Rome and then to many other countries. The Romans discovered that the seeds of anise and other aromatic spices helped the digestion after large banquets, so these spices were incorporated into a special cake which was served at the end of a large meal, such as a marriage feast. This is said to be the origin of today's spicy wedding cake. Aniseed was grown by the monks in monastery gardens during the Middle Ages, for use as a tea.

Cultivation

Because of its spindly nature, this herb needs protection from prevailing winds and, at the same time, plenty of sunshine to promote healthy growth. The seedlings are soft and fragile and do not transplant well, so it is best to sow directly into the ground. Make sure that the soil is well broken up and in fine seed bed condition, adding a little lime if the ground is very acid. Unless the soil is extremely poor, fertilizer is not necessary. Sow the seeds in spring, and again in autumn (fall) in temperate zones, in ½ inch (12 mm) deep drills 12 inches (30 cm) apart. Cover and pack the soil down well, then keep moist until the seedlings appear. Water regularly in hot, dry weather, preferably in the late afternoon or evening, so as not to scorch the plants.

Harvesting and processing

Harvesting the fruit when it is ripe is simple. After the flower-umbels have become heavy with full, brown seeds, cut the heads off before they drop. Store them in cardboard boxes, or on sheets of paper in a dry place, exposing them to direct sunlight when possible, to completely dry out any moisture.

Sun-drying is not good for herb leaves, but is helpful in the drying of seedheads. When they are crisp and dry, rub the seeds between the palms of the hands. The husks and old flowerheads are easily removed by sifting the seeds through a sieve. Store them in labeled and dated airtight containers. For culinary, medicinal, or cosmetic use, the seed will last for many years. But for propagating, germination will be more successful if the seeds are sown the following season.

Culinary

Warmly licorice-tasting aniseed, whether whole or ground, flavors and helps to digest many different types of food, such as breads, pasta, cakes, and biscuits, as well as stewed or baked apples and pears. For the same reason, it is used with some vegetables which can be indigestible, such as cabbages, onions, cucumbers, carrots, turnips, and beetroot. It is used, too, in some rich cheese dishes. The leaves of anise are sometimes used in food — they give a piquant touch to salads. They may also be added to broths and soups while cooking.

Anise is known in Morocco as "habbet-hlawa." It is used in Moroccan cooking because it is believed to aid digestion, and cuts the heavy, greasy effect of some foods.

Piper sanctum, called "hierba santa" or "hoya santa" in Mexico, is a large soft-leaved herb with a strong anise flavor, and is much prized in Oaxaca, Chiapas, Tabasco and Veracruz.

Also in the region of Oaxaca, cooks obtain a slight anise flavor by incorporating avocado leaves into their cooking. The leaves are toasted and crumbled and used like a spice to season that region's famous black bean tamales. The same flavour can be simulated by mixing deveined and crumbled bay leaf with one or two seeds of anise.

ANISE

SOW SEED DIRECTLY
INTO POSITION.
MAKE SURE SEEDLINGS
WILL GET PLENTY
OF SUN AND PROTECT
THE SPINDLY PLANTS
FROM WIND.

The early leaves of anise cuttings are rounded, while those that develop later are fronded.

ANISE FLAVOR

THIS POPULAR AROMA
IS OFTEN SOUGHT
FROM OTHER
COMBINATIONS SUCH
AS AVOCADO LEAVES,
WHERE ANISE IS
NOT AVAILABLE.

Medicinal

Aniseed not only works on the digestive system, but also helps respiratory ailments. The plant's volatile oil contains anethole, the substance which has such a beneficial effect on the digestion. Aniseed tea, taken regularly, is said to allay colds and influenza, relieve flatulence, brighten the eyes, and make the breath sweeter. Anise is used to flavor cough lozenges, some cordials, herb tea blends, and liqueurs, such as Anisette. A little powdered seed added to food for young children will help their digestion, and when some aniseed tea is mixed with warm milk and honey, it helps soothe a fretful child. It is wise to give these simple remedies in moderation to the very young This applies to all medicinal herbs, unless prescribed by a fully trained therapist. The full flavor of aniseed tea is brought out by crushing the seeds before putting them into the teapot. Allow them to draw a little longer than usual.

Cosmetic

The Romans used aniseed in perfumes, as did the Britons in the Middle Ages. Cooled aniseed tea gently sponged onto the face with cotton wool helps to lighten the skin. Anise oil is also a good, fragrant antiseptic and has been used as an ingredient in dentifrices.

Companion planting

The seed of anise will germinate more quickly and grow better if it is sown near coriander seed. It has been observed that the presence of coriander improves the actual seed formation of the anise plants.

N.B. there is another anise called star anise which comes from a tree, *Illicium anisatum*, that is indigenous to China. The oil from these seeds is the same in composition as the annual anise, and equally effective medicinally.

Polygonum

Description

Resembling spearmint, this herb has purplish stems with dark green, tapered smooth leaves growing sparsely along angled stems. It has a strong mint flavor, with overtones of basil. Long, slender flower stems are topped with dense clusters of tiny white or pink blossoms.

History and mythology

The common name of "knotweed" describes the swollen, jointed appearance of the stems of this herb. *Polygonum* literally means "many-kneed," referring to the many angles in the stem. There are over 200 species of *Polygonum*, some of them included in medical Pharmacopeias of Switzerland, France, and Russia since Renaissance times. An important spring food in Northern Europe from early times it was also called "bistort".

> *Polygonum sp*
> Perennial
>
> PROPAGATION:
> *division*
>
> POSITION:
> *sun to semi-shade*
>
> SOIL:
> *very moist*
>
> HEIGHT:
> *12–14 in (30–35 cm)*
>
> PART USED:
> *leaves*

VARIOUS USES

Culinary

Polygonum, sometimes referred to as Asian mint or Vietnamese mint, is popular in Malaysia for use in fish and noodle dishes and features in the characteristic Nonya cuisine. In Thailand the shoots and leaves are eaten raw with nam prik (shrimp sauce) or added to curries. It is known as "daun keson" in Indonesia and Malaysia, and "rau ram" in Vietnam.

Medicinal

The dried rhizome has astringent and anti-inflammatory uses. In Europe, an infusion from the rhizome has been used as a gargle for ulcers and gingevitis, and applied to cuts, sores and haemorrhoids.

There are more than 200 species of Polygonum, a herb which is particularly popular in Southeast Asian cuisines.

Polygonum grows to a maximum height of 12–14 in (30–35 cm).

Purslane (green)

(Portulaca oleracea)
  Portulaceae.
  Annual.

PROPAGATION:
  *seeds, successive sowing
  2–3 weeks apart, late
  Spring to early Autumn
  (Fall).*

POSITION:
  sunny.

SOIL:
  light, rich, well drained.

HEIGHT:
  1³/4 feet (50 cm).

PART USED:
  leaves, stems.

Description

Purslane belongs to the *Portulaca* genus and is a sappy herb. The juicy leaves are attached to short stems growing from a round, succulent, red stalk; the whole plant has a prostrate habit. Tiny yellow flowers cluster on the branches in mid-summer, opening only at noon. Each bloom is followed by a seed case. Purslane was once an important salad and pot herb, and its culinary uses have recently been rediscovered. The smooth small leaves have a refreshing lemony tang — a pleasant surprise to crunch on when eating a mixture of salad greens. Gardeners appreciate purslane's red stems and stalks for color in herbaceous borders, especially when grown together with the contrasting golden-leaved purslane, *P. sativa*. The latter is edible too, but is not as hardy as green purslane.

History and mythology

The *Portulaca* genus is distributed all over the world. Purslane is thought to be native to China, Japan, the East and West Indies, and parts of Europe. The cultivated green (or garden) purslane, *P. oleracea*, is said to have first been developed in the Middle East and, through ancient trade routes, found its way to other parts of the world, including Britain and parts of Australia, where it is now naturalized. I have seen it grow wild in our garden at Dural, in Australia. In the Middle Ages it was recommended as a cure against "blastings of lightenings of planets." It was said to be good for "teeth set on edge with eating of sharpe and sour things." It was believed to be an anti-magic herb, and a protection against evil spirits.

Cultivation

Purslane seed can be sown in late spring to early autumn (fall) in a sunny position. Prepare the ground by digging some compost, or rich loam, into light, well-drained soil. Make drills 7–10 inches (15–20 cm) apart and water well. If seedlings are watered in dry weather, purslane's leafy stems will be ready to pick in four to six weeks. Keep plants free of weeds. Gather purslane before the plant flowers, then after one or two pickings cut it back and it will shoot again. Successive seed sowing every two to three weeks is recommended so that new plants come on when the first ones have finished.

Harvesting and processing

Purslane is eaten fresh and does not dry well. Sometimes thick stems of old mature plants are sliced and pickled for the winter store cupboard. Gather 2–3 inches (5–7 cm) leafy stems as you need them for salads, then when becoming bare cut the plant low and after a short time it will produce a fresh crop of foliage. After doing this once more, the original plant will be depleted and new purslane, having been sown earlier, should be ready to pick.

VARIOUS USES

Culinary

Having tried purslane's leaves and young stems in salads, and sampling their fresh zest, they become an interesting ingredient to mix with other leafy greens. Purslane is the right herb to accompany rich food as the plant's astringent properties help cleanse the palate. Older shoots were traditionally cooked as a pot herb, and the pickled stems were put into winter salads. This herb is an ingredient in some soups, in particular the French soup *bonne femme*, and it is also an important ingredient in the Middle Eastern salad *fatoush*. Add a few leaves to broths and to spinach while cooking. Thinly sliced brown bread sandwiches with cream cheese and a few purslane leaves have a peppy taste.

Purslane is a popular salad ingredient in Syria and Lebanon, and goes into raw vegetable salads in Greece and Cyprus; this succulent herb also features in a typical Armenian cucumber and yogurt salad. Its Arabic names are "ba'le," "bakli" and "farfhin," in Armenian it is "perper," in Greek, "glystiritha."

Purslane is a salad and pot herb whose uses have been only lately rediscovered, especially for salads.

Medicinal

Historically, purslane had medicinal uses for many complaints, such as easing dry coughs, assisting the pain of gout, allaying excessive heat in the forehead and temples, and soothing sore mouths and gums. The 16th-century herbalist and writer John Gerard advised that purslane eaten in salads with oil and vinegar "cooled the blood and caused a good appetite." Today it is known that purslane contains calcium, iron, and phosphorus, another good reason for eating this herb.

Cosmetic

Herbal beauty experts say that healthful herbs work just as effectively on the inside as they do on the outside: they aid the working of bodily functions while also helping to clean the skin. Purslane leaves and buds are recommended for salad. Mix them with many other herbs including rocket, hyssop, broom buds, and grapevine tendrils for a delicious, interesting, and healthy salad.

Companion Planting

There is no evidence at present that purslane has a specific advantage for companion planting, but remember that growing as many herbs as possible is good for the vitality of the whole garden.

> # PURSLANE
>
> A 16TH-CENTURY HERBALIST SAID THAT PURSLANE "COOLED THE BLOOD AND CAUSED A GOOD APPETITE."

Rosemary

Rosemary, Upright:
(Rosmarinus officinalis) Labiatae.
Perennial,
Rosemary, Prostrate:
(R. prostratus) Labiatae.
Perennial.

PROPAGATION:
seeds, cuttings. Spring (Autumn (Fall) in mild climates). Layering also for Prostrate Rosemary.

POSITION:
open, sunny.

SOIL:
average, well drained.

HEIGHT:
upright rosemary: 5 feet (1 .5 m); prostrate rosemary: 12 inches (30 cm).

PART USED:
leaves.

Description

The blossoms and leaves of these two rosemarys are similar in appearance. Both have the same kind of delicate-blue flowers and long, narrow leaves which are dark green on top and silver-striped underneath. The leaves of upright rosemary grow to over 1 inch (25 mm) long, while those of the low-growing or prostrate rosemary are smaller and narrower. There are several other unusual kinds of rosemary which are not often seen, including a white-flowering variety, one with gold-edged leaves, and a double-flowering type. The growth habit of the two rosemarys mentioned here is entirely different. Upright rosemary has a stiff, bushy habit, making it an ideal subject for hedge-work, while prostrate rosemary is grown more for ornamental purposes, as a ground cover, or to hang decoratively over the edge of retaining walls. It is excellent in rockeries and also in tubs, where it will spill toward the ground in a most attractive way. One landscape gardener told us that she had planted a sweep of prostate rosemary on a sloping bank leading down to a swimming pool, where the blue of the flowers and the blue water seemed to reflect one another. Both varieties start blooming in the autumn (fall) and continue on through the winter until spring.

History and mythology

Rosemary is another aromatic plant which first grew in the warm countries of the Mediterranean region and it seems to be the upright variety which is referred to historically. It has great beneficial properties which are still highly respected today. Of the many legends about rosemary, there is a popular one telling how a rosemary bush will never grow taller than the height of Christ — 5–6 feet (1.5 –2 m) — when He was a man on earth, and that after 33 years the plant increases in breadth, but not in height. Some stories tell how

TOP: *Upright rosemary*
BOTTOM: *Prostrate rosemary*

rosemary was used to try to awaken the Sleeping Beauty. The Sicilians tell their children that young fairies taking the form of snakes lie amongst the branches of rosemary bushes.

Cultivation

To propagate upright rosemary, sow the seed in spring, or in autumn (fall) where the climate is mild, in a prepared seed box. Plant out when the seedlings are 3 inches (8 cm) high, leaving about 2 feet (60 cm) between plants. Six inch (15 cm) long tip cuttings may also be taken in late spring, when the soft spring growth has hardened. The prostrate variety can only be satisfactorily propagated by taking cuttings, using the same method as for upright rosemary, or by layering, which is done by pinning down a stem from the parent plant to the soil, using a piece of U-shaped wire and covering the stem with a little soil. When the layered branch has developed a good root system, cut it away from the parent bush and plant out in a sunny position.

Harvesting and processing

Rosemary can be used fresh at any time, the upright variety being the most suitable for culinary purposes as the flavor is better. For drying, cut the branches before the plant begins flowering (when the flavor is at its best), shaping the bush at the same time. Then hang in bunches in a shady, airy place. When dry, strip the leaves from the stalks, crumbling them into small pieces. When stored in airtight containers, the flavor will remain intact over a long period. For freezing, strip the leaves carefully from their woody stalks and chop finely. Mix with a little water and put them into ice cube trays in the freezer. Sprays of fresh rosemary may be wrapped in foil, sealed, and kept in the deep freeze for some weeks. Rosemary butter may also be frozen. Chop the fresh leaves, incorporate them into softened butter, allow to set in the refrigerator, then cut into squares and seal into small polythene bags or other suitable containers.

VARIOUS USES

Culinary

Rosemary is one of the most strongly pungent plants; the taste and scent of the crushed leaves are warmly vital, yet freshly resinous as well. This herb helps the digestion of rich and starchy food. It gives a delicious, savory tang to beef, lamb, veal, pork, rabbit, goose, duck, and sometimes chicken, if it is a highly seasoned dish. Rosemary is used in liver pâté, and in spiced sauces for pasta. It goes well with eggplant, zucchini, lima beans, Brussels sprouts, and cabbage. It is excellent in herb bread and in biscuits (scones). Try stirring a tablespoon of the finely chopped leaves into your usual plain biscuit (scone) mixture before adding the liquid. The

Because of its wiry, bushy growth habit, upright rosemary is very suitable for growing as a hedge.

Prostrate rosemary has a delicate trailing habit and looks most graceful when grown over a wall.

The saying,"Rosemary for remembrance" dates back to Ancient Greece, and herbalists still believe that drinking rosemary tea can aid a poor memory.

Like other aromatic plants, rosemary is a good influence in the garden.

flavor is subtle and piquant, and when freshly buttered and hot from the oven, every morsel quickly disappears. The flowers can be candied.

Rosemary is used in Middle Eastern and Mediterranean countries in several ways, especially when cooking lamb dishes. In Greece it is "thendrolivano," in Turkey it is "biberiye."

Medicinal

It was believed since the earliest times, that rosemary stimulated the memory. Students in ancient Greece entwined the green sprigs in their hair while studying for examinations. This is the origin of the saying "rosemary for remembrance." Herbalists today recommend rosemary tea to strengthen the memory for those who suffer from forgetfulness, and to relieve headaches. In herbal medicine it is used as a nerve tonic and also for the digestion. Rosemary is also reputed to strengthen sight, and there is in old saying that "it comforts the heart and quickens the spirit." Rosemary wine is a quietening cordial for the nerves and is stimulating for the kidneys.

Cosmetic

Rosemary's main attribute is its association with all functions of the head. Extract of rosemary in shampoos and hair tonics revitalizes the scalp, prevents dandruff, and encourages new and healthy hair growth with a shining luster. These occurrences have been experienced personally by ourselves and our family. A few sprays of rosemary, or oil of rosemary, in the morning bath makes a bracing start to the day. But do not use it in an evening bath before going to bed; substitute lavender for its sedative qualities. Oil of rosemary also goes into eau-de-Cologne and the leaves and flowers are a fragrant addition to potpourri.

Companion planting

Rosemary and sage are good companion plants, having a stimulating effect upon each other. Rosemary repels carrot fly. Like other aromatic herbs, rosemary is a good influence in the garden. It attracts honey bees when in flower. Honey made from rosemary is delectable, like eating nectar. In the house, dried sprays of rosemary help to repel moths in drawers and cupboards.

French Sorrel

Description

There are several species of sorrel, most of which are found growing wild. These kinds are very sour and acid-tasting. The variety known as French sorrel is milder in flavor and is the type cultivated for culinary use. French sorrel grows in thick clumps like spinach. The broad, oval leaves are approximately 6 inches (15 cm) long and 3 inches (8 cm) wide, and are joined to reddish stems, resembling a thin rhubarb. The small, greenish flowers appear in summer, near the top, and on either side, of long, scarlet-streaked stalks.

History and mythology

French sorrel is native to the south of France, Switzerland, Italy, and Germany, and is closely related to mountain sorrel, sheep's sorrel, English or garden sorrel, and to the dock family. Long ago, all these plants were valued salad and pot herbs, and were once gathered wherever they were found growing wild, to be taken home and put into bubbling stew-pots, or mixed with other green leaves, for salads. Sorrel has a reputation for sharpening the appetite and was highly regarded in the time of Henry VIII. John Evelyn thought much of its addition to salads, saying that it: ". . . imparts a grateful quickness to the rest as supplying the want of oranges and lemons . . ."

Cultivation

Plants can be cultivated by sowing seed in a prepared box in spring (and in autumn (fall) in mild climates). When seedlings are big enough to handle, they should be planted out, leaving 6 inches (15cm) between each one. Alternatively, seed can be sown directly into the ground where the plants are to grow, then thinned out later to 6 inches (15 cm) apart. Root division of the clumps in the autumn (fall) is also a satisfactory method of increasing French sorrel. In summer, as soon as the flower stalks begin to rise, they should be cut off at the base to prevent the plant from going to seed. If this is done, sorrel will continue to flourish for many years. A small application of manure is beneficial occasionally

(Rumex scutatus)
  Polygonaceae.
  Perennial.

PROPAGATION:
  seed, root division.
  Spring (again in Autumn – Fall – in mild climates).

POSITION:
  sun, or semi-shade.

SOIL:
  average, light.

HEIGHT:
  1 1/2 feet (45 cm).

PART USED:
  leaves.

French sorrel has small, greenish flowers which grow on long stalks. These stalks should be removed as soon as they appear to stop the herb from going to seed.

In moderate climates the broad, oval leaves of French sorrel are available throughout the year.

and keeping the plants watered in dry weather is a necessity. Watch for snails before they eat away the young, succulent leaves. Caterpillars too, are fond of this plant.

Harvesting and processing

The fresh leaves are available throughout the year in moderate climates, so drying should not be necessary. However, if wishing to dry them, place freshly picked, unblemished leaves flat on a wire rack in a cool, dark place where the air can circulate around them. Store in airtight containers. Whole, washed young sorrel leaves may be carefully wrapped in foil, sealed down with the fingers at the edges, and deep frozen for some weeks. Sorrel sauce may also go into the deep freeze packed in sealed containers, then thawed before using. Another method, which was published in an old French cookery book of 1796 (and which I have not tested myself, but considered a good idea), was to preserve the leaves by cooking them over a slow fire with salt and butter until all moisture had evaporated. When half cold, the sorrel was pressed into pots. When quite cold, tepid melted butter was poured over the top and the pots were sealed down and kept in a dry place. Once opened, the contents would not keep for more than three weeks.

VARIOUS USES

Culinary

Formerly, one of the favorite culinary uses for sorrel was to cook and eat it like spinach, with the addition of well-beaten eggs and butter, or cream, to mellow the sharp flavor. Another well-known use for French sorrel, still popular today, is in soup. Sorrel sauce is a delicious accompaniment for cold poultry, fish gelatine moulds, hot boiled potatoes, and as a filling for omelets. Tender shortloin lamb chops, or lamb cutlets, bathed in a thin sorrel sauce are delicious. The young leaves torn into a tossed green salad give a pleasant, appetising bite.

N.B. Sorrel, like spinach, should not be cooked in aluminium.

Medicinal

Sorrel leaves were eaten to assist the kidneys and digestion. They were made into a spring tonic for the blood and a cooling drink for fevers. As there is some oxalic acid present in the plant, the leaves should not be eaten too frequently. Culpeper writes: ". . . it is useful to cool inflammation and heat of the blood in agues, pestilential or choleric, or sickness and fainting, arising from the heart; to quench thirst and procure an appetite in fainting or decaying stomachs . . ." indeed, sorrel leaves were often eaten by

French sorrel in a garden plot.

country folk to allay thirst, although it would have been one of the various wild sorrels and not the cultivated French sorrel.

Cosmetic

Sorrel contains calcium and because of this is listed as one of the herbs which retard the signs of old age, helping to keep the skin firm and wrinkle-free. Many herbs are recommended for use in a facial steam, different herbs being suited to various skin types. Sorrel is suggested for dry, sensitive skins. Sorrel is also one of the herbs used in herbal cosmetics for healing acne. I have used an astringent cream based on sorrel. It is also recommended to be taken as a tea to help clear the skin.

Companion planting

We have found in our own herb garden, that French sorrel has been growing happily in three large clumps for 20 years next to oregano, the oregano almost engulfing the sorrel. Neither herb has had any disease and they are exceptionally healthy plants. Snails and caterpillars are the worst enemies of sorrel.

Rue

(Ruta graveolens)
Rutaceae.
Perennial.

PROPAGATION:
cuttings, seed, root division. Spring.

POSITION:
sunny, sheltered.

SOIL:
porous, well drained.

HEIGHT:
to 3 feet (90 cm) or more.

PART USED:
leaves.

Description

Rue is one of the most ornamental of all herbs. It has unusual, deeply cut, smooth leaves which are quite blue in color; in ideal conditions when the plant grows vigorously, the foliage is thickly massed in graceful layers. In summer and early autumn (fall) small posies of acid yellow blooms gather at the tips of each flower stalk. There is also a rare type with variegated leaves. One would expect such a pretty plant to have a delicious flavor, but this is definitely not so: the taste is extraordinarily bitter.

History and mythology

Rue originated in Southern Europe and was introduced to Britain by the Romans. It is one of the historically well known bitter herbs, the others being tansy and wormwood. It is said that brushes made of rue were once used for sprinkling holy water at solemn church ceremonies before High Mass, thus earning its other name of "Herb of Grace." Ophelia says to Hamlet: "There's rue for you and here's some for me, we may call it herb of grace o' Sundays." Rue was relied on as a cure for a host of physical ills, as well as being an effective insect repellent. It also had a reputation for warding off black magic, and according to legend was a component in witches' spells. One authority says it was an ingredient in the making of mead in far-off times.

Cultivation

Rue cuttings may be taken in spring and inserted in river sand as described in the propagating chapter beginning on page 195 of this book. Seed is also sewn in spring in prepared boxes, and we have found this the easiest and quickest way of increasing it. Young plants are ready for potting, or setting out in the garden, when their root systems have formed. Root division is also effective in spring, the separated pieces being put into the open ground immediately. Grow rue in the sun in well-drained soil. It makes a distinctive border; is effective when grouped in rows as low hedges; or can be interspersed, as foliage contrast, with other herbs. Do not let it flower too soon or plants will quickly look thin and sparse; nip off flower stalks at the base when they first shoot to ensure thick, bunchy foliage, and then allow blooming later on. Water the plants regularly in very dry weather to ensure healthy growth and appearance.

Harvesting and processing

Cut plants near the base (they will shoot again) for drying just before flowering in the morning when the dew has gone. Hang in loose bunches, or spread out on airy racks in a shady place. When the leaves are dry and brittle, crumble them into airtight containers to store for later use.

VARIOUS USES

Culinary

This herb is not sought after for culinary use because of its acrid, bitter taste. However, in ancient Rome it was eaten for the preservation of sight, and we have been told that to this day a little fresh rue is added by some Italians to their salads.

Medicinal

Ancient and modern herbalists agree on the potency of rue in helping to remedy several maladies. As it is very powerful, all the experts warn laymen on its use — it should be administered only by a qualified therapist, and doses should be taken strictly as directed. Pregnant women are advised against taking it, and large amounts can be toxic. When given in the right doses, rue relieves colic and indigestion, has been useful in eliminating worms, and has improved the appetite. It has been found valuable when made into an ointment for external use to help relieve the pain of sciatica, rheumatism, and gout. It also has a use in skin disease.

Cosmetic

Oil distilled from rue has a use in perfumery. This may seem contradictory as we have emphasized its peculiar bitterness: when judiciously employed, an opposite scent or flavor can intensify the potency of other ingredients in many different kinds of blends, whether in fragrances or in food.

Companion planting

It has been noted that rue and basil plants do not grow well near each other. Rue has been esteemed since earliest times as a natural disinfectant; a tea made from fresh or dried rue and sprinkled liberally in a flea-infested area will effectively repel them. Rue plants also repel flies and it is recommended to grow plants around the compost heap or manure pile. Rub some cooled rue tea into the coat of a dog or cat to help rid them of fleas.

Rue is a vigorous, ornamental herb with smooth and deeply cut leaves. It is one of the so-called bitter herbs: the others are tansy and wormwood.

RUE

DESPITE RUE'S BITTERNESS, THE DISTILLED OIL HAS A USE IN PERFUMES, WHERE IT INTENSIFIES THE POTENCY OF OTHER INGREDIENTS.

Sage

(Salvia officinalis)
  Labiatae.
  Perennial.

PROPAGATION:
  seeds, cuttings. Spring (Autumn (Fall) in mild climates). Position: sunny. elevated.

SOIL:
  light, well drained.

HEIGHT:
  3 feet (90 cm).

PART USED:
  leaves.

Description

A sage bush in the garden is a most attractive sight as well as being very useful. The aromatic, silver-gray leaves are approximately 3 inches (8 cm) long and $1/2$ inch (12 mm) across. However, when they first appear they are pale green, then as the leaves mature and harden they turn gray. Bees are fond of the purple, lipped flowers which start blooming on long stems in the autumn (fall), and sometimes in spring. It has been said that when the flowers open, each one resembles a tiny lion's mouth that drinks in the fire of the sun, the plant's chemistry transforming it into an aromatic volatile oil that courses through it.

History and mythology

Sage originated from the northern shores of the Mediterranean. It has been cultivated for culinary and medicinal uses for hundreds of years in England, France, and Germany. In later years it was taken to America, and later still to Australia. The name of the genus is derived from the Latin *salvere*, to be saved, referring to the curative powers of the plant. An old tradition was to plant rue amongst valuable sage plants to keep away noxious toads. Sage was also believed to assuage grief, and in Pepys' Diary he notes the planting of sage on graves in a country churchyard. One of its earliest reputations was as a preventative against the onslaughts of old age: "He who would live for aye must eat sage in May" is an old English proverb. The ancient Egyptians used sage medicinally as a brain tonic. The Chinese valued it for the same reason.

Clary Sage.

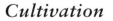

Cultivation

To propagate from seed, sow in spring (in mild climates autumn (fall) sowing is also possible in a prepared seed box). When seedlings have reached a height of 4 inches (10 cm) plant them out, leaving 2 feet (60 cm) between each one in a well-drained and sunny position that is also elevated if possible. Water the plants well

ABOVE: Sage is a most attractive herb to grow in the garden, with its silver-gray leaves and purple-lipped flowers that bloom in autumn (fall) and sometimes in spring.

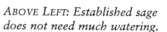

ABOVE LEFT: Established sage does not need much watering.

These sage seedlings have reached a height of 4 inches (10 cm) and are ready for transplanting into pots.

Jerusalem sage.

while they are young. When sage becomes an established plant, water only in dry weather as it will not thrive if conditions are too damp. It is most noticeable that plants with gray leaves do not usually like wet feet or moist conditions. When propagating from cuttings, use 6 inch (15 cm) long new shoots after the leaves have hardened and become gray; this happens in late spring, or possibly earlier, according to the season. Plant out when cuttings have developed roots.

Harvesting and processing

Harvest sage for drying just before the plant flowers. A successful method is to hang loosely bundled long sprays tied together in a cool, airy place. The branches may also be laid out on racks to dry in a warm position, but never in direct sunlight. When dry and brittle, pull off all the leaves and store in airtight containers immediately, as it is unwise to leave the bundles, attractive though they are, to gather dust. By the way, it is important when cutting sage at any time, to prune out any dead twigs and branches, as the plant can become very woody as it grows older. Fresh sage leaves may also be chopped finely, put into ice cube trays, covered with water and allowed to freeze. It will keep for many months like this. When needed, either drop a sage cube into the food you are cooking, or allow to thaw and then use.

VARIOUS USES

Culinary

Sage leaves, whether fresh or dry, counteract the richness in certain foods while assisting the digestion. Use sage on its own, or with other herbs, when cooking pork, goose, duck, veal, and oily fish. It

ABOVE: *Purple leaf sage.*

RIGHT: *Culinary sage in bloom.*

Red flowering sage

Garlic sage.

goes into pea soup, bean soup, and vegetable soup. Cook sage with onions, eggplant, tomatoes, cheese dishes, egg dishes, rich cream sauces, breads, dumplings, and biscuits (scones). Sage is a necessary ingredient in mixed herbs, along with thyme and marjoram.

Medicinal

Sage is believed to restore energy and bad memory, and is known to be helpful to the digestion, having a tonic effect on the liver. Sage tea is still taken today as a nerve tonic, and is recommended as a regular beverage for people who are studying for examinations and need to rely on their memory. This herb has also long been known to be beneficial for the mouth and throat, and is still included by some manufacturers in mouthwashes and gargles. In olden days the leaves have been used for tobacco, for tea, in cheeses, and breads. Because of its antiseptic properties it was used as a strewing herb on floors to keep away unwanted insects and vermin.

Cosmetic

Sage is still used in some commercial hair tonics to prevent hair from going gray. A simple old method for whitening teeth was to rub a fresh sage leaf over them each day. Sage is also used in recipes for cleansing lotions for the skin, in deodorants, hair rinses, and for large pores, in setting lotions, and in neck creams.

Companion planting

In the garden, sage and rosemary aid one another. Sage also helps to repel cabbage butterfly and improve the flavor and digestibility of cabbages if grown amongst them.

Elder

Description

The elder described here (*S. nigra*), the "black" elder (so called because of its dark green foliage), is the most useful kind for the herb garden, although there are other varieties with decorative golden, white, or variegated leaves. However, when these trees carry flowers and berries, they do not have the same therapeutic qualities as the black elder. There is also a dwarf elder with valuable medicinal properties, although it is advised not to grow this one as several parts of the tree can be poisonous if taken internally, especially the berries, which yield a blue dye. The black elder has finely serrated leaves advancing in pairs along supple, pale green stems clinging to bronze, woody branches. It is a deciduous tree, or shrub, and becomes thick and dense as it sends up many suckers. The elder seems to have two distinct seasonal personalities. In summer and early autumn (fall) it is veiled in filmy heads of cream flowers (a nectared haven for bees), looking like a gorgeous bride in billowing lace. Then in late autumn (fall) as the blooms form fruit, the tree changes its appearance and becomes withdrawn and stately, the sprays of ripened berries (a feast for birds) clothing the dowager-tree in a rich garnet robe. Eventually all falls away, and winter strips the branches bare, waiting for spring to bring fresh green buds and a new cycle.

(Sambucus nigra)
  Caprifoliaceae.
  Perennial.

PROPAGATION:
  hardwood cuttings late Winter; tip cuttings late Spring.

POSITION: SUNNY.
  Soil: moist, rich.

HEIGHT:
  14 feet (4.3 m) or more.

PART USED:
  flowers, berries, leaves.

History and mythology

All parts of the elder are useful, it having once been called "the medicine chest of the country people." The close-grained white wood of old elder trees was cut and polished and made into butchers' skewers, shoemakers' pegs, needles for weaving nets, combs, mathematical instruments, and some musical instruments. The stems with pith removed made whistles and popguns for country boys. The elder grows wild in many parts of Europe and belongs to the folklore of a number of countries. The Anglo-Saxons called it Eldrun. Danish legend connected it with magic, believing that in the branches dwelt a dryad, Hylde-Moer, the Elder Tree Mother, and that if one stood under the tree on Midsummer Eve one would see the King of Fairyland and all his train ride by. Russian peasants said that the compassionate spirit of the elder would drive away evil and also give long life. The Sicilians thought that sticks made of its wood killed

Elderberries.

Nectar-bearing cream flowers of black elder veil the trees in summer and early autumn (fall).

ELDER

ELDER TREES HAVE
A LONG FLOWERING
PERIOD, WHICH MAKES
THE HARVESTING OF
THE FLOWERS A
LEISURELY AND
PLEASANT TASK.

serpents and drove away robbers, and in England it was held that the elder was never struck by lightning.

Cultivation

When propagating elder, we have had the greatest success by taking 6 inch (15 cm) hardwood cuttings in late winter before shoots appear, and putting them in a container of river sand. Tip cuttings can also be struck in river sand in late spring when new growth has firmed. When roots appear the cuttings can be planted out, or put into containers with potting mixture. It is also possible to strike cuttings of sprouting wood in early spring in the open ground. Suckers, with some root from the main plant attached, can be dug and transplanted throughout the year, unless winters are harsh, when you may lose them. Elder trees grow almost anywhere but do best in a sunny position in rich, moist soil. If planting a grove of trees, leave at least 10 feet (3.5 metres) between each one.

Harvesting and processing

As elder trees have a long flowering period from summer to autumn (fall), harvesting them may be an ongoing, leisurely task. Gather the blooms when all the tiny buds on each pearly cluster are open, and do this by midday before the sun draws out too much of the flower's etheric substance. Put the heads somewhere shady to dry — a sheet of paper in the linen cupboard will do — and when they shrivel, looking like fine, yellowed crochet, remove them to make room for more fresh flowers. Store the dried ones whole in airtight boxes or jars, or rub them from their frail stalks first. Leave some flowers on the trees for using fresh and to ensure that there will be some fruit later. When the shiny green berries form in autumn (fall), watch them ripen and pick them as they begin to turn reddish purple. If it is not convenient to use the berries at once, allow them to dry, and store in airtight containers. They keep their flavor well and are used like dried currants.

VARIOUS USES

Culinary

A delicious wine is made from fresh elderflowers. Elderflower fritters are an unusual and epicurean dessert. Elder blossoms give a muscatel grape flavor to gooseberry, apple, or quince jelly when tied in a muslin bag and boiled in the fruit syrup for 3 or 4 minutes at the end of cooking time. A friend tasted an elderflower sorbet between courses at a dinner party, and pronounced the flavor exquisite.

Elderberries taste rather like blackcurrants, and flavor some jams and jellies; or they may be used on their own to make jam or jelly, chutney, and ketchup. The berries also give a distinctive sharp taste to fruit tarts and apple sauce. Elderberry wine has long been a favorite country elixir.

Medicinal

Elder tree bark was used long ago as a purgative by Hippocrates, and a soothing ointment was made from the green inner bark. A tea infused from the root was considered the best remedy for dropsy. The uses of the flowers and berries are legion. A strained infusion of the dried or fresh flowers is excellent for alleviating inflamed eyes. Elderflower tea (sometimes together with peppermint leaves) is an old remedy for influenza and, taken every morning, was also popular as a spring medicine to purify the blood; an ointment made from the flowers heals burns and chilblains. The leaves are also used in ointments, and as a wash, to repair and soothe the skin. Elderberry wine has valuable medicinal qualities, including the relief of sciatic pain. Once it was recommended to mix some elderberry juice with port wine for treating rheumatic and neuralgic distress. A cordial known as Elderberry Rob (see page 220), when taken hot before going to bed, was a well-known cure for a cold. Elderberry juice was used as a laxative and for colic.

The flowers and berries of the elder have valuable medicinal qualities.

Cosmetic

A cooled elderflower infusion, or tea, is very effective when patted on the skin to fade freckles and to take the sting out of sunburn. In fact this simple treatment is good for the complexion generally, and if kept up regularly gives the skin a soft, dewy bloom after a week or so. Elderflowers are still used today in the making of many herbal cosmetics.

Companion planting

An infusion of bitter elder leaves dabbed on the face is advised to repel insects such as mosquitoes and flies, a decoction of the leaves sprinkled over delicate plants helps ward off aphids and caterpillars, and the leaves spread about where grain is stored drive away mice. It has been noted that elders growing near compost heaps assist fermentation, and that humus under the trees is especially light.

ELDER

ELDERBERRY WINE
HAS VALUABLE
MEDICINAL USES,
INCLUDING THE
RELIEF OF
SCIATIC PAIN.

Salad Burnet

(Sanguisorba minor)
Rosaceae.
Perennial.

PROPAGATION:
   seed. Spring (again in
   Autumn – in temperate
   climates).

POSITION:
   sunny.

SOIL:
   average.

HEIGHT:
   12 inches (30 cm).

PART USED:
   leaves.

Description

This herb has cucumber-flavored leaves that are small, round, and serrated. They are spaced about 1 inch (25 mm) apart in pairs of 10 or 12 on each side of a slender stem. As the stems become long and heavy, they fall outward from the center, giving the whole plant a weeping, fern-like appearance. The reddish pink, berry-like flowers appear in summer at the top of long stalks that shoot up from the center of the plant. As salad burnet scatters many seeds which germinate easily, it is advisable to cut the flower heads off as the stalks begin to lengthen, or it will take over the garden.

History and mythology

Salad burnet is not well known today, although it is yet another herb highly regarded by the Ancients. It is thought to have originated in the Mediterranean regions, even though for a very long time its natural habitat has been in most of the mountainous areas of Europe, especially where the conditions are moist. It was often used as a border plant in Tudor herb gardens and in knot gardens.

Cultivation

When propagating, sow the seed in spring (and autumn (fall) in temperate climates) where the plants are to remain. Keep the ground moist while the seeds are germinating. When seedlings are 3 inches (8 cm) high, thin them out to 12 inches (30 cm) apart. As it is a soft salad herb and wilts quickly in hot, dry weather, keep the plants well watered at this time. It has no particular soil requirements, is very hardy and will grow strongly all through most winters.

Harvesting and processing

This herb does not dry well for culinary purposes. However, as it is a perennial, fresh leaves are available throughout the year. If wishing to dry it for medicinal use, spread leaf sprays out on a wire rack in a cool, airy place. When they are brittle and dry, crumble and store them in airtight containers. For freezing to go into beverages, pull the small leaves from the stalks and put them whole into ice cube trays. Top up with water and freeze.

VARIOUS USES

Culinary

Add sprays of salad burnet to a tossed green salad, or use them as a garnish for sandwiches, aspics, and any dish for a cold buffet. Whole sprays may also be added to punches, wine cups, and fruit drinks. When the small leaves are pulled from the stalks and left whole, they make an excellent filling for sandwiches, with the addition of a little cream cheese. Or the chopped leaves can be mixed into cream cheese or as a dip.

Medicinal

The Greeks steeped salad burnet leaves in wine cups and other beverages for, like borage, it was said to drive away melancholy. Culpeper endorses this by advising that two or three stalks in a cup of claret will "quicken the spirits" and "refresh and clear the heart." It was also recommended for wounds and was used both inwardly and outwardly. Any part of the herb was considered beneficial for this: the juice, or an infusion, or the powdered root and leaves. Taken as a tea or cordial it is said to promote perspiration and to help cure rheumatism.

Cosmetic

An infusion of salad burnet, cooled and applied to the face regularly, will help clear the skin. A bunch of cucumber-fragrant salad burnet tied in cheesecloth or muslin and put into a hot bath is refreshing and invigorating.

Companion planting

Salad burnet is very nutritious to cattle and sheep and was once grown extensively for this purpose. It has been noted that salad burnet is of particular use to sheep when it is closely cropped, and will give them green feed during the winter when other crops are scarce. In the garden, it mingles especially well with thyme and mint, one early writer pointing out that if these three fragrant herbs are planted together in "alleys," they "perfume the air most delightfully, being trodden on and crushed."

Salad burnet is a hardy plant and will grow in almost any kind of soil. The fern-like foliage looks most effective if planted as a border.

SALAD BURNET

WHEN PLANTING THIS HERB, REMEMBER ITS FRAGRANT COMPANIONS IN THE HERB GARDEN: THYME AND MINT.

Savory

Savory, Winter:
  (*Satureia montana*)
  Labiatae. Perennial.
Savory, Summer:
  (*S. hortensis*)
  Labiatae. Annual.

PROPAGATION:
  *winter savory: cuttings,
  seed. Spring (again in
  Autumn (Fall) in tem-
  perate climates); summer
  savory: seed. Spring.*

POSITION:
  sunny.

SOIL:
  light, well drained.

HEIGHT:
  *winter savory: 12 inches
  (30 cm); summer savory:
  2 feet (60 cm).*

PART USED:
  leaves.

Description

Of these two varieties, winter savory is more popular with home gardeners because it is a perennial. The bush is compact with a rather stiff appearance, making it ideal for low hedges to surround small, formal herb beds. The tiny, lipped, white flowers bloom in late summer and autumn (fall). The glossy, green leaves are thin and narrow, and are approximately 1/2 inch (12 mm) long. The leaves of summer savory are longer and softer and are a bronze green color, while the pale pink flowers bloom at the same time as winter savory. The growth habits of the two types are different. Summer savory has slender, erect stems which snap easily and the flavor is stronger than winter savory, which makes it more satisfactory for drying. Most commercial growers prefer it for this reason, and also because the seed can be scattered over large areas with good results in germination. There is a lesser known form of winter savory, *S. repandens*, a decorative prostrate variety whose leaves are smaller and lusher and the white flowers more thickly clustered than those of upright winter savory. However, because of its matted, close form, it is difficult to gather the leaves for culinary use. It spreads in dense, cushiony mounds, making it a desirable plant for filling pockets in rustic paved paths and terraces and in dry stone walls. It is also suitable for planting in hanging baskets, as the low, horizontal habit of the tiny branches will fall over the rim and hang down.

History and mythology

The savories are native to the Mediterranean countries and their history goes back to the remotest times. They were introduced to Britain by the Romans, and later they were among the first herbs taken to the New World by the Pilgrim Fathers. Their botanical name of *Satureia* is linked with the satyrs of mythology. Virgil wrote in ancient times that it was amongst the most fragrant of herbs and recommended that it should be grown near

LEFT: Winter savory
RIGHT: Summer savory

bee-hives. Savory vinegar (the leaves steeped in vinegar for some weeks to flavor it) was popular with the Romans. Shakespeare mentions savory several times in his plays:

> "Here's flowers for you;
> Hot lavender, mints, savory, marjoram."
> *The Winter's Tale.*

Winter savory, when kept neatly clipped, looks attractive as a low hedge to outline knot gardens and was a favorite plant in Tudor days for this purpose.

Because of its compact, stiff growth, winter savory makes an excellent low hedge around a formal herb bed. The herb flowers in late summer and autumn (fall).

Cultivation

To propagate winter savory, seed may be sown in spring (and again in autumn (fall) in temperate climates) in a prepared seed box, the seedlings to be planted out in a sunny, well-drained position when big enough to handle. Another method is to take small tip cuttings of new growth in late spring when the leaves have hardened, then put them in a pot of wet sand until roots have formed. When setting out in the garden, allow 12 inches (30 cm) between plants. If growing savory as a hedge, put the plants closer together, about 8 inches (20 cm) apart.

Summer savory is propagated by scattering the seed over finely dug soil where the plants are to remain. Successive sowings may be started in spring and carried on into mid-summer, each crop being harvested just as the flowers begin to appear. When a couple of inches high, prick out the seedlings to approximately 6 inches (15 cm) between plants.

Summer savory, Botanic gardens, Geneva.

Harvesting and processing

Both savories can be dried with good results by hanging them in bunches in an airy place just before flowering. When leaves are crisp-dry, they are easily separated from the stalks by running the thumb and forefinger up and down the stems. Stored in airtight

"Shakespeare's garden" in our former herb garden, Somerset Cottage.

Winter savory

Use savory leaves instead of pepper.

SAVORY

BOTH WINTER AND
SUMMER SAVORY CAN
BE USED TO TREAT
COLIC, FLATULENCE,
GIDDINESS AND
RESPIRATORY
PROBLEMS.

containers, the flavor will remain strong for a long time. For freezing winter savory, wait for the new soft growth in spring and summer. Summer savory, with its soft foliage, may be frozen at any time. Strip the leaves from their stalks, then chop them finely, mix with a little water, and put them into ice cube trays in the freezer. Sprays of fresh winter or summer savory may be wrapped in foil and frozen. It will keep like this for some weeks. Savory butter freezes well, too.

VARIOUS USES

Culinary

Both winter and summer savory are used in the same way in food. The finely chopped or dried leaves go with all kinds of cooked beans, either with a little melted butter or in a cream or white sauce. Mix the fresh or dried herb with breadcrumbs for coating fish, pork, and veal fillets before frying. It flavors seafood sauces and cocktails and lentil, pea, and bean soups. Use savory instead of pepper whenever a pepper flavor is needed.

Medicinal

Winter and summer savory both have strong beneficial properties, and they were once used medicinally for treating colic, flatulence, giddiness, and respiratory troubles. Summer savory tea is recommended as one of the herbs to help purify the system. In cooking, both savories help digest many foods, especially leguminous vegetables, in particular all varieties of the bean family. Hence its popular German name of *bohnen-kraut*, meaning "bean herb." The sharp, hot taste of the leaves has also earned it the name of "pepper herb," and it is worthwhile noting that it may be used instead of pepper in the diet where this is desirable.

Cosmetic

Either savory has a tonic and stimulating effect on the skin and may be infused in a muslin or cheesecloth bag in a hot bath for this purpose. An infusion of summer or winter savory freshens the mouth and sweetens the breath. As summer savory tea helps cleanse the system, it has been recorded that it also improves the complexion, making it clear and fresh.

Companion planting

It has been noted that savory seeds inhibit the germination of other seeds when planted nearby. Summer savory is helpful to onions when grown in a border around them. Both summer and winter savories help beans to grow better in the vegetable garden, (as well as being the traditional herb to eat with them). If you are stung by a bee while working in the garden, an old cure is to rub the spot with fresh savory leaves after removing the sting. Honey bees are attracted in swarms to savory when it is in bloom.

Alexanders

Description

This sturdy herb features roundish, dark-green, shiny leaves growing in groups of three. The stalks are thick and furrowed. Yellowish green flowers bloom in summer and are followed by small, black seeds.

History and mythology

Native to the Mediterranean region, this herb was well known to the Greeks and Romans. It was described as a culinary herb by Pliny, Dioscorides, Columella, and Galen. Alexanders is also known as "black lovage", "wild celery" and "horse parsley". It is similar to the rock parsley of Alexandria, hence the name alexanders.

Cultivation

Like lovage and parsley, alexanders likes rich, moist soil and a sunny position. The seed can be sown into prepared boxes, or in forked over and moistened soil in the open ground in spring. When seedlings are 3 in (8 cm) high, plant them out to 1 1/2 feet (45 cm) apart. Keep plants watered in dry weather.

Harvesting and processing

Harvest the seed just before it starts to fall, by snipping off and drying flower-heads. Sift out dried husks and store the seed in airtight containers. Use the leaves for tea, or to store them for culinary use, chop them finely and mix with a little water, then freeze in ice-cube trays. Whole leaf sprays may be stored for several weeks in the freezer when sealed in foil. For drying in a microwave oven see page 193.

VARIOUS USES

Culinary

Young leaves and stems can be finely chopped and added to salads, soups and stews, while the celery-flavored large stems can be cooked as a vegetable, served with butter or olive oil, salt and pepper. The flower buds make an unusual salad when gently steamed for five minutes, cooled, and served with an oil and vinegar dressing. They can be mixed into a lettuce salad for an interesting taste contrast.

Medicinal

The leaves are useful in food for their vitamin C content. The root is bitter, but promotes appetite and stimulates kidney function. The fresh juice was once used on cuts and wounds.

(*Smyrnium olusatrum*)
Umbelliferae.
Biennial

PROPAGATION:
seed

POSITION:
sunny

SOIL:
rich, moist

HEIGHT:
2–5 feet (50–150 cm)

PART USED:
leaves, stems, flower buds

The site of the Wrestling School at Olympia. The great general Alexander, after whom the herb alexanders was indirectly named, maintained his heroic status in the eyes of his army by being as athletic as his crack troops.

Comfrey

(Symphytum officinale)
Boraginaceae.
Perennial.

PROPAGATION:
seeds, root division.
Spring (again Autumn –
Fall – in temperate
climates).

POSITION:
shady.

SOIL:
average, moist.

HEIGHT:
4 feet (1.20 m).

PART USED:
leaves, roots.

Description

There are several varieties of comfrey, the most common being the *officinale*, the kind described here. Comfrey belongs to the same family as borage, and there is a similarity in their appearance, although the hairs covering comfrey's stalks and foliage are much finer than the rough bristles of borage. Comfrey grows to 4 feet (1.20 m) high, and is perennial. A thick-set, bushy plant, the outside leaves can measure 2 feet (60 cm) long and 8 inches (20 cm) wide. The mauve flowers droop in bell-like clusters at the tip of the plant and are in bloom for most of the summer.

History and mythology

Comfrey originally came from Europe and Asia. A variety known as prickly comfrey was highly regarded in the Caucasus as a fodder plant for animals. Historically it has been known amongst country folk for hundreds of years as a wound-healing plant, and in the Middle Ages was a well-known remedy for broken bones. Gerard, a famous herbalist of a bygone age, wrote:
"A salve concocted from the fresh herb will certainly tend to promote the healing of bruised and broken parts."

Cultivation

For propagating, sow the seeds in spring — and again in autumn (fall) where the climate is temperate — in a well-prepared bed, preferably under spreading trees. Keep moist while the seeds are germinating. When the plants are a couple of inches high, thin them out. Watch particularly for snails and caterpillars, which, if not controlled, can shred the leaves of even fully grown plants to a fine lace. Increasing by root division is carried out in autumn (fall), leaving at least 2 feet (60 cm) each way when planting. The roots are persistent and any little piece left in the soil will shoot.

Comfrey, the legendary wound-healing plant.

Harvesting and processing

Comfrey roots and leaves should be harvested as required, as they are more effective when fresh. If this is not possible, select unblemished leaves, lay them on racks, or on paper, in an airy place until crisp, then crumble coarsely and pack into airtight containers. For the roots, dig the required amount for storage, wash, and dry out in an airy place.

VARIOUS USES

Culinary

Herbalists maintain that comfrey leaves are wholesome as a food. The large, outside foliage is rather coarse, so pluck only the succulent, young leaves which have a cucumber taste and a delicious texture. Coat the young leaves in batter, fry them in oil, dust with salt and pepper, and serve as a vegetable. Gently steam the chopped leaves and eat them like spinach, or add a few chopped leaves to spinach during cooking. Put some leaves into the juice extractor together with any vegetable for an extra-nutritious drink.

Medicinal

The leaves and roots of comfrey have long been a country remedy for sprains, bruises, and wounds when made into poultices and applied to the affected parts. An infusion of the leaves or roots has been given successfully for chest colds, for the circulation, and for the intestines. The old name of "knit bone" or "boneset" was given to comfrey because it helps broken bones to mend more quickly. We have a skiing friend who applied comfrey poultices to a broken limb (he drank the tea as well) and to the astonishment of the doctors, his recovery was hastened by six months. The leaves and roots are rich in mucilage — a glutinous substance. They also contain a beneficial element called allantoin, as well as tannin and some starch.

Cosmetic

Comfrey cream, or comfrey ointment, is soothing and healing for the skin, and is especially helpful when applied overnight for wrinkles under the eyes. Comfrey tea helps cleanse the blood stream and clear the complexion. Comfrey leaves in a facial steam help tired and aging skins.

Companion planting

Comfrey is closely related to borage, and is helpful in much the same way if a few plants are grown near a strawberry bed to improve the size and flavor of the berries. Comfrey leaves are an excellent addition to the compost heap. A liquid fertilizer made from large, old comfrey leaves which have been left to rot in water — and then broken down with more water — and applied to the roots of plants has been found helpful (*Esther Deans' Gardening Book*).

For centuries comfrey has been a folk remedy for all kinds of injuries, including sprains and broken bones. It also has a reputation as a very wholesome and nutritious food and can be eaten as a vegetable.

Comfrey leaves.

Tamarind

Tamarindus indica
Leguminosae-
Caesalpinioidiae

Also called *Ma khaam*
(Thailand)

Description

This impressive evergreen tree grows up to 80 feet (25 m) high, with a generous spreading habit. Ten to twelve pairs of small leaves grow along each leaf stalk, giving the leaves a gently drooping appearance. Tamarind is cultivated for its leaves, flowers and seed pods in Thailand and India.

VARIOUS USES

While the seed is used most in India, in Thailand the sour young leaves are served raw with fish salad, or cooked in hot sour soup. The tamarind flowers also add their tart flavor to hot sour soup, and are an ingredient in shrimp paste and chili sauce. The fruit is made into a pulp or juice and sold in jars, to be added to soups and curries.

RIGHT: Tamarind fruit and seeds

The evergreen tamarind tree.

Tansy

Description

Tansy, "buttons," or "parsley fern," is a spreading perennial herb with a strong, creeping root system. It has deeply toothed, green, lemony-camphor scented leaves with a bitter taste. It blooms for a long period in late summer to autumn (fall), growing to about 3 feet (1 m) at this time. The unusual flowers are clustered together on one head looking like a bunch of small yellow buttons, and the stems of quaint, warmly aromatic blooms are useful in posies or in "tussie-mussies," the latter being pretty, tightly bound stalks of fragrant herbs and flowers, each having a message of its own in the language of flowers. The dried flowers go into potpourri too. Tansy dies away to ground level in winter when the roots are dormant, sending up new growth in spring. There is also a lesser known variety of tansy with verdant, curled foliage whose flavor is refreshing. We have not seen any record that this type has similar therapeutic qualities to the tansy described here.

History and mythology

Tansy is native to Europe, and through the centuries has been introduced and become naturalized in various parts of the world. An important herb historically, much has been written about it. Pungent tansy leaves have therapeutic qualities in small amounts, and were believed to help purify the body after winter ills. Traditionally, some of the firmly chopped young leaves were added to other ingredients for making "tansy cakes," which were served on Easter Day as a reminder of the bitter herbs eaten at the Feast of the Passover. One herbalist records that tansy teas were taken during Lent; another says that tansy leaves placed in the sufferer's shoes "cure the ague." It was a valued strewing herb on floors in the Middle Ages, being an effective and aromatic insect repellent.

Cultivation

Tansy will grow in almost any kind of soil, providing it is well drained; it also thrives in most aspects and flourishes in the wild, indicating its sturdiness. This herb is easily propagated by root division in early

---

(Tanacetum vulgare)
Compositeae.
Perennial.

PROPAGATION:
root division: Spring; cuttings: late Spring to early Summer; seed: Spring.

POSITION:
sunny.

SOIL:
average, well drained.

HEIGHT:
3 feet (1 m).

PART USED:
leaves, flowers.

Tansy is a spreading herb with deeply toothed leaves, bitter to the taste, and yellowish flowers.

TANSY

TANSY PLANTS HAVE
INVASIVE ROOTS, AND
AT LEAST 4 FEET (1.2 M)
SHOULD BE ALLOWED
BETWEEN PLANTS FOR
FULL GROWTH.

to mid-spring when new leaves are shooting. Cuttings are taken in late spring once the young stalks are firm, and prepared in the way described for cuttings at the beginning of this book. Seed is sown in spring. When planting, allow enough space, at least 4 feet (1.2 m), for the persistent roots to grow: if becoming invasive, dig out unwanted patches. Tansy stalks begin to shrivel with the onset of winter, and should be cut back to ground level.

Harvesting and processing

Cut leafy stalks for drying in the morning after the dew has evaporated. Do this at any time before the foliage withers and disappears in winter. Hang stalks together in a shady, airy place or spread out on a drying rack. When the leaves are brittle, strip them from their stems and store in labeled containers. Gather flowering stems for drying before the yellow disks become old and powdery from long blooming, and lay them on racks or sheets of paper. When each floweret is moisture-free, snip them away from their tiny stems and store.

VARIOUS USES

Culinary

Tansy is not recommended as a culinary herb because of its harsh flavor. However, it is used in a modern recipe for tansy pudding where 1/2 teaspoon only of the chopped young leaves is an ingredient. A friend often garnishes large serving dishes of sliced, cold meat with decorative tansy fronds; they look attractive and are an effective fly repellent.

Medicinal

This herb should be taken internally only under expert supervision, as an overdose can have a detrimental, irritating effect, and in pregnancy may cause abortion. When administered correctly, it is known to expel worms, is excellent as a spring tonic, aids the digestion, and assists kidney function. For using externally, again care should be taken as some skins react adversely to the leaves or extracted oil: a small area of skin can be experimented on first. Preparations of tansy have been used traditionally for skin eruptions, and for applying to bruises, sprains, and swellings. In aromatherapy, tansy oil has its place in treating some forms of depression.

Cosmetic

As mentioned, tansy can cause an allergic skin reaction, so use it cautiously to begin with. It is an old-time cosmetic, and when steeped in buttermilk for several days, was applied to the face for clearing the skin and making "maids . . . look very faire." This can still be successful if you have the right skin!

Companion planting

One of tansy's greatest virtues is its insect-repellent properties, known and valued since ancient days and up to the present time. In the garden the plant repels flies, ants, and moths. Sachets filled with dried tansy will keep moths at bay in cupboards and drawers. Happily, the pollen-laden flowers are loved by bees. Tansy oil is also a fly repellent. Rubbing the surface of raw meat with tansy leaves will protect it from flies. Massaging a cat's or dog's coat with the leaves helps get rid of fleas. Potassium-rich tansy is excellent for the compost heap. Planting tansy near peach trees is said to protect them from some flying insects.

TANSY

TANSY IS A USEFUL HERB FOR COMPANION PLANTING, BECAUSE IT REPELS FLIES, ANTS AND MOTHS. FORTUNATELY BEES LOVE THE FLOWERS.

Decorative tansy blooms.

Thyme

Thyme, Garden:
(Thymus vulgaris)
Labiatae. Perennial.
Thyme, Lemon:
(T. *citriodorus)*
Labiatae. Perennial.

PROPAGATION:
*seed, cuttings, root
division. Spring.*

POSITION:
open, sunny.

SOIL:
light, sandy.

HEIGHT:
*9–12 inches
(23 cm–30 cm).*

PART USED:
leaves.

Description

Of all the numerous varieties of thyme, garden and lemon thyme are the two kinds which have the most value in cooking. Certain ornamental varieties, like Westmoreland thyme, golden, variegated lemon thyme, and pretty, gray silver posie may be used in emergencies, but their flavor is not as pungent nor as true. There are also a number of creeping, mat-like species, but they have such interwoven, tiny branches, that the tedious job of trying to disentangle a sufficient quantity for cooking is simply not worthwhile. Garden thyme has very small grayish green leaves which are joined to thin stalks projecting in an angular fashion from hard, woody stems that form an erect, bushy plant 12 inches (30 cm) high. The flowers are pinkish white and appear in spring in whorls at the tips of the branches. Lemon thyme has slightly larger and greener leaves than garden thyme and the spring-blooming flowers are deep pink. It has a spreading type of habit and only grows to about 6 inches (15 cm) high. When the foliage is crushed, an unmistakable lemony fragrance overlaying the typical thyme scent is released. This makes it valuable for giving a more subtle flavor to food where required.

History and mythology

The *Thymus* genus is indigenous to the Mediterranean lands, and people declare that it grows with more flavor in its native soil than anywhere else. The tiny, pungent leaves have a primitive form, their outward simplicity belying the great beneficial forces within. Thyme has antiseptic qualities, the name in its Greek form was a derivative of a word meaning "to fumigate." Others say the name comes from the Greek word *thymus*, signifying courage. The ancient Romans liked the aromatic flavor thyme gave to cheese

LEFT: *Garden thyme*
RIGHT: *Lemon thyme*
TOP RIGHT: *Variegated lemon thyme*

Lemon thyme has a spreading habit and is used in the kitchen.

Cat thyme has a creeping, mat-like growth habit and makes an excellent ornamental ground cover.

Westmoreland thyme is a popular ornamental variety.

and to the various alcoholic beverages they made. It was a loved plant in Elizabethan times and was used extensively in garden borders. Shakespeare wrote of herbs many times and obviously appreciated their qualities: "I know a bank whereon the wild thyme blows" is a favorite line from A *Midsummer Night's Dream*. Herb writers of old have told us that "Wild thyme has always been a favorite with fairies."

Cultivation

For garden thyme, the seeds, which are extremely small, can be sown in spring into a prepared seed box, or they can be scattered straight into finely dug soil, kept moist, and thinned out later to about 6 inches (15 cm) between plants. Propagating by root division is another satisfactory procedure and should also be done in spring. Divide the bush into as many pieces as required, making sure each piece has some good rootlets attached, and firm them into the ground. Alternatively, garden thyme can be propagated by taking tip cuttings approximately 4 inches (10 cm) long in late spring, inserting them into a pot of sand, and keeping them watered. This last method ensures good root systems very quickly. Garden thyme, except when young, does not require much watering and no fertilizing at all. Where soil is too poor for cereal crops, garden thyme will grow well and have more flavor than pampered, manured plants which may look healthy and lush, but will lack pungency. Cut the bushes back hard at the end of flowering and renew them every two years or so. Propagating lemon thyme from seed is not recommended, as the seedlings cannot be guaranteed to be as strongly fragrant as the parent plant. For this reason, the seed is not readily available in commercial quantities. Propagation is either by tip cuttings or root division, using the same methods as for garden thyme. For healthy plants, cut them back after flowering has finished and start again with fresh plants every two or three years.

*Gray woolly thyme is another
variety which is not used in
cooking but makes a very
attractive border.*

*Westmoreland thyme is grown
as a decorative garden herb
rather than for use in the
kitchen.*

Lemon thyme in flower.

Harvesting and processing

For drying both garden and lemon thyme, harvest the leafy branches just before they start to flower for fullest flavor, and gather them on a dry day before midday. Hang them in bunches in a shady, airy place, and when crisp-dry, strip off the leaves and seal in airtight containers. The taste and aroma of both these thymes are much more penetrating when dried. As the foliage of thyme is so tiny, we think it a laborious job to strip the stalks for freezing a few leaves in ice cube trays, when this herb dries so well. Washed and dried sprays of thyme can be sealed in foil and frozen whole for several weeks.

VARIOUS USES

Culinary

The special fragrance of garden thyme enhances many dishes and is also a necessary ingredient in many herb blends, such as mixed herbs (the others being sage and marjoram) and in a bouquet garni (with parsley, marjoram, and a bay leaf). The savory, pungent flavor of garden thyme is indispensable for using in soups, stews, casseroles, meat loaf, meatballs, with all kinds of meat, in stuffings, tasty sauces, marinades, and pâté. It gives savor to herb bread and to many vegetables, such as eggplant, zucchini, squash, tomatoes, haricot and lima beans, onions, and beetroot. Lemon thyme, with its milder flavor, is excellent with fish, chicken or turkey mornays, steamed carrots, omelets, and all kinds of food with a delicate or bland flavor. It is sometimes used as an extra ingredient in a "fines herbes" blend, with chervil, chives, parsley, and tarragon.

In the Middle East the word "za'tar" refers to thyme, and this is also the name of a mixed herb blend consisting of dried thyme, marjoram, and sumac (or sumach) and added salt. (To obtain this blend, only the red berries of the non-poisonous species of the sumach tree are used.) "Za'atar" in Morocco is the name both for thyme and a mixture of thyme, marjoram, oregano, and winter or summer savory. A Moroccan story says that goats like to graze on thyme, which is the reason for their warm blood.

Medicinal

Thyme is a plant which absorbs sunlight and converts it into potent volatile oils containing substances that have made this herb a valuable medicine for treating coughs, colds, cramps, colic, poor digestion, and loss of appetite. As mentioned earlier, the plant also has antiseptic qualities. Herbalists also recommend thyme tea for relieving headaches, bowel and bladder disorders, as a nerve tonic, and for toning up the reproductive system. As with sage, it is said to improve the eyesight and clear the brain . Because of its powerful antiseptic qualities, herbalists sometimes recommend thyme to be used with sage as a gargle for sore throats.

Garden thyme has a very small, grayish green leaf.

The leaves of lemon thyme are larger than garden thyme and this variety has a deep pink flower.

ABOVE AND LEFT:
Silver posy thyme is as pretty as its name.

Cosmetic

Thyme is used today in herbal toothpastes, mouth washes, and natural deodorants. It is also used in soaps and herbal bath salts and in facial tonics as it tones up the skin. Thyme may also be used in a facial steam for normal skin.

Companion planting

Thyme, as one of the most aromatic of all herbs, has a beneficial effect in the garden, and associates well with lavender. It helps repel cabbage root fly, and when dried, acts as a moth repellent in cupboards and drawers. Bees have always loved this herb when in flower, and honey made from it is the most delicious and fragrant of all. Thyme was always planted near the bee-hives and the hives were also rubbed with it.

Fenugreek

(*Trigonella
    foenum-graecum*)
Leguminosae.
Annual

PROPAGATION:
    seeds. Spring

POSITION:
    sunny

SOIL:
    light, well-drained

HEIGHT:
    *grows to 2–2¹/₂ feet
    (60–75 cm)*

PART USED:
    leaves, seeds

Description

Fenugreek (sometimes spelt "foenugreek") is a small, slender, annual herb of the pea family, similar in habit to lucerne (alfalfa). It has light green leaves that are trifoliate; each leaflet is oblong and less than an inch (about 2 cm) long. The flowers are yellowish-white and are followed by typical legume fruits that contain the small, furrowed, golden-brown seeds. These release a strong, sweet scent, and are spicy and rather bitter to the taste.

History and mythology

Fenugreek is indigenous to western Asia and south-eastern Europe. It is one of the oldest cultivated plants, having been mentioned in medical papyri from ancient Egyptian tombs. Charlemagne encouraged its cultivation in central Europe in the 9th century. The herb was also a favourite of the Arab peoples. The Latin name *Trigonella* means little triangle, a reference to the shape of the small flowers. *Foenum-graecum* means "Greek hay", the name given to the plant by the Romans when they brought it from Greece. It is also called "bird's foot," "cow's horn," and "Greek hayseed." Fenugreek is cultivated commercially in India and the Middle East.

Cultivation

Sow the seed in spring in the open ground, sprinkling it into narrow furrows after raking and moistening the oil. Choose a sunny position. Keep watered while the herb is growing.

Harvesting and processing

The leaves may be picked when large enough, for culinary use. The fresh leaves can be chopped finely, mixed with a little water and frozen in ice-cube trays. If growing for the seed, the plants will mature three to five months after sowing. Allow the plant to flower and fruit; when pods are ripe collect them as the first few seeds fall from them. Snip off the heads and spread them out on a tray in a dry place. When completely dry, the seeds can be shaken from the pods. They should be stored in airtight containers.

VARIOUS USES

Culinary

In India, aromatic fenugreek leaves, called "methi ka saag," are used as a vegetable and as a flavoring for curries. They are an important

ingredient in tandoori marinades. They are also torn up, or left whole, and mixed into a green salad to give a tang to the palate while toning the system. The seeds ("methi ka beej") are included in curry blends, especially the distinctive vindaloo. In Egypt fenugreek leaves are used as a food flavoring. Sprouts can be grown from the seed, following the same procedure as for alfalfa and other small seed legumes. These sprouts can be added to salads, sandwiches, or eaten on their own with a little oil and lemon dressing. To use leaves which have been frozen in ice cubes, drop about 4 into vegetable soups during the last 30 minutes of cooking.

Fenugreek leaves are used in several Iranian dishes. One speciality is a delectable appetizer consisting of a mixture of fresh herbs: they are usually fenugreek, parsley, garlic chives, tarragon, coriander, mint, and watercress. The herbs are washed, broken up, and crisped in the refrigerator; then they are attractively arranged on a plate. Diners select these herbs buffet-style and eat them with cubes of fetta cheese placed on flat bread which is then folded. In Iranian fenugreek's name is "shambalileh."

Medicinal

Fenugreek's fresh leaves, sprouted seed, and the seed itself have tonic properties. Fenugreek is principally a cleansing, soothing herb. The crushed seeds make a health-giving tea, acting on the liver and intestinal tract, assisting the removal of stale and excess mucous from the body. To reduce the bitter flavor of this tea, add honey and a teaspoon of lime or lemon juice.

Fenugreek is cultivated commercially in India and the Middle East.

FENUGREEK

THE LEAVES OF
FENUGREEK ARE
COMBINED WITH FETTA
CHEESE AND BREAD IN
AN IRANIAN APPETIZER.

Valerian

(Valeriana officinalis)
Valerianaceae.
Perennial.

PROPAGATION:
root division, seeds.
Spring.

POSITION:
semi-shade.

SOIL:
rich, damp.

HEIGHT:
3–5 feet (90 cm–1.5 m).

PART USED:
rootstock.

Description

The valerian used widely in herbal medicine should not be confused with any garden-type valerian, one of which is a popular and decorative small plant with little therapeutic value. It has pinkish red, fluffy blooms clustering at the top of the stems. The true "great" valerian, a tall plant grown for its medicinally important rootstock, can reach a height of 5 feet (1.5 m). The green leaves are oval, "cut" at intervals, and proceed in pairs along narrow stalks. The summer-flowering blooms are pale pink to white, scented, and grow in flat clusters. The rootstock, which is the only part used, has a strong, earthy smell.

History and mythology

Valerian is native to Europe and parts of Asia. Those distinguished recorders of herbal knowledge from long ago, Dioscorides and Galen, wrote of the powerful medicinal properties found in the root system of the plant they named "Phu" — because of its strong smell! Later, scholars were sure they referred to the herb which became known as valerian. It was widely used by Arabian physicians in the 10th century, and by medieval monks, esteemed healers of the sick, who distilled the potent essences from the roots. Valerian has retained its reputation as a relaxing and soothing herb, and in some places still retains its country names of "all heal," "capon's tail," "great wild valerian," or "setwale."

Cultivation

Sow valerian seed in prepared seed boxes in spring, and when plants are big enough to handle, set them about 12 inches (30 cm) apart in a moist, shady position. Dig some manure into the soil first. The roots may be divided and planted out in spring and autumn (fall) in rich, moist soil, at least 12 inches (30 cm) or more apart. Keep new plants watered, as their favorite places in the wild are damp hedgerows, ditches, and wet ground.

Harvesting and processing

Cut flowering tops of valerian as soon as they begin to appear so that the rootstock may develop better. In autumn (fall) the green, leafy tops are cut away and the roots and rhizomes (rootstock) dug and collected. Any clinging soil is brushed away, then the roots are thoroughly dried and stored in airtight containers. However, it is advised to be cautious in using home-grown valerian, as root-drying for medicinal purposes is a lengthy and complicated process which must be expertly managed so that there are no ill effects from this powerful natural drug. It is important to know how harvesting and processing valerian root-stock takes place, even though growing it in the herb garden is mainly for your own interest, knowledge of the plant, and pleasure. Also you can enjoy the flowers instead of removing them.

VARIOUS USES

Culinary

Valerian has no culinary use these days, although in the Middle Ages some dried root was sometimes put into a "broth or pottage" for health reasons.

Medicinal

Preparations made from valerian roots are used in herbal medicine as a sedative, for easing neuralgic pain, muscular cramps and spasms, and various nerve-related conditions. Those with liver problems could feel nauseated when taking valerian because it increases the flow of bile; if this happens do not carry on. We can vouch for its ability as a sleep-inducing tea when wakeful during the night. By the way, the tea has a fairly strong "earthy" taste, liked by some and disliked by others. A suggestion in this case is to mix lemongrass tea with the valerian to offset any aversion to the flavor; the two blend happily together and will not cancel out each other's effectiveness. Respect the value of valerian tea and do not take it in large quantities.

Cosmetic

A soothing herbal bath to promote "beauty sleep" is to put together in a muslin or cheesecloth bag (knotted together at the top if you like) some valerian, chamomile, and lavender, and infuse in a hot bath. Afterward, sip a cup of valerian tea (sweetened with honey if wished) and see how naturally sleepy you feel!

Companion planting

Valerian stimulates phosphorus activity in the soil and is excellent as a border plant for the vegetable garden. It attracts earthworms also. In bio-dynamic composting (a highly specialized and successful type of organic gardening) valerian is one of six herbs specially prepared to influence the fermentation of composts and manures. Stinging nettle grown as a companion plant increases the essential oil in valerian plants.

True Valerian.

Valerian, a native of Europe and parts of Asia, has powerful medicinal properties. Preparations made from its roots are sedatives and relaxants.

Lamb's Lettuce

(*Valerianella olitoria* or
V. locusta)
Caryophylleae.
Annual.

PROPAGATION:
*seeds. Spring, Summer,
Autumn (Fall) for
Winter use.*

POSITION:
sunny to part sun.

SOIL:
light, rich.

HEIGHT:
6 inches (15 cm).

PART USED:
young leaves.

Description

While growing, lamb's lettuce forms itself into a full rosette of layered, light green leaves with a tightly bunched heart, looking like a miniature lettuce. The leaves are flat and rounded and are part of each sappy stem. Pick leaves early before the plant starts to lengthen; young leaves are tender and delicate to the palate, the older ones are surprisingly tough and acrid.

History and mythology

Lamb's lettuce, or corn salad, is so widespread in certain regions that it is difficult to trace its exact origin. It has been cultivated in European, and later British, vegetable gardens for centuries as a valued salad herb. During winter months lamb's lettuce is especially welcome, continuing to grow when less hardy vegetables could not survive. In France it was the custom to eat lamb's lettuce in Lent, so besides being known there as *mâche* and *doucette*, another name for it was *salade de prêtre* (salad of the priest). It self-sows in the wild giving rise to its two most common English names: legend says that new crops of plants not only appeared at lambing time, but were also a favorite food for the lambs, hence the name lamb's lettuce. It was also noticed that the wild plants came up most frequently in corn fields, explaining its other name of corn salad.

Cultivation

Choose an area of light, rich soil in a sunny position for sowing seed, first enriching the soil with some fertilizer if necessary, then clear away any weeds and rake the ground. Sow seed in drills about 6 inches (15 cm) apart in rows; cover drills lightly with soil and gently firm down. Keep the plants weed-free and well watered. Watch for slugs and snails. Seedlings will need thinning out to prevent the spindly growth of crowded plants; the discarded seedlings can be transplanted in another bed. Do not let plants mature beyond the "hearting" stage as the leaves become tough and useless, losing their delicious flavor very quickly as they age. Repeated sowing is recommended at intervals through spring, summer, and autumn (fall).

Lamb's lettuce can be grown in a container together with other salad herbs, purslane, rocket, and mustard. Allow enough room and a large enough pot, window box, or trough for each herb to grow comfortably.

Lamb's lettuce.

Harvesting and processing

It is not possible to dry lamb's lettuce; the aim is to pluck and eat the new green leaves while soft and full of flavor. If a few leaves only are wanted and not the entire head, gather the youngest ones first. For collecting seed to sow again, allow one or two plants to grow tall. Tiny mauve-tinted, greenish white flowers will soon appear and eventually form seeds. Collect ripe seed and resow.

VARIOUS USES

Culinary

Lamb's lettuce or corn salad is essentially a salad herb and at one time was classed as a lettuce. An 18th-century cookery writer gave directions for a "Sallad for Winter" and said to ". . . take corn sallad and horse radish scrap'd fine, dish it handsomely and serve it with oil and vinegar." This delicious herb has been well known and appreciated for many years on the Continent and in Britain. Today it has a wide appeal in many other countries, and packets of seed are readily available. A friend who grows lamb's lettuce once served us the tender young leaves in a subtle dressing at lunch one day; the combination was quite exquisite and seemed to melt in the mouth.

Medicinal

Lamb's lettuce was once popular as a spring medicine.

> ## LAMB'S LETTUCE
>
> THIS PLANT HAS A WIDE POPULARITY AS A SALAD HERB, AND RECIPES FOR ITS USE GO BACK CENTURIES.

Cultivation & Usage

The History of Herbs

THE HISTORY AND romance of herbs are wreathed in the dim mists of time to intrigue and enchant us. Herbs are mentioned in the Bible many times in both the Old and New Testaments. They also appear in Greek mythology, fennel being an example. Legend has it that the god Prometheus went up to heaven holding a hollow fennel stalk in which he concealed some of the sun's fire to bring back to earth for human use.

From the time the written word was set down on papyrus, or incised into wax or stone tablets, the use of herbs in countless different ways was reported. Most of our ancestors' knowledge came from pure instinct, as a result of living close to nature, and it is interesting to learn that today's scientists are proving much of this lore to be correct. Many of these old methods of healing are gaining new followers and are a continuing part of natural therapeutics.

The ancient Egyptians and Greeks were the first people known to write down in technical terms their knowledge of herbs, following their scholarly, systematic observations of plant life. Indian and Asian civilizations, which were very advanced at an early time, also knew the value of plants that grew on their continents.

In Egypt, herbs were used extensively about 2700 B.C. They grew abundantly in the rich soil by the River Nile and were concocted into potions and ointments and, together with rare and exotic spices, were used for embalming the dead. Medical schools began to flourish in Egypt and it is thought that the Greek physician Hippocrates was a student at one of these schools. Another great Greek physician, Dioscorides, who lived during the reign of Nero, was the author of a herbal *materia medica*, and it is said that for a thousand years afterwards, doctors in the known world used the remedies of Dioscorides for healing the sick.

Pliny the Elder (A.D. 23–79), who perished during the eruption of Vesuvius which destroyed Pompeii, and his nephew, known as Pliny the Younger (A.D. 62–113), were Roman historians who left detailed records of life in their times, including many treatises on herbs; however, it is thought that the elder Pliny was the author of the works on herbs. He is still quoted today in herbal encyclopedias.

At historical Ephesus, herbs can be seen growing abundantly and flowering among fallen columns and between paving stones; there is even a small basil plant flourishing bravely in brown, hard, inhospitable ground. This landlocked city of white marble ruins, extensive and preserved enough to captivate the imagination forever, lies glittering in the sunlight as it has done for several thousand years. It was once a seaport where, legend says, Antony and Cleopatra disembarked from their vessel and walked along the lovely streets. Later St Paul visited Ephesus, and it is claimed that the Virgin Mary spent the last years of her life nearby. She was taken there by St John after the Crucifixion for protection.

In Crete, among the green slopes of Knossos, stepping through some of the partially restored and originally enormous Minoan palace, where Theseus slew the fearsome Minotaur in the Labyrinth, is an exquisite wall painting of an immensely elegant azure-blue monkey, sitting with one "hand" poised above a stylized saffron flower. Apparently monkeys were trained to pluck the orange stigmas from the heart of the saffron crocus because of their dexterous fingers and very long nails. Saffron was valued for the delicate taste and golden hue it gave to food (it is highly prized today for the same reason), and its golden-yellow dye was used to color cloth and tint the hair.

In early England it is believed that there were ancient herbal writings which were destroyed during the Danish invasions. Old manuscripts on the subject, now in safe-keeping in Britain, are the 10th-century *Leech Book of Bald* and the Saxon translations of the *Herbarium of Apuleius*. These documents bear out the knowledge that the use of herbs dated from the earliest times. Certain plants were an essential ingredient in charms, spells, and ceremonies, as well as in remedies, and some herbs in particular were believed to ward off treacherous water elves, "the flying venom," trolls and evil spirits. Other herbs were used in remedies, in food, and for dyeing.

When the conquering Romans came to Britain and settled for two hundred years or so, they brought with them the herbs that were essential in their food and medicines. We think of these plants today as being indigenous to Britain but they are actually native to the Mediterranean. Some of these are oregano, marjoram, thyme, sage, rosemary, balm, bay trees, fennel, savory, and mint.

The Vikings in their repeated invasions of Britain brought their own familiar essentails from the northern region, introducing herbs that adjusted to their new suroundings and eventually grew wild. One essential herb known to and used by the invaders was dill, the common name of which stems from the Norse word dilla, meaning "to lull". Dill water, a decoction made from the seeds, was given to babies to soothe them, just as it is today.

Herbs were continually being introduced by newcomers: the invading Normans would have seen to it that their diet in a new land still contained their favourite herbs and that their medicine boxes held the "physics" that they knew were effective.

About one hundred years after the Norman invasion, a group of physicians were known as healers in Myddfai, Wales. They belonged to the highly respected traditional school of medicine flourishing in the twelfth and thirteenth centuries. The interesting story of the "Meddygion Myddfai" was told in the *British Herbal Review* in the summer of 1988. It seems that the remedies provided by this group were gratefully followed by those who sought help. The article points out that much of the physicians' information was derived from earlier sources, such as the writings of Hippocrates, Pliny, Dioscirides and Galen. Here is a Myddfai remedy.

"For a cold: take a pound of garlick, and pound well, adding thereto a quart of good bottled wine, let it macerate well covered, drain under a press and drink lukewarm. If the cold affects a joint, warm the remains of the garlick and apply to the part as warm as it can be borne. It is proven."

Various foreign princesses who became queens of England were influential in importing further herbs; the Countess of Hainault, mother of Philippa, wife of Edward III, sent her daughter a famous manuscript dealing with the virtues of herbs. People who were adventuring to other countries also found new and diverse plants to bring home.

In the Middle Ages monks cultivated herbs intensively and made many advances in their cultivation and use, discovering many more properties, which they recorded. It is well known that the first liqueurs were concocted by monks as potent medicines. A small glass (the forerunner of the liqueur glass), containing the carefully blended precious plant essences, would be administered to the patients who came to the good monks to be healed in body as well as in soul.

Gardens were essential for the the monasteries. Documents describing cloister gardens in

Old fashioned violas border a walled herb garden with a lavender hedge.

detail go back to the ninth century. The oldest plan of a monastery (from about 816–20 AD) is in the abbey of St Gall in Switzerland. This plan shows a section of the cloister and other sections for different kinds of gardens or "garths", a garden for supplying vegetables and herbs for the kitchen, and an infirmary garden providing the herbs for medicines which were prepared by the monks' physician.

The cloister-type herb garden endured in elaborate or simplified forms, with neat geometric beds intersected by pathways for easy maintenance and harvesting. A manuscript from the ninth century written by Walafred Strabo, Abbot of Reichenau on Lake Constance, describes the joy he experienced in his cloister garden:

"Amongst my herbs sage holds the place of honour; of good scent it is full of virtue for many ills. Then there is rue, with its blue-green leaves and short-stemmed flowers, so placed that the sun and air can reach all its parts. Great is its power over evil odours..."

Further on he states, "Mint I grow in abundance and in all its varieties. How many they are, I might as well try to count the sparks from Vulcan's furnace beneath Etna."

A fourteenth-century account tells of an elderly husband, The Goodman of Paris, who was newly wed to a young woman. Because of her inexperience in housekeeping he wrote a complete book of household management for her, including a chapter on gardening. It contains sound advice on caring for plants, including a caution not to water in the sun's heat, to place cinders beneath cabbage leaves against caterpillars, instructions that dead branches of sage be removed in winter, and a warning not to grow marjoram in the shade. He mentions herbs for everyday seasonings that include lavender, mint, hyssop, tansy, parsley, garlic, borage, rue, and rosemary.

Later were to come some other great herbalists like John Gerard (16th century), John Parkinson (17th century), and Nicholas Culpeper (17th century). Other herbalists, gardeners and gourmets have set down their own delightful and helpful observations. Perhaps the greatest person in the history of

the garden was Carl Linnaeus (1707–78) who first classified plants into scientific botanical orders. Latin names were given to every plant, the first name being that of the family to which it belonged, and the second a separate name, thus distinguishing each plant within the same structural group.

Wherever the human race has traded or settled, herbs and spices have been woven into history. It is amazing to consider the ability of herbs to spread and grow in remote corners of the ancient and the modern world.

The Pilgrim Fathers took herbs with them to America. Many of the herbs they used were indigenous to the new land, including bergamot, used by the Oswego Indians as a curative herb. The new settlers soon made "Oswego Tea" a remedy for sore throats and colds, and its soft fragrance made a delicious herbal tea. "Johnny Appleseed," as he was called, helped spread many herbs from his home to families in their new homeland.

The first white settlers in Australia brought with them herb seeds to grow in a new and strange continent to use as flavoring for their food, as medicines, and to make into sweet bags and potpourri to perfume rooms and closets. Stories abound of grandmother's favorite herbal remedies and these pioneers were not afraid to experiment with some of the native Australian flora, such as ti-tree leaves, which it is said they used for making tea, the lemon-scented variety being highly favored. People also learned much in those early days from the knowledge of the Aborigines.

But for many years the popularity of herbs declined and those which were once in everyday use became obscure and their names strange. There are exceptions of course, like parsley, mint, sage, thyme, marjoram, and chives, and in the last 20 years there has been a remarkable world-wide resurgence of interest in herbs.

Herbs have been defined under several different headings: physic or medicinal; flavoring or culinary; fragrant; and those used for dyeing. In many countries they grow as wild as weeds along hedgerows and wasteland. Once a weed has become useful it reaches "herb" status.

Physic herbs were once called "simples" because specific ones contained the effective components for alleviating and remedying simple ills.

Fragrant or "sweet herbs" were those whose aromatic leaves and flowers were strewn on floors to sweeten the air as they were trodden on (and to keep away unwanted insects and vermin). They were picked and dried for a pot-pourri blend, for sweet bags, and for incorporating into numerous other household recipes in the still-room of the mistress of the house.

Herbs and some vegetables were also important for dyeing cloth.

''Pot herbs'' were more like an early form of vegetable. They were used in cooking for the flavor and nourishment in their leaves, roots and stems.

"Salad herbs," eaten raw, were usually leafy and included many chopped-up culinary herbs.

Herbs contain their own particular properties and essence and some medicinal plants if taken in large quantities can be poisonous. If prescribed in the correct proportions and mixtures by a trained practitioner they can be quite effective. Many chemical medicines today have been derived, then synthesized, from herbs. The sedative drug Valium is a synthesized substance found in the root of the herb valerian, long esteemed for its calming and soothing effect. The pretty foxglove (*Digitalis purpurea*) is a plant which is a heart drug, and can be fatal if the leaves are eaten as a salad. A derivative of foxglove is today a chemical orthodox drug and is prescribed with safety by doctors for certain heart ailments.

Medicinal plants are beyond the scope of this book, which deals mainly with culinary and salad herbs which are tasty and healthgiving. When eating them, or taking them as a tea, it is wise to vary them and sometimes blend them, and not eat or drink only one herb many times a day, every day for months, unless prescribed by a professional.

Scented Geranium

The Herb Garden

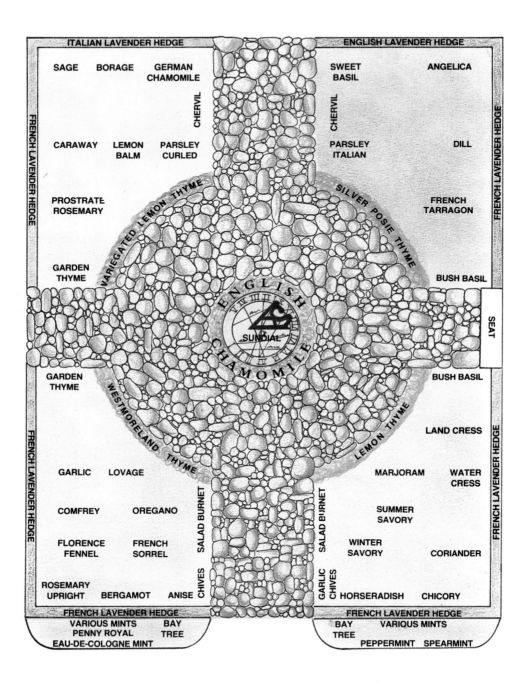

ITALIAN LAVENDER HEDGE

ENGLISH LAVENDER HEDGE

FRENCH LAVENDER HEDGE

FRENCH LAVENDER HEDGE

SAGE   BORAGE   GERMAN CHAMOMILE

SWEET BASIL   ANGELICA

CHERVIL

CHERVIL

CARAWAY   LEMON BALM   PARSLEY CURLED

PARSLEY ITALIAN   DILL

PROSTRATE ROSEMARY

VARIEGATED LEMON THYME

SILVER POSIE THYME

FRENCH TARRAGON

GARDEN THYME

BUSH BASIL

ENGLISH CHAMOMILE

SUNDIAL

SEAT

GARDEN THYME

WESTMORELAND THYME

BUSH BASIL

LEMON THYME

LAND CRESS

GARLIC   LOVAGE

MARJORAM   WATER CRESS

COMFREY   OREGANO

SUMMER SAVORY

FLORENCE FENNEL   FRENCH SORREL

SALAD BURNET

SALAD BURNET

WINTER SAVORY   CORIANDER

ROSEMARY UPRIGHT   BERGAMOT   ANISE

CHIVES

GARLIC CHIVES

HORSERADISH   CHICORY

FRENCH LAVENDER HEDGE

FRENCH LAVENDER HEDGE

VARIOUS MINTS   BAY
PENNY ROYAL   TREE
EAU-DE-COLOGNE MINT

BAY   VARIOUS MINTS
TREE
PEPPERMINT   SPEARMINT

The best aspect for your herb garden is facing the direction in which plants will gain the maximum benefit from the sun's rays. The soil should be light for good drainage.

The Herb Garden

The history of herb gardens

When human beings lived a nomadic existence in an uncivilized state, it was necessary to collect wild plants, berries, and roots for food. When they became ill, instinct led them to the grasses and leaves that had curative properties, in the same way as animals do. When people began to stay in one place long enough to make a dwelling, a garden, however small, became an essential part of life. The tilling of soil and planting of herbs, vegetables, and fruit trees on a plot of ground for easier gathering was a natural outcome. Plants grown for pleasure and beauty became a luxury for the aesthetic senses: special herbs and shrubs were needed for the culinary and healing properties of their foliage, flowers, or fruit, or in the stems and sometimes the roots, and often in the bark. Fragrant flowers and leaves, which were filled with perfumed essences, were made into useful and charming articles.

In ancient Egypt, excavations have uncovered perfect pictures of gardens, complete with graceful birds and brilliant butterflies, reproduced on floor tiles. Egyptian water gardens are said to have been as breathtaking in scale, magnitude, and beauty as the gardens of Versailles, constructed thousands of years later. A colored plan on a splendid manuscript of a formal garden for an Egyptian high official in about 1390 B.C., with geometric beds intersected by paths, is still in existence. Fruit-bearing and other trees and shrubs, waterbirds on ponds, a tangle of grape vines, pavilions,

sculpted-looking plants (which may be herbs), are all depicted in a pleasing, perfect pattern and scale. Reconstructions of the superb formal gardens of early Persia, ancient Greece, and the Roman and Byzantine empires show how old is the urge to make gardens of beauty and of self-sufficiency. Indian gardens were built long before the birth of Christ. Pleasure gardens planted with flowers and trees were made more beautiful by the presence of peacocks and songbirds; there were lakes for fish, the surface starred with lotus blossoms and water lilies where swans and ducks swam. These legendary Indian gardens, some intricately designed with "water ladders" and sparkling water jets, are still to be seen in modern Kashmir.

Old documents illustrated delightful formal gardens of the well-to-do in medieval Europe and Tudor England. They show the dominant impact of early Eastern garden designs. The formality of plant beds divided into precise shapes in monastery cloisters, and in Elizabethan herb gardens and pleasure gardens, has its origins in this Eastern influence.

Simple cottage gardens in Europe and England, and later in America and Australia, possessed their own charm with more random planting, and herbs were placed where they would be within easy reach. If there were hives, perfumed herbs were close by, for bees love the sweet nectar of thyme, lemon balm, rosemary, sage, marjoram, oregano, borage, and many more. Honey flavored with herbs has the most delicate aroma and taste.

Making a herb garden

A simple, neat herb garden is one that is about 12 feet (4 m) square, well drained, and situated in a sunny position. The bed should be prepared by digging in plenty of leaf mold and mushroom or household compost. Add a small amount of coarse river sand if the soil is heavy.

If on the other hand the soil is sandy, and herbs like to grow in this type of soil for drainage, it may be built up with compost for nourishment. Beach sand is not suitable as it contains too much salt, which will kill the plants; river sand bought commercially contains no salt.

Herbs make excellent rockery plants. We once planned a rockery herb garden for friends. It was on sloping ground and herbs were planted on terraces where pathways on each level led down by steps to the small, grassy lawn below.

There are more elaborate herb gardens that one can make, such as modified medieval cloister gardens, and Tudor and Elizabethan gardens reminiscent of the formal ancient Eastern gardens. "Knot" gardens became popular in Tudor times and they were delineated by clipped, dwarf box hedges in complicated patterns. Fragrant culinary and medicinal herbs and favorite flowers were planted within the knot's miniature hedges. Scented lavender or rosemary are excellent for surrounding a garden and may be shaped and pruned after flowering. These kinds of gardens are interesting to plant and are relatively inexpensive to make.

Stone or brick walls around a herb garden cost more, but they give a special, nostalgic feeling of bygone days as you enter them. A sunken garden can be included in a more elaborate herb garden. The sides hold back the earth with paving stones, and between them, in spaces allowed for this, are planted various ornamental perfumed thymes, prostrate rosemary, and small, sprawling, old-fashioned perennials, which all help to bind the soil. Low-growing herbs are planted along stone or brick pathways bisecting conventional geometric beds filled with taller herbs.

However small, herb gardens are a unique place with a definite mystique. It needs an interesting focal point like a sundial, a suitable statue, a bird-bath, or "herb seat." This is made of brick or stone, filled with earth and covered with a matting, scented thyme or starry-flowered lawn chamomile.

Paths of mown grass, paving stones, pebbles, or pine bark make for easier access when picking the herbs. Small plants for edging are chives, chervil, lemon thyme, savory, upland cress, bush basil, and curled parsley. Behind them, for graduated height, can be grown borage, lemon balm, sweet basil, bergamot, marjoram, French sorrel, oregano, Florence fennel, tarragon, coriander, and dill. Some taller herbs for background planting are angelica, lovage, garlic, upright rosemary, Italian parsley, and chicory. Bay trees grow very big if allowed to, and they can be planted on each side of the entrance to the garden; they can always be clipped and shaped to keep them compact. Elder trees and lemon verbena trees may be placed as sheltering and protective guardians just outside the herb garden.

Another way to make a pretty and pleasant herb garden is to buy an old cart wheel. Remove every second spoke and paint the wheel white. Lay it on prepared ground and plant herbs between the spokes radiating from the centre, choosing low-growing herbs that will not sprawl all over the wheel. A similar idea is to use an old ladder, cut in half, painted white, and laid on the ground with a pathway along the centre. Herbs can be planted between the rungs.

If a herb garden as such is not important to you, and yet you would like to have a few of your favorites, grow them among other plants. Gardens edged with curled parsley, or chives, are useful and attractive at the same time. Taller herbs among other flowers add their share of fragrance and foliage interest. The larger herbs can be grown among the shrubs at the back of the garden.

Ingenuity plays a large part in making herb gardens, and imagination can produce some wonderful new ideas. A garden of herbs is extremely useful in many ways, as well as being full of fragrance and delicious flavors, and is always a pleasure to look at. It is worth remembering not to overfeed herbs, as this makes them soft and lush with little taste. (Parsley and chives are exceptions.) Overwatering, or planting them in a place which becomes waterlogged in heavy rain, is disastrous, although watercress is one herb that likes these conditions.

A Shakespeare garden

Shakespeare had a countryman's joy and delight in the herbs and flowers of the hedgerows, meadows, and gardens with which he was so familiar during his rural upbringing. He loved them for the sake of their beauty, meaning, and perfume, and wove many of them into his plays and sonnets.

We made a Shakespeare garden some years ago and beside each herb and flower a small notice was inscribed with the appropriate quotation on it. The size and shape of the Shakespeare plot may follow any of the suggestions for herb gardens already described but the special atmosphere that is evoked in a Shakespeare garden needs a few of Shakespeare's own words to complete the magic.

Our Shakespeare garden is oblong with a paved area in front of it and a garden seat nearby so that one can relax and contemplate at leisure.

A clipped dwarf box hedge gives it a slightly formal air and a statue of a small boy placed under a curved bower of miniature climbing roses is the focal point. In the foreground are low-growing matting thymes:
"I know a bank whereon the wild thyme
blows."
A Midsummer Night's Dream

Clustered in several places are golden clumps of cowslips, oxlips, and primroses.
"The even mead that erst brought sweetly
forth
The freckled cowslip, burnet and sweet
clover."
Henry V

A flower garden in Shakespeare's time

"The wholesome sage, and lavender still gray
Ranke smelling rue, and cummin good for eyes
The roses, reigning in the pride of May
Sharp hishop, good for greens woundes remedies.
Fair marigolds, and bees alluring thyme,
Sweet marjoram, and daysies in their prime,
Cool violets, and Alpine growing still,
Embalmed balm, and cheerful galingale,
Dull popie, and drink quickning setual,
Veyne-healing verven, and head purging dill
Sound savorie, and basil harti-hare,
Fat coleworts, and comforting parsline,
Colde lettuce, and refreshing rosemarie,
And whatso else of vertue, good or ill,
Grew in this garden, fetched from far away
Of everyone, he takes and tastes at will."

from "The Fate of the Butterfly" by Edmund Spenser

And "bold" oxlips, which seem to look half-way between a cowslip and a primrose:
" . . . Bold oxlips and
The crown imperial."
The Winter's Tale

Shakespeare describes primroses many times, especially noting their ethereal beauty:
*"Pale primroses
That die unmarried ere they can behold
Bold Phoebus in his strength."*
The Winter's Tale

Pretty *Bellis perennis*, or pink and white English daisies, are grouped together in a rosy glow:
*"When daisies pied and violets blue,
And lady-smocks all silver-white,
and cuckoo-buds of yellow hue
Do paint the meadows with delight."*
Love's Labour's Lost

Columbines are planted in front of the box hedge and their old-fashioned blue bonnet flowers nod above their delicate foliage:
"There's fennel for you and columbines."
Hamlet

Gray-leaved carnations and "gillyvors" (a smaller type of carnation) are in this collection near the columbines, their flowering time sometimes coinciding — according to the season:
*". . . the fairest flowers o' the season
Are our carnations, and streak'd gillyvors."*
The Winter's Tale

The early form of pansy, before it became a giant hybrid, was *Viola tricolor*, and thank goodness it is still with us, and goes by many names — heartsease, love-in-idleness, Johnny-jump-up, and Cupid's flower are a few. The plant is massed with tiny pansy-like flowers of purple and gold in spring; it self-sows readily and since it is an annual its little pod of seeds, which ripen after flowering, burst open and fall on the ground, the welcome seedlings appearing again year after year. We let it grow unchecked, and remember that it was the

flower Oberon told Puck to find to put Titania to sleep in *A Midsummer Night's Dream*:
*". . . And maidens call it Love-in-idleness.
Fetch me that flower: the herb I show'd thee once;
The juice of it, on sleeping eyelids laid,
Will make or man or woman madly dote
Upon the next live creature that it sees."*

A silver-gray wormwood hedge surrounds the garden, and appropriately it was the herb Oberon used to awaken Titania, and called more delightfully by Shakespeare, "Dian's bud":
*"Be, as thou was wont to be:
See as thou was wont to see;
Dian's bud o'er Cupid's flower
Hath such force and blessed power.
Now, my Titania! wake you, my sweet queen."*
A Midsummer Night's Dream.

There are many more herbs and flowers to plant in a Shakespeare garden. The white Florentine iris, *Iris germanica*, or "Fair Flower-deLuce," as described in *Henry V*, can be included. All the herbs mentioned in this line from *The Winter's Tale* are in the garden:
"Hot lavender," mints, savory, and marjoram.
There is a rosemary bush for Ophelia:
"There's rosemary, that's for remembrance; pray you love, remember."
Hamlet

and also rue, the "Herb of Grace:"
*"There's rue for you;
And here's some for me;
We may call it herb-grace o'Sundays:
O you must wear your rue with a difference."*
Hamlet

Honeysuckle, the early form with small, scented creamy flowers, and often called "woodbine," is a reminder of Titania's bower "overcanopied with lush woodbine" in *A Midsummer Night's Dream*.

There must be roses in a Shakespeare garden. As well as the rose arch which enshrines the small statue in our garden, there are other historic old roses planted outside its confines to catch the sun and air. They include the white rose of York and the red rose of Lancaster, which historically eventually became united in the red and white Tudor rose:

"We will unite the white rose and the red. Smile, heaven upon this fair conjunction."
Richard III

The cuckoo-bud or buttercup we did not plant because of its invasive root system, nor do we have ladysmocks, harebells, or eglantine, simply because there is no more room! Daffodils are in other parts of the garden, as are violets, fennel, and marigolds.

There is a crabapple tree in one corner of the Shakespeare garden. A favorite drink of the day was roasted crabapples dropped into ale:

"When roasted crabs hiss in the bowl Then nightly sings the staring owl."
Love's Labour's Lost

Hemlock, fennel, and crowflower, or ragged robin, are a few more of the many other "Shakespeare" plants.

Bible gardens

We have always intended to create a "Bible garden," especially after reading about one in an overseas magazine some time ago. Like a Shakespeare garden, the herbs, flowers, and trees of a Bible garden need notices next to them with the appropriate Biblical quotation and the name of the herb clearly written on them.

A garden such as this need not be large, although the design would be important — a simple square with a suitable central focus, such as a birdbath or a small statue, would suffice. Paths could radiate outwards from the centre, with plants set in beds bordering the paths.

Some of the herbs quoted in the Bible are the bitter herbs such as dandelion, chicory, and sorrel. Bitter herbs have a symbolic use in the Jewish annual Passover ceremony. Fennel, cumin, and rue are some of the other herbs referred to in the Bible. Wormwood is mentioned in Amos 5:7:

"Ye who turn judgment to wormwood, and leave off righteousness in the earth."

Aromatic coriander seed appears in Exodus 16:31:

"And the house of Israel called the name thereof Manna: and it was like coriander seed, white; and the taste of it was like wafers made with honey."

Leeks, onions, and garlic, all members of the Allium family, appear in Numbers 11:5:

"We remember the fish, which we did eat in Egypt freely; the cucumbers, and the melons, and the leeks, and the onions, and the garlick."

Other plants that could be put in or around a Bible garden, and which are all named, are broom, lilies, the cedar of Lebanon, grapevines, fruit trees, and in the right areas, date palms, sycamores, and of course, spices:

"Spikenard and saffron; calamus and cinnamon, with all trees of frankincense; myrrh and aloes, with all the chief spices." (Song of Solomon 4:15)

It would of course be difficult or even impossible to include the larger species, and tropical plants bearing spices, because of lack of space or unsuitability of the climate, but creating a garden with a meaning and a story behind it would give pleasure and satisfaction to both the beholder and the creator of the garden.

It was a wonderful experience to see the re-creation of a true 17th-century Culpeper garden at romantic Leeds Castle in Kent, on a perfect summer's day. We wandered through paths set between beds of herbs, both culinary and medicinal, as well as flowers, surrounded by low hedges trimmed in different patterns. We were grateful to the person who had so faithfully recreated this garden that it looked exactly as it would have in Culpeper's day.

Companion planting

Plants and trees, whatever their size, are all individual, each one being a composition of many complex parts, besides the roots, trunk, stems, leaves, flowers, bark, or fruit that are visible to the naked eye. Within the make-up of each plant or tree are fine substances that are either alien to other plants, trees, and countless insects, or sympathetic to them and which therefore assist their growth and attract desirable insects to them. Companion planting is the science of finding out which plants are compatible with one another so as to eliminate the use of chemical sprays.

Root excretions and the microlife of the soil are all-important factors and the subject is a very intricate one. There are books that deal exclusively and in depth with companion planting but we will include here a few of the facts and findings for those who would like to know something about this fascinating aspect of gardening and farming.

The impact of companion planting is not immediate, as with contact or systemic sprays. Sometimes one has to wait for a year or two before the results are manifested. For instance, if a fruit tree is susceptible to a specific disease, and a plant known to be particularly resistant to it is planted underneath, in time the fruit tree will absorb some of the root excretions and other benefits from the plant. The tree will then become unattractive to its enemy. In the same way it has been found that the roots of the French marigold (*Tagetes patula*) give off a substance which kills soil nematode worms in rose beds, the nematodes being especially harmful to the health of roses. Rachel Carson wrote of this in her book *Silent Spring*.

In their book *Companion Plants* (Stuart and Watkins, London), Helen Philbrick and Richard B. Gregg tell us that not only the French marigold, but the African marigold too, has the same properties to combat other soil nematodes, including potato nematodes. When marigolds are planted in a tomato bed, they combat white fly and the tomato plants grow better and bear more fruit. Even the smell of marigold foliage and blossoms is effective as an insect repellent.

We have found that a strong wormwood tea poured around the haunts of snails and slugs is an effective repellent. Another remarkable insect repellent is pennyroyal. Sprigs of it under a dog's mat will combat fleas, and during a flea plague sprigs of pennyroyal liberally spread around the house will get rid of the fleas.

Pennyroyal growing in the garden effectively repels mosquitoes and ants.

GARLIC GARDEN SPRAY

We have tried the following garlic spray against aphids, snails, cabbage moth, caterpillars, and mosquitoes, with considerable success, especially when carried out at two-weekly intervals.

3 oz (85 g) (about 3 big knobs) garlic, unpeeled
6 tablespoons medicinal paraffin oil
1 tablespoon oil-based soap, grated
1 pint (500 ml) hot water

Roughly chop garlic, put into blender with paraffin oil and pulverize. Scrape resulting pulp into a bowl, cover, and leave for 48 hours. Stir grated soap into hot water until melted. Stir soap and water into garlic mixture. When cool, strain into screw-top jars and store in refrigerator. For spraying in the garden, use 2 tablespoons of garlic solution to 4 pints (2 L) water.

Herb gardens in containers

Many people living in apartments have little or no garden in which to grow their favorite plants, much as they would like to.

Herbs are easily grown in containers, provided they have plenty of sun and air, such as on a balcony or a window sill. Herbs should never be treated as houseplants, otherwise they will become disappointingly leggy and yellow, then die.

There are many types of suitable pots to buy for container growing: popular and easily obtainable are strawberry jars which are made in various sizes. They are mainly of terracotta and are sometimes glazed on the outside in attractive colors. Terracotta containers always need to be placed on a saucer because the pots are porous, and during dry, hot weather the saucer should be filled with water so that the pot draws up moisture which keeps the plants alive.

An average size strawberry jar has five or six lipped holes in the sides and one large aperture in the top. This would be suitable for a balcony. Troughs are also popular containers for herb

A small herb garden with a sundial as a focus

gardens and are made in various sizes out of many different materials, such as terracotta (some with pleasing neoclassic designs on them), cement, crushed marble, and polystyrene. A fairly small trough would be practical for a kitchen window sill, the size depending on the depth of the sill.

Other types of containers that may be used for raising herbs are large, round tubs made of cement, terracotta, or old wooden wine casks cut in half. We were once offered a large, ancient Roman sink which would have looked superb planted with herbs, but unfortunately it was much too expensive!

Excellent and unusual alternatives are wire baskets lined with damp paper bark (wetting makes it pliable), which when filled can be hung from an overhead beam on a terrace or a balcony. There are also terracotta hanging pots, some with holes in the side. The attractive wicker lobster pots have become much sought after as planters: they vary in shape and size and have suitably heavy chains for hanging. Line these with damp newspaper before filling with soil and herbs. The paper eventually rots into a firm compost while preventing the soil from falling through the cane.

Yet another alternative for growing herbs in a confined area is a novel attachment for a window, which resembles a miniature glasshouse.

When looking for a suitable container for your herb garden, make sure that it has a hole, or holes, in the bottom for drainage; if the hole or holes look rather large, as they sometimes are, cover each with a rough, unevenly shaped stone. This will stop the soil in the pot from falling out and at the same time will allow any excess water to gradually drain away. Do not use a flat stone that will completely cover the hole, seal in the water, and kill the plant in the waterlogged soil.

When planting out herbs from their growing pots, knock them out gently, first making sure that the soil is moist so that it does not fall away from the roots. Small-growing culinary herbs with compact root systems, such as thyme, chives, marjoram, sage, oregano, parsley, and chervil, can be planted fairly close together and still flourish. A trough approxi-

mately 2 feet (60 cm) long and 8 inches (20 cm) wide will comfortably hold five herbs, especially if they are staggered when arranging them. A shallow azalea pot 16 inches (40 cm) in diameter holds up to seven plants.

Planting a strawberry jar with herbs is really quite easy once you know how. Whichever size you choose, start by putting a fairly large, uneven stone on top of the hole in the bottom and then fill the jar with potting mix to the level of the lowest lipped holes. Knock a plant from its pot and pass it down through the large opening at the top, pushing the foliage part of the herb through one of the side holes and leaving the roots intact within the pot. When all the side apertures are planted at this level, fill the pot with more soil to the next level of apertures and repeat the same process as before. When the top has been reached, plant with one of the larger herbs, like rosemary, leaving about an inch (2.5 cm) from the top for watering. Never fill a strawberry jar with soil and sow seeds in the lipped holes because they will wash out when watering.

To water a strawberry or herb jar, fill the pot to the very top, let it soak through the porous soil and repeat this about three times. By doing this you will ensure that the lowest plants in the side will get sufficient moisture.

Much as we all like to grow mint, this herb, with its invasive root system, is better off in its own pot, otherwise before long it will take over the whole container and strangle all the herbs in it.

Harvesting and drying herbs

When drying herbs it is important that the watery element should evaporate, leaving behind the fragrant essential oils which contain many other components as well. The reason that dried herbs have a stronger taste than fresh herbs is because the oils are concentrated in the shrunken, demoisturized leaves. In cooking, if you are using dried herbs instead of fresh herbs, use only half the amount suggested in the recipe.

There are several ways of drying your own herbs. If you are drying them for their aromatic

In this herb garden, the herbs have been attractively grouped and named.

foliage, a general rule is to gather them on a dry day, before noon, when they are at their peak. After that, the sun will have drawn up most of the aromatic essences. Early autumn (fall), just before flowering, is the usual time for harvesting. Oregano is the exception. An Italian friend told us that, in his Sicilian homeland, oregano is harvested and dried when it is in flower. The most intense flavor is in the flower heads, and these are used as well as the leaves for their extreme pungency. (Never hesitate to eat culinary herb flowers, fresh or dried, as well as the leaves: thyme, marjoram, and savory are three that come to mind – they have a lightly honeyed, as well as aromatic, taste and they harmonize perfectly with their foliage.) When harvesting herbs, cut each plant off at ground level, and if they are perennials they will appreciate the pruning.

The simplest way to dry herbs is to bundle them together neatly in bunches, tie with string or raffia, and hang them in an airy, shady, dust-free place until brittle. Then strip off the leaves and put them into clean, airtight containers; do not use plastic, it causes "sweating." We used to recommend that herbs be washed first, but on reading one knowledgeable writer's comment that some of the natural essences clinging to the plant would be lost, we no longer advocate this, unless of course the herbs have been sprayed with insecticide. There is also a chance of mildew setting in if the foliage is damp.

For really efficient, natural drying, branchlets of herbs can be laid on airy, mesh trays in a warm, dry atmosphere where the air can circulate around them. Spreading the herbs on sheets of clean newspaper and leaving them in a shady area is also an excellent method. If the leaves are the type that retain moisture, to prevent mold or mildew from forming, place them so that they do not have any contact with each other. Never dry foliage in the sun, it will draw out all the flavor; neither should they be dried in a *hot* oven. A warm oven is satisfactory provided the leafy

stalks are constantly turned and carefully watched. Drying in a microwave oven can be successful and this method is described below.

If the heads of herbs are to be dried for the seed, as in the Umbelliferae family, which includes fennel and dill, then final sun drying is excellent.

Washed sprays of fresh herbs, as well as chopped fresh herbs, can be wrapped in foil or plastic film and stored in the refrigerator for a week. They may also be deep-frozen for up to three weeks. To keep them fresh for longer, wash the herbs, chop finely, and freeze in ice cube trays with a little water. When needed, defrost the frozen herbs, or drop the ice cubes into the cooking pot where the ice will soon melt. Herb butters are another way to keep your herbs fresh. Most culinary herbs are suitable for herb butters. Wash each batch and chop finely before incorporating into softened butter, with a few drops of lemon juice added. Spread the herb butter onto a fairly deep saucer or plate, and refrigerate. When hard, cut into circles or cubes, put them into a covered container, or a plastic bag, secure the top, and freeze until needed.

Basil is the least satisfactory herb to freeze, it is inclined to discolor and become bitter. Pesto, a superb thick basil sauce, is the most delicious way of preserving fresh basil (see page 249).

Herb vinegars, for use in French dressings, are a pleasant way of capturing summer flavors. These are described on page 210.

Drying herbs in a microwave oven

We sought the advice of an expert on microwave cookery who considers microwave drying a very efficient and quick method of drying herbs. It is advisable first to do a few trial runs, leaving the herbs that have been microwave dried for two or three weeks in airtight containers to establish that they have dried and not developed mold. For future reference, it is important to make a note of how long each herb was in the oven.

After picking the herbs, wash and pat dry with a paper towel. Turn the oven on to full power and lay whole herb sprays, or stripped, fresh foliage, on two layers of absorbent paper in an ovenproof dish. The paper helps to absorb excess moisture. Most herbs seem to dry in about four minutes. Feel them, and if they are not crisp, leave them a little longer, making sure they do not discolor. Each herb varies in drying time, so even half a minute could be crucial. Chervil takes as little as one minute to dry, and chives a little more than four minutes. Parsley is particularly rewarding, becoming an even brighter green than when picked from the garden. Dried, whole sprigs look very attractive.

Holy basil growing in pots on a Greek sidewalk.

Propagating & Cultivating Herbs

Cuttings

When taking cuttings from a parent plant, always keep them in water, or wrapped in a damp cloth until ready to put in the sand. Do not let them wilt.

Use coarse river sand for striking cuttings, never use beach sand as it is too fine and probably contains salt.

When preparing cuttings, always pull off leaves with an upward pull, or use pruning shears to avoid tearing the bark of the plant.

When removing leaves from cuttings, one-third of the foliage should be left on top.

Never push a cutting into the sand; always make a hole first with a knitting needle or skewer slightly thicker than the cutting.

Trim cuttings with a sharp knife or pruning shears just below a leaf node. Moisten the ends of the cuttings, then dip lower $1/2$ inch (1.2 cm) into a suitable cutting powder. Shake off excess powder and insert cuttings one-third of the way into the sand. Try to cover at least two leaf nodes, and more if possible.

When cuttings are first put in sand, flood with water so the sand will pack tightly around the cuttings, then keep sand moist at all times.

Rooted cuttings can be taken from the sand and planted directly into the ground, but to obtain best results with a minimum amount of loss, grow them in small separate pots in semi-shade for several weeks first.

Cuttings must be watered daily.

To help cuttings make roots in cool climates, place them in a glasshouse, or if this is not possible, lay a sheet of glass over a box, making sure the glass is painted with whitewash to prevent the plants being scorched by the sun's rays.

Seeds

When sowing seeds always keep the seed bed, or box, moist at all times, as drying out even for a short period can cause germination to cease.

Put seed box on a level surface, as accidental overwatering or heavy rain can wash the covering soil and seed to one end of the box.

Pots or tubs must be filled to about $1/2$ inch (1.2 cm) from the top to allow for easy watering.

Cultivating Herbs

A well-drained porous or sandy soil is preferred by nearly all herbs, unless stated otherwise in their sections. They do not like soil enriched with fertilizers and manures, although garden compost is always helpful. If the ground is heavy, dig it well first, and if sour add some lime before planting. Rockeries are excellent places for growing herbs.

A sunny, open situation suits most herbs best. Where this is not so it has been stated.

Cut the old growth and dead wood away

Cuttings should be planted in coarse river sand to strike. First make a hole slightly thicker than the cutting with a sharp object such as a knitting needle.

The correct way to take a cutting is just below a leaf node, snipping with a sharp knife or pruning shears.

A rosemary cutting has made good roots and is ready to be put into a small pot of potting mixture.

For the best results, rooted cuttings should be put in small, separate pots in semi-shade for a few weeks.

When inserting cuttings into the sand, they should be packed closely together and the sand kept moist.

regularly to give new growth a chance and to improve the appearance of the plant.

Herbs in our experience have remained free from diseases. However, many of them are vulnerable to leaf-eating pests such as slugs, snails, caterpillars, and small beetles. Snail bait will look after the slugs and snails and a routine twice-weekly dusting with Derris Dust (a non-poisonous old remedy) on dampened foliage should take care of the caterpillars and beetles. For those who wish to build up the strength of their gardens so as to try and eradicate all pests, we recommend a comprehensive book on this subject, *Companion Plants* by Helen Philbrick and Richard B. Gregg, published by Stuart and Watkins, London. This book deals with the placing of certain plants near one another or not, according to their make-up, for compatibility, and as insect repellents.

When preparing a seed box, furrows for the planting of the seeds can be made with a piece of timber.

Seed boxes should be placed on a level surface and the seeds sown along the furrows.

The soil on top of freshly sown seeds should be firmly pressed down.

When covering seed in a box, the soil should be rubbed through the hands so that it is fine and powdery and any hard lumps should be discarded.

A tray of healthy young sage seedlings which have reached a stage where they can be potted up.

As well as being useful, fresh herbs are also very decorative. Different varieties can often be successfully grown together and make an attractive display in a stone tub in the garden or in a patio.

This clump of pennyroyal is being prepared for propagation by root division. The herbs are divided up into sections using sharp pruning shears.

This rosemary is a well-established plant which was potted as a cutting and has grown to a stage where it can be transferred to a garden bed.

When clumps of herb seedlings are separated for propagation by the root division method, it is very important to ensure that each section has an adequate piece of established root attached.

During the weeks that it has been in the pot, the rosemary cutting has developed a good root system. In cool climates roots can be encouraged by placing cuttings in a glasshouse or under glass sheets.

Herbs for Beauty

SINCE TIME IMMEMORIAL men and women have adorned their bodies with colored stones, polished bone, and the like, and have used plant dyes on their faces and bodies to enhance their appearance. Today we wear jewelery and use make-up and try to make ourselves look as attractive as possible. Making the most of ourselves enhances our self esteem, and a clean, glowing skin, bright eyes, shining hair, and a healthy, cared-for body all create a pleasant impression. An awareness of the advantages of a healthy lifestyle and basic skin and hair care ought to be nurtured in the young so that as they grow older these attributes, together with the self-assurance and wisdom gained through the experience of living, will give them added appeal.

There are many natural and inexpensive ways to beauty, and in the following recipes we suggest just a few. Different herbs have various components which are helpful for skin, hair, teeth, and eyes, and some of the foods we eat also have these properties so that they, too, can be used as beauty products. Some dairy products, fruits, vegetables, and other natural foods, which also assist surface skin function, are excellent rejuvenating sources from the outside as well as from within. There are stories of how the legendary Cleopatra bathed in asses' milk to keep herself beautiful. Venetian ladies dyed their hair with saffron and henna (a natural substance) for golden or auburn locks. Kohl, mainly composed of powdered minerals, was introduced in Neolithic times and became an early Egyptian cosmetic for the eyes; nowadays it is used in a more refined form as an eyeliner. One of the latest beauty and health phenomena to re-emerge from ancient times is aloe vera (*Aloe barbadenisis*), a native of North Africa and the Mediterranean region of Southern Europe; it was known to the ancient Egyptians and is recorded in the Ebers Papyrus of 1500 B.C.

Facial steaming

Herbal facial steaming is a well-tried and proven aid to a fresher, clearer skin. Dry skin brushing on the body is important too as a daily routine; for this, a long-handled brush, especially made for the purpose, is used. Brushing removes dead skin cells, eliminates acid, stimulates circulation and helps to maintain the body skin's elasticity. Inner cleansing is also important for a glowing skin and clear, sparkling eyes. Apart from drinking at least six glasses of water a day, and ensuring regular, complete, bowel evacuation by eating foods high in dietary fiber, certain herbs are particularly helpful for a clear skin. Lemongrass, for example, taken as a tea or in tablet form, is good, and garlic, eaten either raw or in the form of garlic oil capsules, which can be bought with the addition of parsley to make them odorless, is another.

For a herbal facial steam, the herbs or flowers are simmered in water so that the volatile essences and the medicating, cleansing properties are released. Steaming with herbs induces perspiration, which deep cleanses the pores of the skin, helps to eradicate blackheads, and improves circulation. As well, the facial tissues absorb moisture which has the effect of "plumping up" the skin. After steaming the face, the skin should be rinsed with warm water, gently patted with cotton wool soaked in a cold herb tea to close the pores, and then lightly dried. Allow an hour after a steam treatment for the pores to close completely before going outside. There are various steams to use for different types of skins, but the basic method of preparation is the same for all.

Thoroughly cleanse the skin before starting the treatment. Now put 2 tablespoons of fresh herb leaves or flowers (1 tablespoon if using the dried) into 5 cups (1.25 L) of water in a saucepan (not aluminium) and, with the lid on, slowly bring to boiling point. Lower the heat and simmer the liquid for 2–3 minutes. Turn off the heat, put the saucepan onto a flat surface, and remove the lid. Cover your hair with a shower cap, or wrap it in a towel, envelop your head and the saucepan with a towel and lower your face over the saucepan to within about 8 inches (20 cm). Close your eyes and let the steam circulate around your face by turning your head from side to side. If your skin is fine, or if you have close surface capillaries, 5 minutes should be enough. If you have broken capillaries, do not attempt a facial steam; instead, try cooled, soothing herb teas made from comfrey leaves, comfrey root, chamomile flowers, or elderflowers applied to the face with cotton wool. For normal skins, allow 10 minutes' steaming. One or two facial steam treatments a week should be enough, as too many may destroy the skin's natural moisture and oils.

Here are some suggestions for facial steams according to skin type:

Normal to dry skins

Chopped comfrey leaves, chopped comfrey root, and whole chamomile flowers mixed in equal quantities to make 2 tablespoons. Add to 5 cups of water and follow the general directions given above.

Normal to oily skins

Chopped comfrey leaves and comfrey root, chopped lemongrass, crushed fennel seeds, and crumbled lavender flowers mixed in equal quantities to make 2 tablespoons. Add to 5 cups of water and follow the general directions given above.

Problem skins

To help overcome acne, try chopped comfrey root, crumbled lavender flowers, and chopped lemongrass mixed in equal quantities to make 2 tablespoons. Add to 5 cups of water and follow the general directions given above.

To tighten and stimulate the skin

Chopped peppermint leaves, chopped comfrey leaves, crushed aniseed and rosemary leaves mixed in equal quantities to make 2 tablespoons. Add to 5 cups of water and follow the general directions given above.

To moisturize and soothe the skin

Chopped orange peel, whole orange blossoms, chopped comfrey root, and crushed fennel seeds mixed in equal quantities to make 2 tablespoons. Add to 5 cups of water and follow the general directions given above.

BEAUTY TREATMENTS

Fresh strawberry mask

An old beauty treatment for refreshing and revitalizing the skin was to apply a mask of fresh strawberries to the face and neck. After cleansing the skin, or after a facial steam, cut up and mash to a pulp enough strawberries to spread all over the face and neck, leaving the eye area clear. Lie down for 20 minutes. For extra benefit, soak cotton wool pads in a cold tea made from crushed fennel seeds and put them on your closed eyelids. Rinse the mask off with warm water, then splash cold water all over the face and neck.

Beauty face pack

Natural face packs and lotions work magically on the skin, giving a dewy glow and lovely texture. Fennel seed helps smooth lines away; chamomile is astringent and anti-inflammatory; sage is cooling and astringent; elder flowers lighten and soothe the skin and are especially good for helping to fade freckles. Yogurt and honey feed, clear, and stimulate the skin. Fuller's earth contains minerals. For dilated capillaries on the face, do not use a face pack or extremes of heat and cold. Bathe with tepid milk, leaving it to dry on the face before gently washing off with lukewarm water.

1 cup water
2 teaspoons of any of the following herbs:
  fennel seeds
  chamomile flowers
  sage leaves
  elderflowers
3¹/2 oz (100 g) plain yogurt
1 tablespoon honey
1 tablespoon Fuller's earth (available from pharmacies)

Simmer herbs in water for 15 minutes. Strain into a small bowl (makes about 1 tablespoon strong liquid). Add yogurt, honey, and Fuller's earth. Mix well together. Cool in the refrigerator. Cleanse face thoroughly. Apply pack lightly with cotton wool, all over the face and neck. Lie down for 15 minutes. To remove pack, rinse well with cotton wool, repeatedly dipped into warm water or a strained herb tea of your choice. Pat dry.

Honey and milk rejuvenating lotion

1 cup clear honey
1/2 cup milk
2 teaspoons rosewater (available from a pharmacy or continental delicatessen.)

Warm the honey gently in a saucepan. Add the milk and rosewater, turning off the heat at the same time. Stir until the ingredients are amalgamated. Allow to cool, then pour the lotion into a container and store it in the refrigerator. Before using, stir again if the mixture has separated, and pour a little into a saucer. Soak cotton wool balls in the lotion and pat onto the face and neck. Use this lotion every night and do not rinse it off until the next morning.

Avocado face and neck freshener

Avocado oil is an excellent moisturizer to use under make-up, particularly in drying winds. Fresh avocado on the face and neck is especially nourishing for the skin.

Scoop out the flesh from half an avocado and mash it to a pulp. Spread the pulp on the face and neck and lie down, if possible, for 20 minutes. Remove with tissues, then dampened cotton wool.

Flower-scented facial cleansing oil

1 cup olive oil
1 tablespoon avocado oil
1/2 cup apricot kernel oil
1/2 cup walnut oil
1/4 teaspoon essential flower oil
(e.g. lavender, rose, jasmine, violet, lotus, or ylang ylang — available from specialist herbal stores)

Pour all the oils into a screw-top jar and shake it vigorously. Store in the refrigerator. To use, pour some of the oil onto a piece of cotton wool and gently apply to the face and neck until clean, using an outward and upward movement. Remove oily residue with an alcohol-free toning lotion, or witch hazel, by pouring a little onto slightly damp cotton wool and using the same upward and outward motion. Use this cleanser to remove make-up, city smog, perspiration, and so on.

Herbal after shave

1 tablespoon chopped sage leaves
1 tablespoon chopped comfrey leaves
1 tablespoon rosemary leaves
1½ cups apple cider vinegar
1½ cups witch hazel

Put the herbs and vinegar into a stoppered glass jar and stand it on a sunny windowsill to infuse for 1 week. Strain, then stir in the witch hazel. Store in an airtight container in the refrigerator.

Elderflower lotion for the eyes

Make an infusion as described in Elderberry Lotion but be sure to strain it through fine muslin or cheesecloth before using. Bathe the eyes several times a day with the lotion.

Hand lotion

5 parts glycerine
15 parts rosewater

Mix well together. Soft water or elderflower water can be used instead of rosewater. When using herb water, add a pinch of borax.

Balm tea for strengthening the memory

1 oz (30 g) balm
1¼ pints (600 ml) boiling water

Infuse the balm in the water for 15 minutes. Allow to cool. Drink freely. Sugar and lemon juice give this infusion a pleasant taste.

To whiten the teeth

Rub with sage leaves.

SCENTED BATHS

From *The Scented Garden*
by E.S. Rohde

A cosmetic bath

Take two pounds of Barley or Beanmeal, eight pounds of Bran, and a few handfuls of Borage leaves. Boil these ingredients in a sufficient quantity of spring water. Nothing cleanses and softens the skin like this Bath.

An aromatic bath

Boil, for the space of two or three minutes, in a sufficient quantity of river water, one or more of the following plants; viz. Laurel, Thyme, Rosemary, Wild Thyme, Sweet Marjoram, Bastard-Marjoram, Lavender, Southernwood, Wormwood, Sage, Pennyroyal, Sweet-Basil, Balm, Wild Mint, Hyssop, Clove-july-flowers, Anise, Fennel, or any other herbs that have an agreeable scent. Having strained off the liquor from the herbs, add to it a little Brandy, or camphorated Spirits of Wine.

Jasmine oil

Nothing more is required than to dip the finest cotton wool in clear olive oil, which must be spread in thin layers, in a tall glass vessel, with alternate layers of jessamine flowers which, in a few days, will impart the whole of their perfume to the cotton. The oil may then be pressed out for use: and the cotton itself may be laid in drawers or band-boxes, where its perfume is wished for.

LOTIONS FOR SUNBURN AND FRECKLES

These are very easy to make and do wonders for any skin, especially if used regularly for several weeks. Not only do they soothe sunburn and eliminate some of the redness, they also fade freckles and give the complexion a fine-textured luster.

Elderflower lotion

We have made this lotion with dried elder-flowers, and if you have a tree (*Sambucus nigra*) you can collect the heads of the frothy, creamy blossoms and use them fresh; or dry them on sheets of paper in a dry, airy place until they shrivel into fragile, filigree-flowers, the color of old ivory, then store them in air-tight containers.

Pour 2 cups boiling water onto 2 table-spoons of crumbled, fresh elderflowers or 1 tablespoon fragmented, dried elderflowers. Cover and leave for at least 15 minutes, then strain the lotion into a screw-top jar and store in the refrigerator. (Otherwise it will develop an unpleasant odor.)

Instead of washing your face in the morn-ing, pour some elderflower lotion into a small bowl, and, with cotton wool, pat it all over the face and neck and allow it to dry on the skin. This quantity should be enough for one week if the lotion is kept in a cold place, and it will stay fresh enough to use for that length of time.

Anti-freckles cream

1 fl oz (28 ml) lemon juice
1/4 teaspoon powdered borax
1/2 drachm (3.5 ml) oil of rosemary

Mix the ingredients well and let stand for a few days before using. Rubbed on the hands and face, the cream will lighten, and finally disperse freckles.

Anti-freckles lotion

2 oz (60 g) tincture of benzoin
1/2 drachm (3.5 ml) oil of rosemary
1 oz (30 g) tincture of talc

Mix the ingredients well together in a corked bottle. When required for use, add a teaspoon of the mixture to a wineglass of water and apply the lotion where required night and morning, gently dabbing it in with a soft cloth.

HAIR TREATMENTS

Wash for the hair

4 fl oz (120 ml) lavender water
1/2 oz (15 g) borax
3 fl oz (90 ml) rosewater
1/4 oz (7 g) tincture of cochineal

After washing the hair in this solution, rinse well with a little borax in the last water. This wash is particularly good for oily hair.

Tonic and restorative for hair 1

Infuse in vinegar: rosemary, sage, southern-wood. Allow to stand in bottle in a sunny win-dow for seven or eight days before straining.

Tonic and restorative for hair 2

Infuse in olive oil: sage, thyme, marjoram, and balm. Prepare as for above recipe. Rub a little into scalp before shampooing.

Sage hair tonic

1 tablespoon each of tea and of dried sage

Put into 2 lb (1 kg) jam jar, cover with boiling water, and simmer for two hours. Cool and strain. Rub into scalp four or five times a week. Gradually grayness will disappear, and hair will become dark brown. Tonic will keep for a week. Add 1 tablespoonful of rum, gin, or Eau-de-Cologne for longer keeping.

Rosemary hair rinse

Shampoos and hair lotions containing pure extract of rosemary revitalize the scalp and hair and help to prevent dandruff. Herbal cosmetic manufacturers produce these shampoos, but if you have a rosemary bush in the garden you will be able to make this lotion yourself.

Gather about 4–6 leafy rosemary stalks and simmer them in 5 cups of water for 30 minutes. Keep the lid on the saucepan to prevent the pre-cious vapor from evaporating. Strain and cool, then use as a final rinse after washing your hair, rubbing the lotion well into the scalp.

Herbs as Gifts

MANY CHARMING, UNIQUE, and useful gifts may be made from herbs and flowers. Always appreciated are piquant, aromatic herb vinegars, delectable jams and jellies fragrant with roses or scented herb leaves, preserved sugary flowers, and savory, crumbled "bouquet garni" rolled into small cheesecloth or calico balls tied with string for casseroles, soups, or stews.

Hair rinses, lotions for the face, and other cosmetics are made with bounty gathered from the garden. Nostalgic perfumes of leaves and blossoms, redolent of glowing sunlit gardens, are evoked by various types of potpourris. Exotic scents of the East are contained in a spicy pomander ball. Among many other delights are herbal "bath balls" for tying under a hot running tap, "moth bags" containing a special mixture of sweet and bitter herbs and pungent spices to repel unwanted marauders in cupboards and drawers, and of course, lavender sachets, forever a beloved favorite. Sleep pillows filled with soothing lavender, balmy lemon verbena, and gentle rose petals release a mingling of Nature's tender opiates for untroubled slumber.

Potpourris

The name "potpourri" is French for "a hotchpotch or medley of all sorts of flowers in a jar", according to our dictionary. The "hotchpotch" should be a subtly fragrant mixture of dried scented flowers and leaves, with the addition of aromatic spices to give a warmly contrasting depth to the blend. Top-quality essential oils are combined with orris powder as a fixative for a longer lasting potpourri. Orris powder is the finely ground root or rhizome of the Florentine iris (*Iris florentina*); it "takes up" the moist oils and is distributed right through the mixture, at the same time preventing the potpourri from becoming damp and mildewed. Various methods for making this time-honored mixture have been handed down in some families for generations. At Sissinghurst Castle, famous for its garden, a treasured recipe from the Sackville-West family was made, and is said to have originated in the time of King George I.

There are recipes for "wet" potpourris containing salt and brandy; they are not as straightforward to make as the "dry" variety. Some very old "receipts" include bay salt (sea salt) which can cause a potpourri to become mouldy in damp weather. Gum benzoin, storax, civet, ambergris, and benjamin are either unobtainable or hard to find. A mixture made without these exotic components is still deliciously fragrant.

The first step in making a potpourri or "sweet pot" is to gather perfumed roses and other fragrant flowers on a dry day after the dew has left them; miniature blooms are left whole, bigger flowers are gently pulled apart. Spread the flowers and petals onto sheets of newspaper in a shady but airy place, turning them every day. When petals and flowers are paper-dry, put them into a crockery or glass vessel with an airtight lid. At the same time, gather perfumed foliage, cutting off the stems for quicker drying: scented geranium leaves (particularly the rose-scented), leaves of French lavender (*Lavandula dentata*), bay leaves, lemon-scented verbena, eau-de-Cologne mint, citrus leaves, and any fragrant foliage from a tree, shrub, or plant. Dry them in the same way as the flowers. A microwave oven can be used for drying potpourri ingredients, and this method is described on page 193.

Many different components can be added to the basic assemblage of flowers and leaves, thus giving visual delight as well as fragrance. While flowers and foliage are drying, press flat some whole flowers like violets, tiny roses and carnations, jasmine and mignonette, wall flowers, orange blossom, and rosemary flowers. Interesting colored leaves dry well when pressed. For added scent and effect, stud crabapples with cloves and let the fruit harden; dot cloves into wide strips of orange, lemon, or lime peel; collect glowing ripe rose-hips, nuts, and tiny cones. Add the pleasing shape of star anise, 2 or 3 whole nutmegs, some coriander seeds, pieces of cinnamon bark, and whatever else pleases you.

Basic method for preparing potpourri

The following measures are a guide and can be doubled or trebled. Assemble all the dried flowers and leaves that have been gathered, as well as the orris powder, spices, and any of the extra embellishments suggested. Small bottles of essential oils should be at hand. Choose perfumes that complement one another, but with opposite qualities: some oils and their individual scents are explained below. These essences are available from health food stores and are also used in the art of aromatherapy.

To go with 4 cups of dried flowers and leaves you will need 1 tablespoon of orris powder, 1 teaspoon each of the oils of your choice, and 1 teaspoon each of ground cinnamon and ground coriander seed. Mix orris powder and spices together in a small bowl, then add oils and amalgamate. Sprinkle this crumbly mixture over the measured dried flowers and leaves in a larger bowl, stir well with your hands or with a wooden spoon, put back into the crockery vessel, and close up for 2–3 weeks to mature, turning the potpourri over occasionally. The blend is now ready for putting into one wide attractive bowl or several smaller ones. Finish with the collected and prepared pressed blooms and leaves, clove crabapples, 2 teaspoons of whole cloves, some cinnamon bark, rose-hips, nuts, cones, and citrus peel. You can add more dried flowers to the potpourri at any time.

SOME OILS AND THEIR PROPERTIES

Sweet: honeysuckle, hyacinth, lavender, geranium, jasmine, neroli, rose.
Sharp: boronia, lemongrass, lime, lemon, mandarin, petitgrain, pine.
Lingering: ylang ylang, sandalwood, frankincense, cedarwood, amber, lotus, bergamot — from the fresh peel of the bergamot orange (*Citrus bergamia*).

Here is a list of essential oils and their supposed influence on moods—an idea worth trying in various potpourris. For use as an inhalant or as a massage oil, or for burning as incense, choose only one oil at a time.

Concentration and Willpower: bay, cedarwood, ginger, sage.
Meditation and tranquility: bergamot, lavender, rose, sandalwood, patchouli, ylang ylang, jasmine.
Relaxation: coriander, lavender, pine, lemongrass.
Devotional: neroli, rose, ylang ylang, boronia, jasmine.
Psychic mood: bergamot, lavender, lemongrass, petitgrain, sandalwood, verbena.
Healing: bay, rose, sandalwood, wintergreen, mandarin.
Memory and mental stimulation: rosemary,

pine, thyme, sage.

Wedding and festivities: neroli, rose, boronia, jasmine.

Femininity: bergamot, rose geranium, lavender, rose, jasmine.

Masculinity: cedarwood, pine, ginger.

For soothing sleep: lavender, valerian, rose, lemon-verbena.

For clearing sinuses: pine, eucalyptus, rosemary.

N.B. Do not expect to have all the flowers and leaves ready at the same time. It is usual to collect and dry them while they are at their peak and then store them in covered containers until you are ready to make the potpourri.

Crystallized flowers

The following method is the simplest and quickest way to crystallize flowers. Whole small blooms or single petals may be used, the most suitable being violets, borage flowers, rosemary flowers, English primroses, rose petals, and small, whole rosebuds. (The various scented mint leaves are excellent too.)

Put the white of an egg into a saucer, break it up with a fork, but do not whip. Take a dry flower, or a single petal, and with a small paint brush dipped into the egg white, cover it completely, then shake powdered (caster) sugar through a fine sieve over the flower, first on one side, then the other. As they are finished, spread them out on greaseproof paper laid in a small oven dish. Put the flowers in a very slow oven with the door open for approximately 10–15 minutes, gently turning them as the sugar hardens. Do not leave too long or they will go brown. Store the candied flowers between layers of greaseproof paper in an airtight box.

Rose-petal jam

A small glass jar, or a special pottery bowl, filled with fragrant rose-petal jam, is a very special and quite exotic gift. Use the jam to spoon over ice cream, or to spread on thin, crustless triangles of bread and butter, or on hot, buttered scones.

To 50 fully opened, fragrant red (or red and pink together) roses, allow 2 pints (1 L) of water and 3 lb (1.5 kg) of powdered (caster) sugar. Boil the sugar and water until it is slightly candied. Add the juice of a lemon and the rose petals, which have been gently pulled from the flowers. Stir well and bring to a boil. Put in a pat of unsalted butter to clear the scum and then simmer for approximately an hour. It is necessary to stir frequently, every five minutes or so, or the color will be brown instead of a translucent, ruby red. Cool, pour into clean pots or jars, and cover when cold.

If the mixture seems a little too thin, add some fruit pectin (available from health food stores or grocers), following the instructions on the packet.

Clove apple (or orange)

To keep away moths

It is important to start with a fresh, firm apple, or a ripe, fresh, thin-skinned orange. Stick the fruit full of cloves, starting from the stalk end and going around as many times as is needed to cover it, leaving a small space between each clove. Now roll the fruit well in 2 teaspoons of orris root powder and 2 teaspoons of ground cinnamon mixed together. Wrap the fruit in tissue paper and put it away in a dark cupboard for a few weeks. A staple may be pressed into the top at this stage so that when the fruit has hardened, ribbon may be threaded through it. Alternatively, ribbon can be passed around the fruit four times, giving a "basket" effect, and then more ribbon can be attached to the top so that the clove apple can be hung from a clothes hanger in a wardrobe, or, using a pretty idea from the past, on a door handle. Velvet or corded ribbon in colorful shades makes a charming contrast with the snuff-brown of the pomander. Once the fruit has hardened, it will last indefinitely, gradually shrinking over a period of time. We do not know what happens to the inside. We once broke one open, using a cleaver because it was iron-hard, and there was no sign of anything at all, not even a pip!

Peppermint-geranium jelly

This is another unusual and delicious-tasting conserve that will make a unique and very special gift. Other types of scented geranium leaves may be used instead.

*1 small bunch stalkless peppermint-geranium
    leaves (about 1 cup)
5 cups powdered (caster) sugar
juice of 2 small lemons or 1 large lemon
4 cups water
4 oz (125 g) powdered pectin
green food coloring or Crème de Menthe*

Wash the geranium leaves and steep them in the sugar and lemon juice for 1 hour. Place in a saucepan with the water and bring to a boil. Strain, add the pectin (follow the instructions on the package), and boil again, stirring for about a minute. Add the food coloring or Crème de Menthe. Pour into clean jars or pots, placing a small peppermint-geranium leaf in each one. Seal the lids. This will keep in the refrigerator for several weeks.

Bath sachets

Soothing lavender

These are made with the dried flowers of English lavender. French lavender flowers may be used instead but they do not have the highly incensed perfume of English lavender. The sticky, oily leaves of French lavender give an excellent, strong fragrance. Both of these lavenders soothe the nerve endings of the body, and the best way to do this is to lie in a bath permeated with the essential oils, either released from the bath sachets or from drops of the essential oil, or a lavender "bath milk." (Smelling lavender flowers for some time when packaging it acts as a soporific.)

As these sachets are disposable after several uses, do not buy expensive material for them; select a pretty, sprigged, thin cotton, or other suitable fabric in lavender colors.

Cut the fabric into small squares, put a small pile of lavender in the middle, and tie into a ball, securing it with a long piece of string; use pinking shears to prevent fraying. Tie about six

together with a little card, saying: "Soothing Lavender Bath Sachets: tie to the hot tap and run hot water over the sachet to release the natural essences. May be used two or three times."

Revitalizing Rosemary

Use the same idea for rosemary bath sachets, which, instead of being sleep-inducing, are revitalizing. A rosemary bath is an excellent way to start the day, or before going out again at night. For these sachets use green or blue sprigged material since rosemary flowers are blue.

Bouquet garni

This is a useful gift for people who like to use a bouquet garni in little sachets, which are removed after cooking. Buy, or make, a bouquet garni of crumbled, dried bay leaves, dried thyme, dried marjoram, and dried parsley. Put a little pile of the herbs in the middle of a muslin square and tie with a long piece of string for easy removal at the end of cooking time. Put about six sachets into a celluloid box, or a cellophane bag, attractively tied with ribbon.

Herb vinegars

There are many different uses for the herbs in your garden, so while they are still bountiful making herb vinegars is a very satisfying and useful task, and they make delightful and unusual gifts. The vinegar may be flavored with various herbs, or a combination of compatible-tasting herbs. Tarragon, rosemary, savory, basil, thyme, marjoram, oregano, garlic, and lemon balm, as well as dill and mint, all make strongly flavored vinegars on their own. Parsley and fennel combine well, as do parsley and peppercorns, or parsley and garlic. Rose-petal vinegar is an unusual and colorful vinegar with several uses.

Herb vinegars make delicious vinaigrette dressings. One tablespoon of herb vinegar to three tablespoons of oil is the usual mixture. There are many interesting oils on the market, as well as the time-honored olive oil. A few to choose from are walnut oil, hazelnut oil, apricot-kernel oil, sunflower-seed oil, or pumpkin-seed oil. Some of these rather rare oils may only

Roses, rose geranium, and lemon geranium growing together. Dried, these make an equally lovely combination.

be available from specialist delicatessens or health food stores, but they are well worth ferreting out.

Making the vinegars is simple. Pick and wash the herbs to be used and dry them well on absorbent paper. Pack the leaves into clean bottles or jars with lids, and fill with white wine vinegar, replacing the lids firmly. Another method is to heat the vinegar first to hasten the release of the oils from the leaves before pouring it over them. Stand the infusing vinegars on a sunny windowsill for about two weeks. The warmth from the sun releases the flavor and perfume of the herbs. If there is no sun during this time, let them stand for two more weeks. Some herbs lose their color and become pallid-looking after soaking in the vinegar and giving out their color and flavor. If this happens, strain the vinegar into a clean bottle and put in a fresh, washed sprig of the herb. This not only improves the appearance but adds flavor. Replace the lids and label the bottles. If using red rose petals, the vinegar will gradually turn a most beautiful rich crimson. This is a valuable ingredient for subtle

salad dressings but may also be used to relieve headaches. An old remedy is to soak a cloth in the vinegar, wring it out, and apply the wet cloth to the forehead. Repeat until the vinegar in the bowl is used up.

WAYS WITH FRESH AND DRIED HERB FLOWERS

Harvesting and drying herbs from a scented garden for decoration, means continued enjoyment of their color and fragrance long after the growing season has passed. Pick long stems of English lavender in full bloom before the flowers begin to fall, and arrange the collection in various ways: a compact group of lavender flower spears, vessels full of perfume, will dry naturally and make a subtle and original embellishment to a window ledge, a garden room, or a kitchen table. To do this, fill a small terracotta trough with floral foam and press into it rows of lavender stalks, until the trough is full — a charming contingent of lavender "at attention!"

Crystallized flowers and leaves (see page 209).

Whole, barely opened miniature rosebuds hold their color and shape when picked in dry weather and carefully hung by their stems in a warm, airy cupboard until crisp; or strew the roses onto sheets of newspaper and leave until dry. When ready, cluster the papery roses together on their own in posies, or mix with dried lavender heads. Any colorful flowers and fragrant leaves that you would prepare for a potpourri, but with their stems intact, can also go into a dried herb-flower assortment.

A tight bunch of fresh herb flowers gathered as you walk around the garden becomes one of the prettiest and most fragrant of flower posies. As the assemblage grows, one remembers the "language of flowers", a delightful means of communication between lovers in a more romantic age. Roses signified love; rosemary was, and is, for remembrance; sweet basil expressed good wishes; four-leaved clover said "be mine", and mint meant virtue. Lavender is always welcome in a posy, so are eau-de-Cologne mint's plump, purple-tinged flowerheads. Pluck velvet-textured peppermint-geranium leaves and their frail flowers; add a brilliant flourish of nasturtium blooms; rob the bees of a few red or pink bergamot flower tufts; cut stems of rosy betony and bistort, and choose some sages in a dazzling color spectrum of blooms from deep blue to purple, red, pink, and white, the size of the flowers varying as much as the colors. Sage foliage differs widely too; several kinds are grown especially for their variegations. Cousins of the common gray sage, they have leaves streaked with white or with gold and others have purple- or red-flushed leaves. Golden marjoram, and green and white-pied applemint do not lose their fragrance or their flavor just because their leaves are ornamental. Don't forget to include chives' mauve pincushion-flowers when in bloom and the fairy-like blossoms of thyme on tiny leafy stalks, or yellow button-heads of cotton lavender. Sky-blue borage flowers on their sappy stems need plenty of water, so when your bunch is in a vase, keep it topped up. Float the star-like single borage blooms in finger bowls, a punch bowl, or on top of a jug of fruit juice.

Taller herb flowers are spectacular and last well when picked: showy spires of acanthus, (the oyster plant or bear's breeches) lofty foxgloves, large round heads of garlic flowers, and shining, pale lemon mullein, the candelabra plant, are a few, and although these are not culinary herbs, except for garlic, all are medicinal plants. A vase massed with the flowers of one of these herbs will look stunning and takes very little effort. Dill, fennel, or angelica flowers are also well suited to this treatment, as is their relative, Queen Anne's Lace, which is thought to be a wild carrot.

A lavender bottle

Creating a lavender bottle is a traditional craft known to European countryfolk and practiced for generations. This art continues, as evidenced in Rome recently, where we saw a *contadina* sitting on a wooden stool by a street corner deftly weaving ribbon in and out of bent lavender stalks, a full basket of freshly picked lavender by her side.

To make a lavender bottle: pick English lavender in full flower but before it begins to drop. When the lavender is fresh the stems are pliable, a necessary condition for this task. Take about 10 heads (an even number is desirable) with stalks that are as long as possible. You will need a length of mauve ribbon (or another suitable color) about 1/4 to 1/2 inch (6–12 mm) wide. Tie the heads tightly together just below the flower spike, leaving one end of the ribbon about 9 inches (23 cm) long and the other end as long as possible. Bend the stems carefully over just below the ribbon knot, spacing evenly over the flower spikes. Interweave the long end of ribbon through alternate stalks, going round and round the stems until the flowers are enclosed. At this point, twist the ribbon several times round the stalks to secure them, and tie in a bow with the short end (which must be brought down with the flower heads) underneath the weaving. For a plumper bottle, add loose lavender to the inside before finally tying the ribbon. Squeeze gently to release the perfume.

Herbs as Medicine

THE BENEFITS OF orthodox (allopathic) medicine are undisputed, and advances in scientific research and modern technology are bringing new and dramatic lifesaving discoveries every day. In spite of this, alternative forms of healing and prevention of illness are becoming more widely recognized and accepted. One of the reasons for this is that many practitioners of orthodox medicine, and people in general, are concerned with the side effects of chemically manufactured drugs and are turning to natural forms of healing where possible.

Treatment by alternative (or "traditional") medicine need not be a complete break-away from the orthodox, but allied with it. A partnership of both, one taking over where the other is unable to complete a cure, or a combination of both, is happening already. Some clinics, as well as private practitioners of orthodox and alternative medicines, work in conjunction with each other. A selective use of both when needed is an individual choice. A number of people have, however, found renewed health by following alternative methods only.

Most alternative medicines have in common a *holistic* philosophy, which profoundly, yet subtly, activates the healing of the entire person, that is body, mind, and spirit. Nearly all these forms of healing use herbs in certain ways during treatment. Meditation is essentially part of holistic philosophy also. Different types of natural therapies are an integral part of the curative routine prescribed in alternative medicines, and you will find that treatment is combined with one or more therapies to achieve the final goal.

Specialized books provide detailed explanations of particular alternative medicines and therapies. Amongst these methods are acupuncture, the Alexander technique, medicine, aromatherapy, biochemics, Bach remedies, color therapy, chiropractic, crystal healing, the Feldenkarais method, homeopathy, macrobiotics, hydrotherapy, naturopathy, osteopathy, psionic medicine, pyramid healing, shiatsu, tai-chi, and yoga. Three are discussed briefly here.

Naturopathy is one form of alternative medicine. After diagnosis, the patient is advised on diet and inner cleansing and is treated with herbal medicines, tablets, ointments, teas, and special oils. These treatments are sometimes used in conjunction with various other therapeutic skills including massage, manipulation, aromatherapy, and others mentioned earlier. The ancient Egyptians practiced the art of aromatherapy, where skilled practitioners prescribe certain oils, which according to the ailment, may be used internally, massaged into the skin, or used to purify the air. Physiotherapists who are trained in this therapy claim to be able to change a person's mood by using oils with different aromas – some oils are said to improve the memory, others help concentration and meditation, induce tranquillity, influence recovery from illness, and so on.

Homeopathy, another form of healing, is very highly regarded and has also the Royal seal of approval. In the 18th century Dr Samuel Hahnemann, a German physician, after long observation and study, and successful treatment of patients, revealed this particular form of medicine. "Like cures like" is one of the basic principles of homeopathy. Medicines are made from plants, trees, flowers, weeds, minerals, and some animal products. They are individually prepared so that they may be given to patients in small, diminishing doses, until the "trilogy" of mind, body, and spirit is generated into the healing process. People on homeopathic treatment keep a range of these medicines, which they use every day, and even have a special kit to use when traveling.

Bach remedies, discovered by Dr Edward Bach in the 1930s, also have a distinguished reputation; they are made from the essential energy found within flowers and trees. The essences are extracted in a unique way and are meticulously prepared for individual use, in a way that is similar to homeopathy. There are a great many specialist homeopathic doctors throughout the world today, many of whom have also completed their orthodox medical training, who prescribe homeopathic and Bach remedies for their patients. As with any form of healing, it is important to seek the advice of a registered, experienced, and reputable practitioner.

The remedies and cures detailed in this chapter are merely household "simples" and are not intended to replace any medication that may have been prescribed by a doctor or other registered practitioner. Some of these household remedies have been quoted from *Lotions and Potions* and some are from Dr Kunzle's *Herbs and Weeds*. Naturopathy, homeopathy, and Bach remedies require study, training, and a thorough background knowledge, which takes many years to acquire.

OLD AND WELL-TRIED REMEDIES

Many years ago, when we first decided to make the growing and processing of herbs our livelihood and way of life, a very kind English aunt, the late Mrs Thomas Dodd, sent us a most enchanting little book called *Lotions and Potions*, which was a collection of "Recipes of Women's Institute Members and their Ancestors," edited by Gwynedd Lloyd and printed in England by Novello and Co. Ltd, in 1956. This delightful book, with its cheerful blue and yellow cover depicting a country cottage surrounded by flowers, a many-paned window left invitingly open, birds perching on the sloping, thatched roof, and pet cats on the path, has been a great source of interest and knowledge, and a number of the household remedies within its pages have been quoted, and acknowledged, in books we have written. It is still treasured amongst our reference books, and is now showing signs of all the thumbing and reading it has had through the years.

Imagine our delight when, visiting Culpeper's fascinating and charming shop in Cambridge recently, we saw a new edition of this book on their shelves, printed by Bournemouth Press Ltd, Bournemouth — this time with an evocative musk-pink cover. Naturally we bought it immediately. We should like to borrow a few more of the common-sense and useful recipes from a favorite book.

A lotion for baldness

"Take of box leaves four handfuls. Boil in eight pints of water in a tightly closed pan for fifteen minutes. Add an ounce of Eau-de-Cologne. Wash the head every evening."
N.B. Box leaves come from *Buxus sempervirens*.

To cure corns

"Wash the feet in hot salted water. Squeeze a drop of the juice of the greater Celandine (*Chelidonium majus*) onto the corn and leave to dry. Two applications are usually sufficient. This cure can also be used for warts."

N.B. The book attributes this cure to an "old herbal."

Bruise oil

"Balm, rosemary, chamomile flowers, rose-buds, feverfews, sage, lavender tops, southern-wood betony, wormwood.

Take of each a handful and chop them small, put in a stone jar with sufficient salad oil to cover them. Stand for a fortnight, stirring often. Then boil gently until oil is extracted (till ingredients become crisp), but do not exceed the heat of boiling water. Strain through linen, and keep in a well corked bottle. A well tried receipt."

Infusion for nervous headaches and bad memory

"One ounce fresh or dried rosemary, infused with one pint of boiling water. Cool and strain. Dose: a wineglassful 4 times a day — hot."

Rheumatism

"Boil 1 oz of celery seed in 1 pint of water until reduced to half. Strain, bottle and cork careful-ly. Take 1 teaspoonful twice a day in a little water for a fortnight. Repeat again if required."

Chilblain mixture

"Mix one tablespoonful of honey with equal quantity of glycerine, the white of an egg and enough flour to make a paste — a teaspoonful of rosewater may be added. Wash the affected parts with warm water, dry and spread on paste. Cover with piece of linen or cotton material."

So many people have been sincerely interested and generous to us during the long years of our rewarding "herbal experience." One person in particular, whom we have never met, has a special place in our thoughts. He is the gentle-man who sent us a dear and quaint little book, full of wisdom and sound advice, called *Herbs and Weeds*, by "Father John Kunzle, Herbalist." The new copy we have been able to find was printed by Salvioni and Co. SA., Bellinzona, Switzerland, in 1975.

John Kunzle was born in Switzerland in 1857. He wished to devote himself to God's service and was ordained after graduating from the seminary of St. Gall. He then, through various circumstances, continued studying botany, a favorite subject, and soon became aware of the healing powers of herbs. After many case histories, and a rigorous examination by a board of physicians, which he passed brilliantly, he was acknowledged by the authorities as a Father-herbalist and became world famous. He was able to understand man in his entirety, taking into account the interaction of body and soul; he also had an intuitive flair for the hidden healing powers of herbs and was a pioneer in the science of poisonless herb healing. His booklet *Herbs and Weeds*, edited in 1911, was published in German and has been translated into several languages.

In 1945, at the age of 87, Father Kunzle died of a heart attack, "but still in rare mental vigour . . . he passed to the better world, to the blessed Kingdom where the most beautiful alpine flowers and the finest herbs will flourish and smell sweet for him."

The following cures are from Father Kunzle's booklet.

A simple remedy for corns

Many people cut onions in slices, lay them in vinegar, and place a slice on the corn every night. It helps many. But usually vanity is to be blamed for all these corns because people wear too small shoes.

Influenza tea

To prevent influenza, drink a sip of a tea prepared from the following mixture in the morning and evening: one handful each of wormwood, sage, Alpine speedwell, and liquorice root. People who are sick with influenza should take a spoonful of this tea every half-hour. They will recover in two days.

Sage tea has many medicinal properties (see page 276).

Orange blossoms – *Flores aurantil*
Orange blossoms are considered to be a very pleasant and absolutely harmless sedative for the nerves which explains why they are mainly used as an ingredient for teas to calm the nerves and to encourage sleep. They are also suitable for correcting the scent and taste in remedies.

Wild pansy – *Herba violae tricoloris*
Wild pansy blossoms are a blood-purifying remedy in case of skin diseases (eczema, milk-crust, acne, furunculosis). They stimulate both urination and metabolism and are therefore used for stomach and bladder troubles, weakness of the kidneys, micturition, gravel, articular rheumatism, gout, and arteriosclerosis; also in case of heart disturbances, hysteria, chronic bronchial catarrh, and cramps.

N.B. This pretty little wild pansy, an annual, is often known as heartsease, Johnny-jump-up, and love-in-idleness.

SIMPLE HOME REMEDIES AND HINTS

• For simple household burns, caused by touching a hot iron in the wrong place, or grasping an overheated saucepan handle, and the like, gently pat lavender oil over the sore part. This will not only take away the pain, but will help to heal the skin tissue.

• For a sweet-smelling bathroom, pour a few drops of a flower oil on to the spout of the hot tap and turn it on for a few moments to release the fragrance. The floral aroma will fill the room for some time.

• During a flea plague, fresh pennyroyal sprigs should be rubbed into the coats of dogs and cats and placed wherever you can around the house, even under mattresses. If you do not have fresh pennyroyal, pennyroyal oil can be used with caution—a single drop behind each ear and at the base of your pet's tail.

• Insect bites are alleviated by rubbing the skin with fresh sage leaves. The pain of a bee-sting is lessened if the area is rubbed with fresh leaves of winter or summer savory — after first removing the sting.

• Lavender oil rubbed into some of the furniture, or bunches of fresh lavender in vases, helps to keep houseflies at bay. A posy of rue, tansy, wormwood, and elder leaves is excellent for this purpose too.

• Chewing strawberries will prevent the formation of tartar on your teeth.

• Cinnamon bark pieces, dried wormwood leaves, and the dried leaves of tansy and mint crumbled together and put into muslin bags will help keep moths and silverfish away from cupboards and drawers.

• For restless legs syndrome, during the night, put your legs in a bath of hot water up to the calves and pour in a few drops of soothing lavender oil. Soak them for five minutes, rubbing gently with a washer. Dry your legs and go back to bed. It helps the condition, but does not cure it.

• Plant tansy near entrances to the house to prevent the small, black summer flies that somehow find a way inside, in spite of fly screens. (This has been proved effective by us.) Tansy, together with rue, wormwood, lavender, and a small elder tree planted around a barbecue area has the same effect. Sprays of tansy placed on an outdoor buffet also help to repel flies. Unfortunately it is too bitter to eat.

• A strong wormwood tea, cooled, and poured on the tracks of slugs and snails in spring and autumn (fall) will deter them.

• *Bronchitis and tightness of the chest*

Chop a garlic small and put into a jar of petroleum jelly (vaseline). Stand on a warm hob for a few days. When cold, massage freely into back and chest.

• *To cure corns*

Take equal parts of a roasted onion and soft soap. Beat well together and apply them to the corn on linen, as a poultice.

• *To relieve a heavy cold*

Grate horseradish and inhale the fumes that arise.

• *Anti-moth herbs 1*

A handful each of dried and crumbled santolina, wormwood, mint, tansy; half a stick of cinnamon cut up small. A few dried pyrethrum flowers.

• *Anti-moth herbs 2*

A handful each of lavender, rosemary, southernwood, thyme. A little pennyroyal, 1/2 oz (14g) crushed cloves, small piece of dried lemon peel.

• To lose weight

"For the normal healthy person who is falling into flesh the safest and best method of slimming to adopt is to eat much less of all food taken as a usual thing at meals. It is also necessary to refrain from eating between meals." From *The Coronation Cookery Book*, compiled for the Country Women's Association of NSW, Australia, by Jessie Sawyer OBE and Sara Moore-Sims.

And from the same book:

• A good eyewash

"One dram boracic powder, 1/2 oz witchhazel, 2 grains sulphate of zinc, 8 oz rose water. Dilute with two or three parts of warm water, and apply by means of eyebath."

• A doctor's preventive for influenza

"Take 2 drops of oil of cinnamon on sugar daily."

• For cleansing the digestive system

A herbal tea made from the fresh or dried leaves of lovage taken twice a day for one or two weeks. To be included in fresh green salads as well.

• Elizabethan or Elderberry Rob

A recipe from *Lotions and Potions*, with a note that it is a very old recipe, well tried.

Put 5 lb (2.5 kg) of washed, ripe elderberries with 4 lb (500 g) of sugar into a saucepan and simmer until it is the consistency of honey. Strain and bottle. One or two tablespoonfuls to be taken at bedtime in very hot water. It is a mild aperient, will stop a cold and bring on a sweat. It relieves all chest troubles. A tablespoonful of whiskey may be added if liked.

• A comfortable cordial to cheer the heart

"Take one ounce of conserve of gilliflowers, four grains of the best Musk bruised as fine as flour, then put into a little tin pot and keep it till you have need to make this Cordial following: Take the quantity of one nutmeg out of your tin pot, put to it one spoonful of Cinnamon water, and one spoonful of the Sirup of Gilliflowers, Ambergris, mix all these together, and drink them in the morning, fasting three or four hours, this is most comfortable." A *Choice Manual of Secrets in Physick*, Elizabeth Grey, Countess of Kent, 1653, in *A Garden of Herbs*, Eleanour Sinclair Rohde, published for the Medici Society Ltd, London, by Philip Lee Warner.

Saint Fiacre, the patron saint of gardens.

Cooking with Herbs

THE FOLLOWING RECIPES contain ingredients which are not unusual in everyday cooking except for the inclusion of certain herbs or edible flowers. These give flavor, color, nourishment, digestive qualities for easier assimilation, and piquancy to the palate.

It is astounding how the varied tastes of herbs can alter the character of any dish, and experimenting is always recommended. However, there are excellent traditional reasons for combining many foods and herbs. For instance, some herb seeds (which are usually listed as spices once they are dried) have remarkably therapeutic digestive-aiding oils locked into them, like dill seeds, caraway seeds, fennel seeds, coriander seeds, anise seeds (aniseed), and cardamom seeds. Some are incorporated into special recipes for helping to dispel flatulence — cabbage dishes with dill or caraway seeds, starchy yeast cookery with any of the above seeds, and succulent, fatty pork, duck, or goose with dry, aromatic sage leaves to counteract too much richness, are some examples.

The use of a special herb, or a combination of herbs, occurs in various recipes and in the alphabetical listing of herbs we have given their medicinal and culinary properties, so that the reasons for using them in a given dish are clear. Once again, a favorite herb flavor of your own choice should, through testing, be tried as well.

The employment of fragrant, silky-petalled flowers is a nutritious, delicate way of sampling some of the rarefied essences within the heart of blooms, usually only enjoyed by butterflies and bees. "Cookery . . . means the knowledge of all herbs and fruits and balms and spices, and all that is healing and sweet in the fields and groves, and savory in meats . . ." (Part of a quotation by Ruskin from *The Gentle Art of Cookery* by Mrs. C. F. Leyel and Miss Olga Hartley, Chatto and Windus, London, 1925.)

Salad Herbs

Today's meals often include a light, healthy salad, and some of the herbs in this book will find their way into your own salads. Salad herbs have been grown for centuries in traditional cottage gardens and in the kitchen gardens of grander establishments. Quite recently it has been discovered that some types of lettuce were almost extinct owing to a temporary preference for larger hybridized versions with a more subtle taste; but now the older varieties, with their interesting textures and tastes, are being appreciated again. John Evelyn, a prominent 17th-century culinary expert, herbalist, and author of the book *Acetaria*, wrote fascinating discourses on the variety of components for "sallets."

Most greengrocers display a choice of different kinds of lettuce which can be bought singly or as mesclun, where their leaves are torn up and mixed together with herbs which may include rocket, cress, purslane, chervil, and red chicory as well as some whole flowers or their petals. With the following information you can make your own mesclun as well as unique and interesting salads, containing herbs freshly picked from your own garden.

There are a great number of herbs in this book whose young foliage, tender tops, and flowers enhance a salad, although it is not suggested that too many be used at the same time. Some of them are basil, chervil, chives, cress, dill, garlic, salad burnet, sweet cicely, parsley, garlic, balm, bergamot, borage, chicory, coriander, hyssop, marjoram, and mint. There are also specific herbs which are lesser known but make an interesting foundation, or partnership, with lettuce for innovative, delicious salads: they are purslane, rocket, lamb's lettuce (also known as corn salad), and mustard greens. Purslane, rocket, lamb's lettuce, and mustard greens are available in seed packets and are occasionally found already started in punnets.

You may like to add a few wild dandelion leaves to a salad for their rather bitter contrast to the other ingredients and for their influence on the kidneys. Also cleansing to the kidneys are violet leaves (if in flower add a few of these too). Edible peppery nasturtium leaves are nutritious and rich in vitamin C, and their flowers are edible as well. Chickweed is another wild herb which can be used.

Nasturtium flowers and leaves make excellent salad ingredients.

Soups

PARSLEY SOUP

SERVES 6

This is an excellent and nourishing soup, rich in vitamins.

1 large bunch of parsley
about 4 oz (125 g)
1 lb (500 g) potatoes
1/2 lettuce
1 medium-sized white onion
2 teaspoons salt
8 cups water

Wash the parsley, reserve a little for garnishing, and cut the rest up coarsely, removing the stalks. Peel and wash the potatoes; cut into small chunks. Wash the lettuce, discarding any discolored leaves, and chop roughly. Peel onion. Put all these ingredients into a large saucepan with the salt and water, and bring to a boil. Simmer with the lid on for 45 minutes to 1 hour. Purée the slightly cooled soup in a blender, or press soup through a sieve. Return to the saucepan to reheat. Garnish each serving with the reserved parsley, either chopped or in small, whole sprigs, and serve hot. In summer, chill the soup and add a spoonful of sour cream to each serving before decorating with the parsley.

MRS GODDARD'S CHERVIL AND AVOCADO SOUP

SERVES 6

2 medium-sized ripe avocados
1 clove garlic, crushed
1 tablespoon lemon juice
2 1/2 cups cold chicken stock
salt
freshly ground black pepper
1 1/4 cups sour cream
1 tablespoon chopped chervil
(or 2 teaspoons chopped green dill)

Halve the avocados, remove the stones and set them aside, scoop out the flesh, including all the green part next to the skin. Chop the flesh roughly and purée in a blender at high speed with the garlic, lemon juice, half the stock, the salt, and the pepper. Pour the mixture into a large bowl and stir in the cream and the remainder of the stock; whisk until blended. Fold in the chervil, add the stones (to prevent discoloration), cover, and chill for 2 hours. Garnish with a small spray of chervil (or dill) and serve with a slice of lemon and an ice cube in each bowl. Accompany the soup with Shrimp and Parsley Rolls (page 232).

PUMPKIN AND BASIL SOUP

SERVES 6

2 lb (1 kg) pumpkin, peeled and roughly chopped
2 potatoes, peeled and roughly chopped
1 onion, chopped
1 tablespoon chopped basil
salt and pepper
2 chicken stock cubes
5 cups water
sour cream

Boil all ingredients (except sour cream) until tender. Cool and purée. Return the soup to the saucepan and simmer for 30 minutes until thick. Serve with sour cream.

SORREL SOUP

SERVES 4

4 oz (125 g) butter or vegetable margarine
1 small bunch, 4 oz (125g) sorrel leaves,
shredded
8 cups water
1 lb (500g) potatoes, washed, peeled, and diced
1–2 teaspoons salt
pepper to taste
2 egg yolks

Melt the butter in a saucepan, stir in the shredded sorrel, and simmer until softened. Add water, potatoes, salt, and pepper. Bring to a boil, then simmer with the lid on for 1 hour. Press the soup through a sieve, or purée in a blender. Reheat in the saucepan. Blend a little of the hot liquid into the beaten egg yolks, pour into the saucepan of soup, and stir well without boiling. Chill. Serve with a spoonful of cream in each bowl and a little chopped parsley. Serve hot in winter.

GREEN CRESS SOUP

SERVES 4

1 lb (500 g) potatoes, peeled and diced
2 green outside lettuce leaves, chopped
1 onion, peeled and chopped
2 1/2 cups water
2 cups milk
1 cup firmly packed cress leaves, any variety,
chopped finely
2 teaspoons salt

Simmer potatoes, lettuce, and onion with water in a covered saucepan for 1 hour. Purée soup in a blender or press through a sieve, return to saucepan on a low heat. In a separate pot, heat milk, then stir into purée until thoroughly blended. Add cress and salt, remove from stove, and serve. For cold cress soup, chill in refrigerator, pour into cold glasses or bowls, top with a spoonful of sour cream and a cress leaf.

LOVAGE SOUP

SERVES 4

1 oz (30 g) butter or vegetable margarine
2 tablespoons wholemeal flour
2 1/2 cups chicken stock (may be stock cubes)
2 1/2 cups milk
1 tablespoon chopped lovage leaves
2 teaspoons lemon juice
salt
1 tablespoon chopped chives
yogurt or sour cream

Melt the butter in a saucepan, add the flour and blend to a smooth paste. Gradually pour in the warmed stock, stirring until thickened. Still stirring, add the milk, lovage, and lemon juice. Simmer for 15 to 20 minutes and add the salt. Purée the soup and return it to the saucepan. Stir in the chives and cook for a few minutes only.

Serve either hot or chilled and garnish with a swirl of plain yogurt or sour cream, topped with a sprig of fresh lovage.

BLENDER BORAGE SOUP

SERVES 4–6

1 cup mashed potato (may be made with instant potato)
1 bunch, or 4 oz (125 g) borage leaves, washed and roughly chopped
½ teaspoon salt
4 cups chicken stock (may be made with 2 chicken cubes)

Put potato, borage leaves, and salt into blender with as much stock as will fit into it. Turn onto high for a few seconds, or until borage is finely chopped and soup is blended. Pour into a saucepan and stir in the rest of the stock, adding more salt if necessary. Heat and serve. In summer this soup is delicious chilled and served cold.

LENTIL AND SAVORY SOUP

SERVES 4

1 cup green lentils
5 cups water
1 onion, chopped
2 carrots, chopped
1 parsnip, chopped
1 teaspoon salt
sprig of savory
1 tablespoon all-purpose (plain) flour
3 teaspoons finely chopped savory

Wash lentils and put in a saucepan with water, onion, carrots, parsnip, salt, and a sprig of savory. Simmer until soft. Press the soup through a sieve, or purée in a blender. Return to the saucepan with flour smoothed in a little cold water, and stir until boiling. Add finely chopped savory and serve hot.

Blender borage soup.

Savories & Snacks

CRAB COCKTAIL IN HERB YOGURT SAUCE

SERVES 4

1 cup plain yogurt
1 teaspoon tomato paste
2 teaspoons finely chopped savory tops
2 teaspoons tarragon, dill, or chervil, finely chopped
2 teaspoons lemon juice
8 oz (250 g) crab, flaked (remove any sharp pieces)

Mix all the ingredients together, except the crab. Chill. Fold the crab into the sauce and serve in individual glasses garnished with a sprig of savory. An excellent accompaniment is thin, crustless, brown bread sandwiches filled with herbs.

AVOCADO, CRESS, AND CAVIAR MOLD

SERVES 8

2 tablespoons gelatine melted in a little hot water – stir briskly until clear
3 avocados, peeled, stoned, and sliced
1 tablespoon lemon juice
4 cups canned beef consommé
1 tablespoon finely chopped onion
3 tablespoons black lumpfish roe (often called caviar)
1 tablespoon chopped cress

Purée the avocados, lemon juice, consommé, and onion in a blender or food processor until smooth. (Do it in batches so as not to overload the appliances.) Transfer the mixture to a bowl and fold in the gelatine mixture, lumpfish roe, and cress. Pour into individual molds, or a shallow dish, and leave to set in the refrigerator. To serve, unmold, or cut into squares, and accompany with sour cream and sprigs of cress.

HERB SANDWICHES

Fresh herb sandwiches are both nourishing and delicious. A thin coating of cream cheese or yeast extract on the bottom slice of buttered bread will help to bring out the flavor of the herbs without being overpowering. Unsalted, "sweet" butter is recommended, unless margarine is preferred. There are other spreads, or fillings, which seem to complement certain herbs, and some suggestions are given below. It is always interesting to experiment with flavor combinations too.

Herb sandwiches can be served for morning or afternoon tea — with cakes or cookies as well if you wish, although most people nowadays prefer not to eat very much between meals, if at all, so herb sandwiches on their own are usually quite sufficient. They make an excellent accompaniment to a first course. Use a good-quality fresh bread, either white or brown, and cut the slices as thin as possible. Butter the bread first, then cut through with a very sharp knife. Alternatively, sliced sandwich bread may be used.

Cover the bottom slices with your chosen spread, then the chopped herbs, then close the sandwich. When enough have been made, remove the crusts and cut the sandwiches into triangles, squares, or fingers. (The smaller the better for a dinner party.) Put the sandwiches onto an attractive plate and cover with plastic film or foil and store in the refrigerator until needed. Alternatively, roll up each crustless slice of buttered, herb-strewn bread (the bread must be very fresh for this) and secure with a toothpick, which can be removed before serving.

The most delectable herb rolls we have tasted accompanied a first course of iced chervil and avocado soup, for lunch, in an English dining room. We were seated at a gleaming table that reflected the gentle noon light filtering through scented wisteria hanging over open French doors leading to a rose garden. Kind friends had driven us from London to their country house on a warm spring day. Driving through the countryside, we passed lush green and golden fields shimmering in the sun and hedgerows thickly embroidered with starry white Queen Anne's Lace, until we came to a story-book village, and the comfortable, old, elegant house where we were spoilt for the whole weekend. Soft feather beds enveloped us like cocoons at night. In the morning, the butler arrived with steaming cups of Earl Grey tea to awaken us, and Mrs Goddard, the housekeeper, plied us with the most delicious food. She very kindly gave us her recipe for Prawn and Parsley Rolls, and her Chervil and Avocado Soup is on page 225.

Fillings for herb sandwiches

- Thin slices of white, buttered bread, spread fairly thickly with cream cheese spread, and sprinkled with chopped garlic chives.
- Scrambled egg, cooled, mixed with a rasher of cooked, crumbled bacon, and chopped fresh oregano.
- Swiss cheese slices scattered with chopped fresh, stalkless savory.
- A thin layer of yeast extract (vegemite or marmite), and stalkless, soft marjoram leaves left whole.
- Crunchy peanut butter and chopped onion chives.
- Mashed banana mixed with lemon juice, sugar, cinnamon, and chopped mint leaves between crisp lettuce leaves; eat soon after making.
- Thinly sliced, skinned (if preferred) tomato, and chopped basil between crisp lettuce leaves. (The lettuce leaves form a barrier between the moist fillings and the bread, thus preventing the bread from becoming soggy.)
- Sliced cucumber, chopped dill or chervil, between crisp lettuce leaves.
- Salad sandwich — comprising a crisp lettuce leaf on the top and bottom slices of bread, alfalfa (or other) sprouts, thinly sliced tomato, grated carrot, finely chopped chives, and chopped (or whole) mint leaves.
- Cold chicken, sliced or chopped, and *fines herbes* (equal quantities of finely chopped parsley, chervil, chives, and tarragon).
- Chopped cress, with or without cream cheese.
- Flaked salmon mixed with lemon juice and chopped tarragon or chervil.
- Chopped prawns with a squeeze of lemon juice and a sprinkling of *fines herbes*.
- Thinly sliced tongue and a scattering of very finely chopped *fines herbes*.
- Mashed liverwurst mixed with crumbled, cooked bacon and chopped sage leaves.

The herb garden at Chelsea Flower Show.

SAGE WELSH RAREBIT

SERVES 2

1 tablespoon cornstarch (cornflour)
1/2 cup beer
1 cup grated cheddar cheese
hot buttered toast
1 tablespoon butter
2 teaspoons finely chopped sage
salt and pepper

Blend the cornflour and beer together until smooth, put into a saucepan together with the cheese, butter, sage, salt, and pepper. Stir continually over a gentle heat until melted and thickened. Do not overcook. Pour immediately over toast.

ELDERFLOWER FRITTERS

SERVES 4

A slightly altered 18th-century recipe of John Nott, cook to the Duke of Bolton.

8 elderflower heads, washed
1 tablespoon orange-flower water
1 teaspoon ground cinnamon
10 fl oz (250 ml) vegetable oil
1–2 tablespoons powdered (caster) sugar,
or confectioners' (icing) sugar

Batter:
4 oz (120 g) all-purpose (plain) flour
1/2 teaspoon salt
1/2 teaspoon sugar
1 egg, separated
10 fl oz (300 ml) milk

Place the elderflowers in a dish and sprinkle them with the orange-flower water and cinnamon. Make the batter by sifting the flour, salt, and sugar together into a bowl, then drip in the egg yolk and add some of the milk. Stir well and add the rest of the milk, beating until the batter is smooth. Whisk the egg white and fold it into the batter. Heat the oil in a frying pan. Take the elderflowers by their short stalks and dip them one at a time into the batter, covering them completely, then place them in the frypan and cook until crisp and golden, turning them once. Drain on paper, sprinkle with sugar, and serve hot with cream or plain yogurt. When presented on a serving dish, decorate with one or two fresh flowers.

CURRIED EGG MOUSSE

SERVES 6 FOR LUNCH, 10 FOR STARTERS

1 x 15 oz (430 g) can chilled evaporated milk
1 x 15 oz (430 g) can cream-type soup
(e.g. celery, asparagus, vichyssoise, watercress)
1 tablespoon curry powder
2 teaspoons onion powder
1 tablespoon lemon or lime juice
1 tablespoon gelatine melted in a little hot water
8 hard-boiled eggs, chopped
salt to taste
1 tablespoon chopped parsley or chives
2 tarragon or dill leaves

Garnish:
1 small jar caviar or lumpfish roe and
1 lime or lemon

Whip 1/2 can evaporated milk until thick. Put remainder of milk into blender together with soup, curry powder, onion powder, lime or lemon juice, melted gelatine, and roughly chopped eggs. Blend until smooth. Fold this mixture, with parsley, into whipped milk. Add salt to taste. Pour into wetted mold and set in refrigerator. When set, unmold and spread caviar on top. Surround mousse with thinly sliced lime or lemon and sprigs of fresh herbs. Serve with a tossed salad (and cold meat if you wish). This dish can be accompanied by a bowl of chutney.

GARLIC HERB BREAD

1 oblong loaf of rye bread
2 garlic cloves, crushed
1 tablespoon chopped parsley
1 tablespoon chopped marjoram
2 teaspoons chopped sage
1 teaspoon finely chopped thyme leaves
8 oz (250 g) butter or vegetable margarine,
softened

Using a sharp knife slice the bread thinly, almost to the bottom crust. Mash the garlic and herbs into the butter and spread generously on both sides of each bread slice. Wrap the loaf loosely in foil and put in an ovenproof dish in a hot oven (450°F/230°C/Gas 8) for 10 to 15 minutes, until the bread is crisp. Serve hot.

GWENNYTH'S BRAN MUFFINS

MAKES ABOUT 9

2 cups unprocessed bran
1 cup wholemeal flour
1 teaspoon baking soda (bicarbonate of soda)
1/2 teaspoon baking powder
3/4 cup light corn (golden) syrup,
melted in 1 cup milk
1 teaspoon very finely chopped fresh rosemary
leaves

In a bowl, combine bran and the flour sifted with the soda and the baking powder. Fold in the melted golden syrup and milk mixture, then the rosemary, until well blended together. Spoon into buttered muffin pans and bake in a moderate oven for 15–20 minutes. Slice in half and serve buttered and hot, or warm.

MRS GODDARD'S SHRIMP AND PARSLEY ROLLS

Prepare thin, fresh, crustless brown bread slices, butter well, then cover with chopped shrimp (prawns), roll firmly, wrap with plastic film and leave to "set" in the refrigerator. (Use a toothpick to keep the shape if necessary.) To serve, dip each end of the rolls into melted butter, and then into finely chopped parsley, which will stick to the melted butter. This last step can be done in advance, the rolls covered with plastic film again and refrigerated before serving.

CRAB MOUSSE AND CAVIAR

SERVES 4

1 1/4 cups mayonnaise
1 1/4 cups cream
2 teaspoons green dill
salt
pinch of cayenne pepper
1 lb (500 g) crab meat
1 tablespoon boiling water
2 teaspoons gelatine
1 1/2 –2 oz (45–60 g) red or black caviar
sprays of fresh herbs
lettuce or endive leaves

Blend mayonnaise and cream together in a mixing bowl, add green dill, salt, and cayenne pepper. Flake crab meat and fold into the other ingredients. Pour boiling water onto gelatine, stir until clear, combine with crab mixture. Pour into a mold previously rinsed with cold water. Chill in refrigerator until set. Unmold onto a serving plate, place caviar on top of mousse, and surround with sprays of fresh herbs, or with salad greens. Serve with herb sandwiches.

Main Courses

TARRAGON FISH PIE

SERVES 4–5

12 oz (375 g) cooked fish, flaked
1 1/2 cups béchamel sauce
salt and pepper
1 scant tablespoon chopped tarragon
1 tablespoon walnut pieces, mixed with
1 cup fresh brown breadcrumbs
butter, cubed

Stir the fish into the béchamel sauce. Season with salt and pepper to taste and add the tarragon. Pour into a buttered ovenproof dish, top with walnut and breadcrumb mixture, and dot with the butter cubes. Heat through in a moderate oven until the breadcrumbs have browned. Serve with slices of lemon and very thin brown bread and butter, or herb sandwiches.

ELIZABETH'S SPINACH PIE WITH ROSEMARY

SERVES 6 AS AN ACCOMPANIMENT,
4 AS A MAIN DISH

1 bunch spinach (about 20 leaves)
2 teaspoons finely chopped
rosemary leaves
1/2 cup feta cheese, crumbled
1/2 teaspoon ground nutmeg
2 eggs, beaten
salt (optional, as feta is very salty)
pepper
12 sheets filo pastry
1 tablespoon melted butter

Strip all green leaves from the spinach stalks (use the stalks in soup or a Chinese dish). Chop the leaves finely and put them into a saucepan with a little butter and the rosemary; steam lightly until cooked. Drain well in a colander, reserving some of the water. (When cooled, the spinach may be puréed in a blender with some of the reserved water for extra smoothness.)

Put the spinach and rosemary mixture into a bowl with the cheese, nutmeg, and eggs; stir until well mixed. Transfer to a buttered oven-proof dish and cover with filo pastry using 2 sheets at a time and brushing with melted butter until all the pastry is used.

Bake in a moderately hot oven (350°F/180°C/Gas 4) until heated through and the pastry is brown and crisp. Eat while hot. Serve as an accompaniment to a main dish or as a light meal with hot buttered bread or rolls.

COLD SALMON SOUFFLÉ WITH ROSEMARY

SERVES 4–6

1 1/2 cups beef consommé
1 tablespoon gelatine dissolved in a little hot water
5 fl oz (150 ml) thick mayonnaise
1 1/4 cups cream, whipped
2 teaspoons very finely chopped rosemary
1 lb (500g) or nearest weight, red salmon, flaked
and bones removed
1 small jar red lumpfish roe (red "caviar")

Put the consommé, dissolved gelatine, and mayonnaise into a bowl and stir until well mixed. Fold in the whipped cream, rosemary, and salmon. Pour the mixture into individual soufflé dishes and allow to set in the refrigerator. Garnish each soufflé with red lumpfish roe before serving.

HERB AND CHEESE SOUFFLÉ

SERVES 4–5

1 1/4 cups milk
2 eggs, separated
4 oz (125 g) cheddar cheese, grated
3 oz (90 g) soft wholemeal breadcrumbs
1 tablespoon grated onion
1 tablespoon chopped parsley
2 teaspoons chopped tarragon
salt and pepper

Warm the milk and add it to the beaten egg yolks and other ingredients (except egg whites). Allow to stand for 1 hour. Whip the egg whites and fold in the mixture. Bake in a buttered ovenproof dish in a moderate oven (350°F/ 180°C/Gas 4) for 30 minutes.
An excellent, simply prepared luncheon or supper dish.

GARLIC RICE WITH CRISP FENNEL STEMS

SERVES 6–8

2 1/2 cups water
pinch of salt
1 cup brown rice
1–2 teaspoons finely chopped garlic
1 fennel base or bulb, sliced thinly and chopped
2 teaspoons finely chopped fennel leaves
extra salt and freshly ground pepper

Bring the water to a boil in a saucepan, add a pinch of salt and the rice (wash only if dusty). Put the lid on and simmer gently until the water has been absorbed – about 40 minutes. If necessary place on a flameproof mat to prevent the rice from sticking. Since the absorption rate of rice varies, more boiling water may need to be added — a little at a time — if the grains are still hard. When the rice is cooked, and dry, with a fork stir in the garlic and the chopped fennel base and leaves. Add salt and pepper to taste. Serve hot as a vegetable or cold as a salad.

To make a rice salad, let the rice cool, transfer to a bowl, cover with plastic film, and chill. Before serving, toss the rice in a French dressing of 3 tablespoons oil to 1 tablespoon herb or wine vinegar. If a larger amount of dressing is preferred, increase the quantities of oil and vinegar, keeping the ratio of 3 to 1.

N.B. As brown rice is said to help reduce high blood pressure, do not add salt and pepper to this recipe if you suffer from this complaint; include some very finely chopped young borage leaves (natural salt) instead, and some finely cut peppery winter savory.

STEAMED LEMONGRASS CHICKEN

SERVES 4

2 lb (1 kg) chicken
1¹/4 cups water
1 teaspoon salt
pinch of pepper
6–8 lemongrass leaves, coarsely chopped
1 tablespoon cornstarch (cornflour)
milk to mix

Place the chicken on a heavy saucer in a saucepan. Add the water, sprinkle the salt and pepper over the chicken, and heap the lemongrass onto the breast. Put the lid on the saucepan, bring the water to a boil, then lower the heat and simmer for 2 hours, occasionally basting the chicken with the liquor in the saucepan. If the water is evaporating too quickly, place a flameproof mat under the saucepan.

If the chicken is to be eaten hot, remove it to a serving dish and keep hot. Strain the stock into a small saucepan and add 1 tablespoon cornstarch blended to a smooth paste with a little milk. Pour the thickened sauce over the chicken and serve.

If the chicken is to be eaten cold, put it into a deep bowl or dish and pour the strained stock over it. Cool, then cover and chill overnight. Next day, the stock will have jellied and a surface layer of fat will have formed which should be removed. The chicken will be aromatic and succulent.

SPINACH AND BASIL TART

SERVES 5–6

3 cups all-purpose (plain) flour
1 teaspoon salt
2–3 tablespoons iced water
3 tablespoons butter, or vegetable margarine

Filling:
2 packages frozen chopped spinach
1 small can anchovy filets
6 tablespoons milk
1 tablespoon chopped basil
salt and pepper
1 tomato, sliced thinly
3 eggs
a few capers or sliced olives
ground nutmeg

Pastry: Sift flour and salt together, then rub in the butter until the mixture resembles breadcrumbs. Add water gradually to make a stiff dough, then roll out thinly. Take a buttered 10 inch (25 cm) tart plate and line it with the pastry, trimming the edges and pricking it all over with a fork. Put in a moderate oven (350°F/ 180°C/Gas 4) for 15–20 minutes, or until just cooked.

Filling: Thaw the spinach as instructed on the package. Beat eggs with milk, fold into spinach with the basil, add salt and pepper to taste, and pour into the pastry shell. Make a pattern with anchovies, tomato slices, and capers, finish with nutmeg, and put back into the oven (350°F/180°C/Gas 4) for a further 30 minutes, or until the filling is firm. Decorate the center with a fresh basil sprig if available. Serve the tart hot or cold.

OPPOSITE: Preparation for spinach and basil tart

SPINACH FETTUCCINE WITH BASIL AND GARLIC

SERVES 4–6

*12 oz (375 g) spinach fettuccine (spinach spaghetti
or plain spaghetti may be used instead)
4 oz (125 g) unsalted butter
2 cloves garlic, pounded, or very thinly sliced
1/2 cup thin cream
2 tablespoons freshly chopped basil
(or 1 tablespoon dried basil; fresh or
dried oregano may be substituted in the
same proportions)
1/2 cup grated Parmesan cheese
pepper to taste*

Boil a quantity of salted water in a large saucepan. Add fettuccine unbroken, gradually loosening it with a fork as it softens. Cook briskly, uncovered, for approximately 12–15 minutes until tender. Drain in a colander and immediately pour boiling water over the pasta, continuing to let it drain.

Meanwhile, melt butter, sauté garlic in it over a low heat, do not let it brown. Pour this mixture into a bowl and beat in the cream and basil. Now transfer the drained fettuccine into a warmed serving bowl and pour the butter and cream mixture over it with half the Parmesan cheese. Toss well with a spoon and fork, adding extra cheese gradually while doing this, and seasoning with the pepper — freshly ground if possible.

Before bringing to the table sprinkle more grated Parmesan over the cooked fettuccine. Garnish with a few sprigs of fresh basil or oregano (optional). Serve hot with crusty bread and a tossed crisp salad. A bowl of Parmesan should be handed around at the table in case more is needed to sprinkle over the vanishing portions of this fragrant and deliciously soothing dish.

RICE AND HERB SPINACH ROLLS

SERVES 4–6

*12 young spinach leaves
1 cup uncooked rice
1 onion, finely chopped
1/2 green pepper (capsicum), seeded and chopped
1 tablespoon chopped parsley
1 teaspoon each of 2 or 3 other favorite herbs,
chopped: e.g. marjoram, chervil, tarragon, and
bergamot; or sage, dill, oregano, and rosemary
salt and pepper (lemon pepper preferably)
2 chicken stock cubes dissolved in 1/2 cups hot
water, or an equivalent amount of stock*

Wash spinach leaves and trim off stalk edges. Mix together the rice, onion, green pepper, herbs, salt, and pepper. Place 1 tablespoon of rice mixture on each flattened spinach leaf, and roll into neat envelope shapes. Pack into a saucepan. Pour the stock over the rolls. Place a weight over the rolls (a dessert plate will do), and put the lid on the saucepan. Bring the stock to the boil, turn down the heat, and simmer for 45 minutes.

STEAK AND KIDNEY CASSEROLE

SERVES 4–6

1 lb (500 g) steak and kidney, chopped and mixed
3 tablespoons flour
2 large cloves garlic, chopped
1 small onion, chopped
2 medium-sized carrots, chopped
1 outside stalk celery, chopped
2 teaspoons salt
freshly ground pepper
A fresh bouquet garni, made with a stalk of bay
leaves, a spray each of parsley, marjoram, and
thyme tied together with a long piece of string,
or
2 teaspoons dried, crumbled bouquet garni
1¼ cups water or stock

Preheat the oven to 350°F (180°C/Gas 4). Roll the meat in the flour and put into an ovenproof casserole dish with the rest of the ingredients; add the water last. Put the lid on and place in the oven for about 2 hours. (Stir once or twice during this time.) Remove the fresh bouquet garni by pulling out the piece of string holding it together — the stalks will be mostly skeletal by this time, the leaves having floated into the gravy. Serve hot.

Steaming herb dumplings are delicious with this casserole, and should be dropped onto the bubbling mixture 20 minutes before the end of the cooking time.

Herb Dumplings

Sift 1 cup self-raising flour into a bowl, add half a teaspoon of salt, and rub in 1½ oz (40 g) butter or margarine. Add a tablespoon of chopped parsley, marjoram, or oregano and enough cold water to make a stiff dough. Rub the flour onto your hands and form the dough into balls; add them to the casserole. Do not replace the lid. Cook for 20 minutes.

RACK OF LAMB ROSEMARY

SERVES 2

Rosemary stores sunlight in its freshly pungent leaves and this gives a deliciously fragrant tang to food. The leaves are thin and spiky, so chop them as finely as possible before use as swallowing a whole rosemary leaf can be irritating. A food processor is excellent for this.

1 rib of 6 lamb cutlets
salt
2 garlic cloves, finely chopped
1 tablespoon rosemary, finely chopped
2 tablespoons virgin olive oil

Rub the lamb all over with salt, then press garlic and rosemary over the rack. Place in a baking dish and cook in a pre-heated oven (350°F/180°C/Gas 4) for approximately 45 minutes, occasionally basting meat with juices from the pan. Cut the rack in half as individual servings and put paper frills on the end of each cutlet if you wish. Decorate the plates with flowering rosemary sprigs. Serve with your favorite vegetables and redcurrant jelly or mint jelly as an accompaniment.

MACARONI WITH SOUR CREAM AND OREGANO

SERVES 4–6

8 oz (250 g) elbow macaroni
1 cup dairy sour cream
4 eggs, separated
1 tablespoon finely chopped oregano
salt and pepper
1 tablespoon black olives, pitted and chopped

Cook and drain macaroni. Combine sour cream and lightly beaten yolks, season with salt and pepper, add macaroni, oregano, and olives. Whip whites and fold into mixture. Bake in a greased ovenproof dish in a moderate oven, 350°F (180°C/Gas 4) for approximately 30 minutes. The mixture should not be dry, but slightly soft in the center.

SAGE AND SAVORY ROLLS

There are two kinds of savory, known as winter savory (perennial) and summer savory (annual). Winter savory sends up fresh green tops from its stiff-leaved winter stalks in spring, and these are the leaves to use until the plant shrinks back in late autumn (fall). Summer savory grows from late spring until early autumn (fall) and all its leaves are soft. A Tudor custom was to mix dried savory with breadcrumbs giving a "quicker relish" to crumbed fish or meat. The peppery bite of fresh savory and the stimulating taste of sage combined in these rolls makes them not only a tasty treat, but one with a delectable aroma.

MAKES 8

1/2 oz (15 g) dry yeast
3 tablespoons warm water
4 cups all-purpose (plain) flour
1 teaspoon salt
2 tablespoons fresh savory, finely chopped
1 tablespoon fresh sage, finely chopped
2 teaspoons sugar
1 cup warm milk
1 oz (30 g) soft butter
1 egg, lightly beaten

Dissolve the yeast in warm water. Sift flour and salt into a bowl and mix in the savory, sage, and sugar. Melt the butter in the warm milk. Form a well in the center of the flour mixture and pour in the milk and butter, then the egg and dissolved yeast. Mix lightly, turn onto a floured surface, and knead. Put the dough into an oiled bowl, cover with a folded tea towel, and leave in a warm place to rise for 1 hour. Turn out onto a floured surface once more. Knead gently again, cut dough, and shape into oblong rolls, press a few savory and sage leaves on top, and dust with flour. Place on an oiled baking sheet and stand for 15 minutes. Bake in a pre-heated oven (425°F/220°C) for 20 to 30 minutes or until golden.

SALMON AND MARJORAM PIE

SERVES 4–6

4 cups soft breadcrumbs
3 tablespoons butter
3 tablespoons all-purpose (plain) flour
3 cups milk
salt and freshly ground pepper
juice of 1 lemon
1 x 14 oz (440 g) can flaked salmon
1 x 14 oz (440 g) can asparagus cuts, drained
6 hard-boiled eggs, sliced
1 tablespoon finely chopped marjoram
1 tablespoon finery chopped parsley
2 tablespoons cheese, grated

Breadcrumb case: Toss 3 cups of soft breadcrumbs in melted butter until well coated. Reserve 1 cup for later, and press the rest firmly into the shape of an ovenproof plate. Brown in a moderate oven (350°F/180°C/Gas 4) for 5–10 minutes.

Filling: Make a white sauce by melting butter in a saucepan, blend in all-purpose flour, add milk, salt, and pepper to taste. Stir until thickened. Add the lemon juice, flaked salmon, drained asparagus cuts, eggs, marjoram, and parsley. Pour into crumb case, top with the reserved buttered crumbs and 2 tablespoons of grated cheese. Bake in a moderate oven (350°F/180°C/Gas 4) until heated through and cheese is melted.

SALMON AND BASIL LOAF

SERVES 5–6

2 x 14 oz (440 g) cans red salmon, flaked
1 cup dry breadcrumbs
4 tablespoons tomato paste
1 green pepper, finely chopped
1 onion, finely chopped
1/2 teaspoon salt
1 tablespoon finely chopped basil
4 eggs, beaten
3 tablespoons vegetable oil

Mash all the ingredients, except the oil, together in a bowl in the order given above. Grease a loaf tin and pack the mixture into it, then refrigerate for a few hours. Loosen the edges with a knife, turn the loaf into a shallow ovenproof dish, and pour the oil over it. Bake in a moderate oven (350°F/180°C/Gas 4) for 45 minutes. Serve hot with the following sauce.

Tomato sauce: Stew 4 medium-sized peeled tomatoes in a little butter with salt, pepper, a pinch of sugar, and some basil, then thicken with a tablespoon of cornstarch (cornflour) smoothed in a little milk. Serve hot in a jug separately.

THICK OXTAIL AND LENTIL STEW

SERVES 6

This is a tasty and nourishing cold weather dish.

2 cut oxtails
2 tablespoons flour
2 tablespoons vegetable oil
6 cups water
1/2 teaspoon each peppercorns and juniper berries
2 bay leaves
a branch of garden thyme
2 cloves of garlic, chopped
1/2 cup green lentils
3 teaspoons salt
1 large carrot, chopped
1 small turnip, chopped
2 onions, chopped
2 stalks celery, chopped
parsley for garnish

Roll oxtails in flour, then brown all over in a saucepan in the oil. Add water and bring to a boil with the lid on. Add peppercorns, juniper berries, bay leaves, thyme, garlic, lentils, and salt. Lower heat, cover and simmer for 2 hours, skimming off the fat as it rises to the surface. Add all the vegetables and simmer for another hour. Sprinkle chopped parsley over each helping. Serve with steaming-hot boiled potatoes.

HERBED LEG
OF LAMB

SERVES 6

This unusual and delicious recipe was given to us by Gretta Anna Teplitzky, a good friend and a gifted cook.

1 x 4 lb (2 kg) leg of lamb
salt and pepper
4 cloves garlic, peeled and cut into slivers
10 sprigs thyme
10 sprigs rosemary
juice of 2 lemons (optional)
1 cup vegetable oil, or good beef fat

Sprinkle salt and pepper all over the lamb. Make small incisions in the meat with a pointed knife, and press the garlic slivers into them. Place 5 sprigs each of thyme and rosemary in the bottom of a roasting pan and lay the leg on the herbs. Place 5 more sprigs each of thyme and rosemary on top of the lamb, and pour over the lemon juice and the oil. Place in a slow oven (325°F/160°C/Gas 4) for about 3 1/2 hours. (The meat should be just pink where it touches the bone.) Remove lamb to a serving platter, decorating it with all the cooked herb sprigs. Pour off the fat from the baking dish, leaving the essence or juice for making gravy in the usual manner. The joint is brought to the table with the herbs on top, but they are pushed to one side when carving, and are not served.

CHICKEN AND
PARSLEY PIE

SERVES 6–8

1 x 4 lb (2 kg) chicken
3 teaspoons salt
bouquet garni, fresh, or 2 teaspoons prepared dried mixture
3 tablespoons butter or vegetable margarine
4 tablespoons all-purpose (plain) flour
4 tablespoons finely chopped parsley
4 tablespoons finely chopped onion
6 hard-boiled eggs, sliced
2 cups mashed potato

Simmer the chicken until tender in enough water to come half-way up the sides of the bird, with salt and bouquet garni. Remove chicken, slice meat away from bone, discard skin. Skim fat off reserved stock (there should be at least 3 cups of stock; if not, top up with water). Make a sauce with the butter, flour, and stock, then stir in onion and 3 tablespoons of parsley. Put a layer of chicken in an ovenproof dish, then half the eggs and half the sauce; repeat with the same ingredients. Mash 1 tablespoon of parsley into the potato and spread over the top. Heat and serve.

ROAST TARRAGON
CHICKEN

SERVES 4

1 x 4 lb (2 kg) chicken
salt and pepper
knob butter
bunch tarragon, or 3 teaspoons dried tarragon
4 tablespoons vegetable oil
2 bacon rashers

Wash chicken and shake salt and pepper into the cavity, add a knob of butter and a bunch of tarragon (or 2 teaspoons of dried tarragon).

Place the bird in a baking dish, pour vegetable oil over it, sprinkle with salt and pepper, and put a spray of tarragon, or 1 teaspoon dried tarragon, on top. Place greaseproof paper, or a piece of brown paper, over the chicken and put it in a moderately hot oven, (375°F/190°C) for 1½ hours. After 20–30 minutes, take the paper off the bird, baste it with the liquid from the dish, then replace paper. If roasting vegetables, put them into the baking dish now with the chicken. Baste again in another ½ hour. During the last 20 minutes of cooking, remove the paper and cover the breast with bacon rashers.

SAVORY THYME CHICKEN

SERVES 3–4

1½ lb (750 g) chicken pieces
2 tablespoons vegetable oil
15 oz (425 g) can whole tomatoes
1 small onion, chopped
1 clove garlic, chopped
1 teaspoon dried thyme. or several sprays
of fresh thyme
salt and pepper

Arrange the chicken pieces in an ovenproof dish. Pour oil over the chicken, then spread the tomatoes and their juice over the pieces. Top with the onion, garlic, thyme, salt, and pepper, and bake in a moderate (350°F/180°C) oven for approximately 1 hour, or until the chicken is cooked, basting it occasionally with the liquid in the dish. Serve hot.

FISH PIE WITH LEMON THYME

SERVES 3–4

3 cups cooked flaked fish
2 teaspoons dried lemon thyme
1 tablespoon finely chopped parsley
salt and pepper
1½ cups white sauce
breadcrumbs
butter

Stir the fish, lemon thyme, parsley, and salt and pepper to taste, into the white sauce. Pour into a buttered ovenproof dish, top with breadcrumbs and a few pieces of butter, and brown in a 350°F (180°C) oven for about 10 minutes. Serve hot.

BAKED FISH FLAVORED WITH FENNEL

SERVES 2

a bunch of leafy fennel stalks
2 whole cleaned and scaled fish,
each about 1 lb (500 g)
½ cup vegetable oil
1 sliced lemon, or lime
salt and freshly ground pepper

Lay the fennel on the bottom of a baking dish, rest the fish on it. With a sharp knife make several cuts down the back of the fish, then insert the slices of lemon into the cuts. Pour oil over the fish, dust with salt and pepper, and cover loosely with brown paper. Place baking dish in a moderate oven (350°F/180°C) for about 1 hour, or until the fish is cooked, basting from time to time with the pan juices. Remove the brown paper for the last 15 minutes. Do not serve all the fennel with the fish, but allow any particles of leaves adhering to them to remain.

FISH TERRINE FINES HERBES WITH SORREL SAUCE

SERVES 6

Anise-flavored chervil, onion-tasting chives, the unobtrusive subtlety of parsley, and warmly spicy French tarragon have many individual uses. When mixed together they comprise the classic, delicately aromatic and indispensable mixture known as *fines herbes*. The leaves of each are finely chopped separately in equal quantities before combining them. *Fines herbes* season and garnish omelets, broiled (grilled) or baked chicken and fish, salads, soups, mornays, and cooked or uncooked vegetables. The combination is also delicious as a filling for crustless, thin sandwiches to accompany starters. Sometimes lemon, thyme, or other subtly fragrant leaves are added to *fines herbes*.

*2 lb (1 kg) ready ground (minced) fresh fish,
or grind (mince) 2 lb (1 kg) large boneless
fish fillets
1 cup dry breadcrumbs
1 tablespoon tomato paste
1 tablespoon scallions, finely chopped
salt to taste
4 eggs, well beaten
2 tablespoons fines herbes (chervil, chives,
parsely, and tarragon, finely chopped and
mixed in equal parts)
vegetable oil
lime or lemon slices to garnish*

Mix all the ingredients, except the oil, together in a bowl in the order given above. Rub oil over the inside of a 48 fl oz (1.5 L) loaf tin and pack the fish mixture into it. Place the tin in a baking dish half filled with boiling water (a *bain-marie*), cover the fish with brown or greaseproof paper, and place in a preheated oven (350°F/180°C/Gas 4) for 45 to 60 minutes, or until set. Test for firmness by pressing a thin-bladed knife into the middle of the dish. Remove from the oven and cool, then refrigerate. When completely cold, run a knife around the edge of the tin and carefully unmold the terrine onto a long serving plate. Dust the top with *fines herbes* and embellish the plate with whole sprays of chervil, parsley, tarragon, and single "straws" of chives. Paper-thin crescents of lime or lemon add appeal. Serve with Sorrel Sauce (see recipe page 250).

OPPOSITE: *Baked fish flavored with fennel.*

Thai Recipes

Asian food has a wide appeal to Western palates as a change from our everyday fare. For many years Chinese meals were immensely popular, while recently Thai cuisine, with its new and unexpected taste sensations, its fresh ingredients, and unusual combinations, has our palates captivated.

Typical Thai food flavors are created from a carefully selected balance of sweet, sour, salty, and hot elements, while contrasting textures are important as well. Solid ingredients are sliced into small pieces to release maximum taste and aroma. There are a great many indigenous herbs and spices used in Thai food, but there are also others which originally came from different continents and are now relied on to contribute their individual fragrances to standard Thai dishes. Chilies originated in South America; several varieties of mint, fennel, and coriander, which are used extensively in this cuisine, have their source in Mediterranean countries. Basil is native to India, and three different kinds are found in Thai cooking. Of course, the ancient trade routes were responsible for the exchange of herbs and spices: over the centuries Chinese, Indians, and Portuguese have all influenced what we know as distinctly Thai tastes.

The following recipes are inspired by The Thai Cooking School at The Oriental, in Bangkok, Thailand. The quantity of dried chilies has been reduced from the original amount to suit unaccustomed palates, so increase the amounts if you prefer. If you need to counteract unpleasant burning sensations from eating hot chilies, chew a teaspoon or two of palm, brown, or white sugar. Do not sip cold water as it does not help at all.

Asian food stores stock the packaged ingredients. Specialist greengrocers keep the fresh herbs, if homegrown ones are not available. When Kaffir lime leaves are hard to find, lemon leaves may be substituted.

THAI CUCUMBER SALAD

SERVES 3–4

1/2 cup white rice vinegar
2 tablespoons white sugar
1 teaspoon salt
*1 teaspoon finely chopped red chili,
seeds removed*
1/2 cup thinly sliced shallots
*1 cup thinly sliced small pickling cucumber,
unskinned*
cilantro (fresh coriander) leaves to garnish

Measure vinegar into a container, stir in sugar and salt until grains disappear. In a bowl combine chili, shallots, and cucumber. Pour vinegar mixture over the salad and put in refrigerator. Leave for 1 to 2 days, to allow the flavors to amalgamate and the cucumber to crisp. Strew cilantro leaves picked straight from the stem over the salad, for decoration and flavor. Serve as a side dish.

SPICED CALAMARI SALAD

SERVES 3–4

*2 cups sliced calamari, quickly boiled,
drained, and chopped*
2 tablespoons lime juice
2 tablespoons fish sauce
1 teaspoon pulverized dried chilies
*2 tablespoons finely sliced lemongrass
(from the bulbous base upward,
not including the green top)*
2 tablespoons finely sliced shallots
2 tablespoons finely sliced scallions

Box tree gets an unusual treatment to make these topiary elephants in Bangkok.

(spring onions)
2 tablespoons shredded Kaffir lime leaves
1 tablespoon palm sugar, or brown,
or raw sugar
chili and sweet pepper (capsicum) shreds, mint,
and coriander leaves to garnish

Stir lime juice and fish sauce together, then add the dried chilies. Add lemongrass, shallots, scallions, palm sugar, and lime leaves.

Mix lightly before adding calamari. Taste the salad and if too hot stir in more sugar, if not hot enough judiciously add pulverized chilies. Turn onto a serving dish and garnish the salad with red chilies, peppers, whole mint, and coriander leaves.

N.B. Cooked squid or any other seafood, chicken, or meat may replace the calamari in this salad.

Sauces

AIOLI

12 garlic cloves, peeled
salt
3 egg yolks
1³/4 cups best olive oil
a few drops lemon juice

Mash the garlic cloves to a cream on a board with a little salt, using a sharp knife, then transfer to a bowl. Stir in the egg yolks with a wooden spoon, and when well blended start beating in the oil drop by drop. As the mixture thickens, and when about half the oil has been used, add the rest of the oil a little more quickly, in a steady stream, still beating. Add the lemon juice last. If the aioli separates – and this applies to any mayonnaise – put a fresh yolk in another bowl and slowly add the curdled sauce to it.

HORSERADISH SAUCE

1 cup white sauce
pinch mustard powder
pinch salt
pinch sugar
2 teaspoons lemon juice
1 tablespoon cream
2 tablespoons freshly grated horseradish, or 1 tablespoon dried horseradish grains

White sauce:
3 tablespoons butter
3 tablespoons all-purpose (plain) flour
3 cups milk
salt and freshly ground pepper

Make sauce by melting butter in a saucepan, blending in all-purpose flour, adding milk and salt and pepper to taste. Stir until thickened. Add remaining ingredients to sauce and mix thoroughly. If using dried horseradish, leave sauce for 1 hour before serving.

PAW PAW SEED DRESSING WITH PARSLEY

Here is an adaptation from Hawaii of an unusual and healthy salad dressing featuring pawpaw seeds. These peppery seeds have a traditional reputation for assisting the digestion. An added advantage is knowing that you are going to use most of those glistening black seeds when cutting open a pawpaw, instead of scooping them out and throwing them away. Vitamin-rich parsley and tasty spices go toward making this dressing a delectable taste treat.

2 teaspoons sugar
1/2 teaspoon salt
3–4 tablespoons lemon juice
(according to taste)
1 tablespoon onion, chopped
1/2 teaspoon crushed garlic
1 tablespoon freshly chopped parsley, chervil, or dill leaves
1 cup any cold pressed salad oil (walnut oil makes an interesting change)
2 tablespoons fresh pawpaw seeds

Place all dry ingredients and lemon juice in blender. Gradually add salad oil while blending. When thoroughly blended add pawpaw seeds. Blend again until seeds are the size of coarse ground pepper. Store dressing in sealed container in the refrigerator.

CUCUMBER AND GREEN HERB SAUCE

1 cucumber, peeled, seeded, and diced
salt
1 small bunch seedless grapes,
picked from their stalks
1 tablespoon parsley or chervil,
finely chopped
1 tablespoon chives, finely chopped
2 teaspoons spearmint, finely chopped
1 cup low-fat sour cream
pinch of ground chili or a little pepper

Mix all ingredients together in a bowl. Chill. Serve with curries, or put on a buffet table as an accompaniment to other dishes.

PESTO

Pesto is an excellent way to preserve and freeze basil. Use it as a spread, or fold it through freshly cooked, drained pasta. This recipe comes from Mrs Clare Wilmot of the Triad Health Clinic.

1 large bunch of sweet basil, or a smaller
bunch of bush basil
4 oz (125 g) grated Parmesan cheese
4 oz (125 g) pine kernels
4 cloves garlic, peeled
a little sea salt
cold pressed oil

Wash the basil and strip the leaves from the stems. Place all the ingredients in a blender, with a little oil. Turn the blender to high, adding more oil if necessary, until the ingredients are pulverized. The mixture should have the consistency of thick, running cream. Use immediately, or store, covered, in the refrigerator, or seal down in small jars and deep-freeze.

OREGANO AND BELL PEPPER RELISH

3 red bell peppers (capsicums)
3 green bell peppers (capsicums)
2 onions, peeled and chopped
2 cloves garlic, peeled and chopped finely
1 cup white wine vinegar
1 cup raw sugar
2 teaspoons salt
1 tablespoon chopped fresh oregano leaves
2 tablespoons seedless raisins

Wash the peppers, cut into small pieces, discarding the seeds. Put all the ingredients together in a saucepan and bring to a boil, then simmer with the lid off for 1 hour. Seal into jars when cold. Refrigerate once the jar is opened.

SORREL SAUCE

²/₃ oz (20 g) butter or margarine
3¹/₂ oz (100 g) young sorrel leaves,
washed and finely chopped
1 heaped tablespoon all-purpose
(plain) flour
1¹/₄ cups chicken stock
(made with 2 cubes)
1 tablespoon cream (optional)
1 egg yolk (optional)

Melt the butter in a saucepan and gently cook the sorrel until soft. Blend in the flour and gradually add chicken stock, stirring well until thickened and smooth. The sauce should have the consistency of thickened cream. Add salt to taste and serve cold with a small ladle. For a more subtle taste to this tart sauce, mix the cream and egg yolk and beat it into the sauce immediately it comes off the stove. Do not put the finished sauce into a blender because the finely chopped sorrel gives it an interesting texture.

N.B. It is advisable not to cook sorrel in an aluminium saucepan: like spinach, its acid content reacts with the aluminium and it becomes harmful.

Vegetables

BEETROOT IN CARAWAY PORT JELLY

SERVES 8–10

1 bunch beetroot
2 teaspoons salt
1/2 cup sweet port wine
3 tablespoons lemon juice
2 teaspoons honey
1 teaspoon caraway seed
7 rounded teaspoons gelatine

Cut the tops off the beetroot, putting any unblemished leaves aside to use later in salads or in soups. Wash the beets well and place in a saucepan with salt and enough water to cover. Simmer until tender. Peel beets, cut them into dice, circles, or quarters and arrange in a dish. Measure 1 1/2 cups of the liquid and return to the saucepan on a low heat with the port, lemon juice, honey, and caraway seed, adding more salt if necessary. Pour some of the hot liquid onto the gelatine, stir until clear, pour back into the saucepan, and stir again, then cover the cut-up beets with the tasty, crimson broth. Cool, then chill in refrigerator until set.

SPICED WHOLE GRAPES

A delicious accompaniment to grills, baked meat, poultry, fish, or curry.

2 lb (1 kg) seedless white grapes
1 lb (500 g) raw sugar
4 fl oz (120 ml) cider or white vinegar
2 teaspoons mustard seed

1 teaspoon ground ginger
1 teaspoon ground allspice
2 bay leaves
1 oz (30 g) powdered fruit pectin

Wash grapes and remove stalks. Place sugar and vinegar in a saucepan and add mustard seed, ginger, allspice, and bay leaves. Bring to boil, then simmer gently, uncovered, for 15 minutes, stirring at intervals. Remove bay leaves. Add grapes, sprinkle in pectin. Bring to boil again and simmer for a further 3 minutes, skimming off any foam and giving the mixture an occasional stir. Remove from heat and allow to stand for 10 minutes, stirring frequently to prevent a film from forming on the top. Spoon into jars and seal. Use within 4 weeks.

GRETTA ANNA'S POTATO FANS WITH OREGANO, CHEESE, AND BACON

SERVES 6

This recipe was given to us by a kind and close friend.

Take 6 medium potatoes all the same size. Peel and cut away a thin horizontal slice from the bottom of each, so that they will all sit flat. Slice each potato downwards all along in 1/8 inch (3 mm) slices, but do not cut right through to the base. Place potatoes in a roasting pan. Sprinkle the slit potatoes with salt, pepper, 1 tablespoon fresh chopped oregano (or 3 teaspoons dried oregano), 6 teaspoons grated cheese, and 6 teaspoons finely chopped bacon.

Roast the potatoes in a little oil to barely cover the bottom of the pan in a moderate oven

(350°F/180°C) for approximately 1¹/4 hours or until golden brown and cooked through (test with a skewer.) Roast potatoes flavored and adorned like this are unusual and delicious.

CAULIFLOWER CHEESE TEPLITZKY

SERVES 6–8

This recipe is dedicated to Gretta Anna (a well-loved, inventive cook with tremendous flair) and her husband, David Teplitzky, their daughter, Anna, and Gretta's ageless and enchanting mother, Mrs Schneideman. Sunday evening is a special time for us all to relax together and enjoy a simple but tasty meal, and these dear friends say that this is their favorite cauliflower cheese. The original recipe was my late, wonderful, mother's. We serve this fairly substantial dish with cold meat and mustard, a tossed green salad, and hot herb bread, followed by fresh fruit.

1 medium to large cauliflower,
cooked whole in salted water until just soft
(test the stalk with a skewer; it should be crisp,
but cooked)
4 cups béchamel sauce (not too thin)
2 tablespoons chopped parsley
1 tablespoon chopped chives
¹/2 tablespoon chopped dill or chervil
1 cup grated melting cheese
(Gruyère, or similar)
1 cup dry breadcrumbs

Turn the whole, cooked cauliflower into a colander to drain. Transfer to a fairly deep, buttered, ovenproof dish, flower side up. Mix the herbs into the sauce and coat the cauliflower with it, letting the excess run into the dish. Mix the cheese and breadcrumbs and sprinkle them over the cauliflower. Put the dish into a moderate oven (350°F/180°C) for approximately 30–45 minutes until the cheese has melted and the cauliflower is hot. If the cheese begins to burn, cover with a piece of brown paper or foil.

BAKED BROCCOLI WITH DILL SEED AND SOUR CREAM

SERVES 4

1 lb (500 g) broccoli, cooked,
or 1 small cauliflower, cooked
2 teaspoons dill seed
salt and pepper
1 cup sour cream
1 cup breadcrumbs
green dill for garnish

Place cooked broccoli (or cooked cauliflower) in an ovenproof dish. Sprinkle with dill seed, dust with salt and pepper, cover with sour cream, and top with breadcrumbs. Bake in a moderate oven (350°F/180°C) until crumbs are brown. Garnish with a few sprays of green dill if available.

OREGANO AND GARLIC CHIVES ZUCCHINI (COURGETTES)

SERVES 4

1 lb (500 g) zucchini (courgettes), thinly sliced
1 tomato, peeled and chopped
2 teaspoons finely chopped garlic chives
(or onion chives)
2 teaspoons finely chopped oregano
salt and pepper
2 tablespoons virgin olive oil

Thinly slice the zucchini and place in a saucepan with tomato, garlic chives, oregano, salt, pepper, and oil. Cover and simmer gently for a few minutes until the zucchini are lightly cooked and still crisp, stirring frequently in the beginning to prevent the vegetables from catching.

ROSEMARY ZUCCHINI

SERVES 4

1 lb (500 g) zucchini
1 tomato, peeled and chopped
1 tablespoon finely chopped onion
2 teaspoons finely chopped rosemary
salt and pepper
2 tablespoons vegetable oil

Thinly slice the zucchini and place in a saucepan with tomato, onion, rosemary, salt, pepper, and vegetable oil. Cover and simmer gently until soft, stirring frequently in the beginning to prevent the vegetables from catching.

HEALTHY
BROWN RICE AND
MINT SALAD

SERVES 6

2 cups brown rice, cooked
1 cup raw slivered almonds, browned in oven
2 medium-size ripe tomatoes, peeled and chopped
1/2 teaspoon salt
1 tablespoon finely chopped onion or shallots
2 tablespoons finely chopped mint
4 tablespoons finely chopped parsley
4 tablespoons lemon juice
4 tablespoons vegetable oil

Mix all ingredients together in the order given. Serve.

FRENCH BEANS
AND SAVORY

SERVES 4

1 lb (500 g) French beans
1/2 teaspoon salt
2 teaspoons finely chopped savory
2 teaspoons finely chopped shallots
or onions
4 tablespoons sour cream

Cook prepared French beans in water until tender. Drain. To the beans in the saucepan add salt, savory, shallots or onion, and sour cream. Steam gently with the lid on until heated through. Serve hot.

COMFREY FRITTERS

comfrey leaves
batter

Strip the comfrey leaves from the plant. Dip them in cold water, then into batter. Fry in sizzling fat to make unusual, but delicious fritters.

FENNEL BULBS WITH CHEESE SAUCE

SERVES 4
FOR A LIGHT LUNCH

Trim and wash 2 fennel bulbs, cut in halves, and simmer in boiling water for 20 minutes. Drain well, then lay the bulbs cut side down in an ovenproof dish and pour 1 cup of white sauce over them. (Some finely chopped fennel leaves stirred into the sauce first is an excellent addition.) Sprinkle 2 tablespoons of grated tasty cheese over the top and place under the griller until the cheese has melted. Serve hot.

CHICORY CASSEROLE

SERVES 4

4 chicory heads
butter or vegetable margarine
2 teaspoons dried thyme
salt and pepper

Wash and trim the chicory. Cut it into circles and pack into a buttered casserole dish with the thyme, salt, pepper, and pieces of butter between the layers. Put the lid on and bake in a moderate oven (300°F/150°C) for about 1¹/₂ hours.

TOMATO AND BERGAMOT LOAF

SERVES 4

1¹/₂ cups canned tomatoes with juice
2 tablespoons water
2 tablespoons chopped bergamot leaves
1 cup celery, chopped
1¹/₂ cups packaged breadcrumbs
1 cup grated tasty cheese
2 tablespoons vegetable oil
2 tablespoons grated onion
¹/₂ teaspoon salt
2 eggs, beaten

Break up tomatoes, mix together with all the ingredients in the order given, spoon into an oiled ovenproof dish, and bake in a moderate oven (350°F/180°C) for 20 minutes. Serve hot.

BAKED TOMATOES WITH MINT

SERVES 4 AS A SIDE DISH

2 medium-size tomatoes
1 shallot, finely chopped
2 teaspoons finely chopped mint
salt and pepper
pinch of sugar
2 cups breadcrumbs
knob of butter

Cut tomatoes in halves and scoop out pulp into a bowl. To the tomato pulp add shallot, mint, salt, pepper, and sugar. Stir, then spoon mixture into tomato cases. Top with breadcrumbs and butter. Bake in an oiled ovenproof dish in a moderate oven (350°F/180°C) for approximately 20 minutes.

BRAISED CHICORY WITH DILL

SERVES 4

1 lb (500 g) chicory heads
1 tablespoon chopped chives
2 teaspoons chopped green dill
(or chervil, fennel, or oregano)
butter or vegetable margarine
salt and pepper

Wash and trim the chicory. Cut into thick circles and pack into a buttered ovenproof dish with the herbs, salt, pepper, and pieces of butter between each layer. Put the lid on and bake in a moderate oven (350°F/180°C) for 1 1/4 to 1 1/2 hours.

N.B. The chicory must be of the best quality, the leaves white, without any trace of green. If you like, the heads can be boiled in water first for a few minutes to help remove any bitterness.

Salads

SALADS WITH HERBS AND EDIBLE FLOWERS

Green salads that are generously laced with aromatic herbs have an appealing relish and help to stimulate the appetite, as well as being packed with health-giving properties. Some of the lesser known "salad greens" to use as a base include mignonette lettuce, cos lettuce, chicory or witloof, celery tops, torn up leaves of English spinach (not as coarse as silver beet), finely sliced heads of raw young cabbage, and young cauliflowers. If you don't grow these yourself, they are readily available from most greengrocers.

Green dill, finely cut and mixed into a coleslaw with a few dill seeds, makes the cabbage more digestible, and imparts its subtle anise flavor.

Quantities of fresh parsley and mint, chopped finely, are included in that nutritious and delectable Lebanese salad, tabbouleh.

Borage leaves add a natural, salty flavor to salads, and the brilliant blue flowers are edible too. Because of the hairy texture of the leaves, they should be very finely chopped, almost minced.

Nasturtium leaves are often added to salads and sandwiches. Their keen, hot taste makes them a useful replacement for pepper in many dishes. Pick young, tender leaves and eat them whole in salads: put a cluster of jewel-colored flowers in the middle of a salad niçoise, and eat them too.

Fresh winter and summer savory can be used instead of pepper in salads. Basil, bergamot, cress, chervil, chives, tarragon, fennel, mint, balm, comfrey, angelica, lovage, small quantities of coriander, marjoram, oregano, finely chopped fresh rosemary and sage, are excellent herbs to mix into a green salad; they all grow through summer, into autumn (fall), and some even later. There are numerous wild plants you can use in salads, including chickweed and dandelion leaves, so when you are weeding, don't dig them all up; keep some for the kitchen. Of course, not all weeds are edible, so if in doubt do not eat them.

A FLOWER SALAD

A "flower" salad doesn't necessarily have to be made from flowers; it can be made from many ingredients, but because of the way it is arranged it looks like one large flower, and tastes quite heavenly. It has been said that: "In eating flowers we partake of the more refined essences of the plant, the final stage before returning to seed and completing the circle of plant life. So the flower offers a more subtle energy, as well as sweet nectar . . . flowers can speak to us and contain special healing powers. To gather and make flower salads is one way of being with flowers and learning how they express the harmony of nature." *(Jeanne Rose's Herbal Guide to Inner Health*, published by Grosset and Dunlap, New York.) Not all flowers are edible, so make sure the ones you choose *are.*

Many blooms of old-fashioned cottage plants may be eaten, like pinks and carnations, nasturtiums, violets, most jasmines, English marigolds, violets, primroses, rose petals, and orange and apple blossoms. Never eat foxgloves, however, as they are toxic in spite of their medicinal properties.

WHOLE FLOWER SALAD

To make this flower salad, you will need a flat, large, round china or glass platter, or a round tray. On it make a bed of some of the larger herb leaves, for instance angelica, lovage, comfrey, nasturtium, chicory, or dandelion. In the center put a mound of grated carrot, and circle it with small, broken sprigs of washed, raw young cauliflower florets. Next, make a circle of colorful nasturtium flowers interspersed with honeyed bergamot flowers and leaf sprigs, then a surround of alfalfa, or any other favorite sprouts. Around this, make a rainbow circle of sky-blue borage flowers, purple violets, pink or red rose petals, and yellow stars of dill or fennel flowers. Surround the plate with sprays of curly parsley and spearmint tops. If there is still room, add radish "roses" and crisp curled celery to the flowery platter. Pour a light dressing over all before bearing it to the table. This salad may be made an hour ahead of time and kept fresh in the refrigerator, but do not add the dressing until the very last moment.

LIGHT SALAD DRESSING

Put 6 tablespoons of a fine salad oil (walnut or hazelnut oil) into a clean bottle or jar with a lid, add 2 tablespoons of herb or wine vinegar (or lemon juice), salt, freshly ground pepper, and a small teaspoon of clear honey. Put the lid on, shake well, and pour a sufficient amount over the salad without drowning it. Store any left-over dressing in the refrigerator.

MIXED FLOWER SALAD

SERVES 5–6

This recipe is a collection of tender green leaves and fragrant blossoms sprinkled with the lightest of dressings. When completed it looks and tastes quite heavenly. The colorful petals sparkle like confetti among the fresh greenery.

suggested salad greens:
wild dandelion leaves
spicy sorrel leaves
whole young bergamot leaves
2 or 3 nectar-rich bergamot flowers

8–12 borage flowers
3 nasturtium flowers
2 small roses (1 pink and 1 red)
3 tablespoons of walnut oil
1 tablespoon of herb vinegar, or fresh lime juice

Wash and dry a favorite selection of salad greens, including wild dandelion leaves if they are available, some spicy sorrel, and several whole young bergamot leaves. Put them into an attractive bowl. Wash the flowers only if necessary, for some of the fragrance may disappear. Now toss the leaves in a well-blended mixture of the oil and herb vinegar, or fresh lime juice if preferred. Pluck the bergamot petals into the bowl, sprinkle in the whole borage flowers, pull the nasturtium petals apart, and add them, then the carefully torn-off rose petals. Give the salad another gentle turn and serve.

N.B. These flowers may be replaced, or added to, by other edible blossoms.

GREEN HERB SALAD

QUANTITIES ARE YOUR CHOICE

spearmint leaves stripped from their stalks
watercress leaves
cos lettuce
chives, finely chopped
chickweed
young dandelion leaves

Wash and thoroughly dry all the ingredients. Tear up the larger leaves, and put all the greens together in a salad bowl. Cover with plastic film and crisp in the refrigerator for a few hours, or overnight. Before serving, pour on some Light Salad Dressing and toss well.

HERBED POTATO AND BANANA SALAD

SERVES 5–6

*3 cups diced, peeled, cooked potatoes (boiled in
their skins and peeled while warm)
1 cup sliced banana
a little fresh lemon or lime juice
salt and pepper
1 cup finely chopped scallions (spring onions),
including the green part
1 tablespoon chopped basil, dill, tarragon, or
chervil
1 cup mayonnaise
2 hard-boiled eggs, shelled and sliced*

Sprinkle lemon or lime juice over the banana
slices to prevent discoloration. While the potatoes are still warm, season them with salt and
pepper and add the banana and scallions. Blend
the chopped herbs with the mayonnaise and
mix gently through the salad. Add the egg
slices. Chill before serving.

GREEN DANDELION AND BORAGE SALAD

SERVES 4–6

Dandelion leaves are a natural health food. They are
a blood cleanser, and are beneficial to the liver, gall-
bladder, kidneys, and digestion. It is best to use the
tender young leaves.

*8 young dandelion leaves, washed and dried
1/2 lettuce, washed and dried
1 tablespoon each finely chopped borage leaves
and chives
1/2 thin-skinned orange, unpeeled
and finely sliced
4 tablespoons vegetable oil
1 tablespoon white vinegar or lemon juice
1 clove garlic, finely chopped
1 teaspoon salt
pepper*

Tear dandelion and lettuce leaves into a salad
bowl, add borage leaves, chives, and orange.
Blend oil, vinegar, garlic, salt, and pepper
together and toss through the salad. Scatter the
borage flowers over the top and serve.

CHICKEN SALAD

SERVES 2

*1/2 cup natural yogurt
1/4 teaspoon dry mustard
1 teaspoon lemon juice
1/2 teaspoon garlic salt
dash of pepper
1 tablespoon chopped chives
2 teaspoons chopped sage
1 cup diced cooked chicken
1/2 green cucumber, peeled and diced
lettuce leaves*

In a bowl stir together yogurt, mustard, lemon
juice, garlic, salt, pepper, chives, and sage.
Fold into this mixture cold diced chicken
and cucumber. Serve the salad in crisp, curved
lettuce leaves.

SALAD MARIE LOUISE

SERVES 5–6

Take equal parts of sliced boiled cold potatoes
and raw peeled and sliced apples. Add oil, salt,
and pepper. Mix at the last moment and place
in a mound in the center of the salad bowl.
Sprinkle with crushed hard-boiled eggs.
Surround with alternative small mounds of
corn and violets, stems removed. (Alice B.
Toklas, *Aromas and Flavors*, 1958.)

GREEN LIMA BEAN AND BASIL SALAD

SERVES 4

This salad may be flavored with any one of your favorite herbs. Basil is particularly suitable, but, if it is out of season, oregano, marjoram, rosemary, mint, tarragon, dill, chervil, or fennel can be substituted. A discreet amount of chopped fresh coriander leaves gives the salad an unusual and piquant flavor.

2 cups frozen or canned small green lima beans
1 tablespoon finely chopped basil
2 scallions (spring onions),
finely chopped
salt and pepper
4 tablespoons vegetable, or walnut,
or hazel nut oil blended with 1 tablespoon
white vinegar or lemon juice

Boil the frozen beans in salted water until cooked. If using canned beans, drain and rinse, then drain again. Put the beans into a bowl and add the basil, scallions, salt and pepper to taste, and the oil and vinegar mixture last. Toss well.

CHRYSANTHEMUM SALAD

SERVES 5–6

Clean and wash in several waters about 20 chrysanthemum flowers picked from the stalks. Blanch them in acidulated and salted water; drain them and dry them in a cloth.

Mix the flowers well into a salad composed of potatoes, artichoke bottoms, shrimps' tails, and capers in vinegar.

Arrange this in a salad bowl, and decorate it with beetroot and hard-boiled egg. A pinch of saffron may be added to this salad for seasoning.

The dark yellow chrysanthemums are best. In Yokohama the flowers, already prepared, are sold in the greengrocers' shops.

The Gentle Art of Cookery, by Mrs C. F. Leyel and Miss Olga Hartley (Chatto & Windus).

Desserts

CONTINENTAL POPPY SEED CAKE

SERVES 6

1 1/2 cups ground poppy seed
6 eggs, separated
1 cup sugar
1/2 cup mixed candied fruit peel
1 teaspoon allspice
whipped cream, mascarpone,
or fresh neufchâtel to garnish
grated orange peel to garnish

Grind the poppy seed in a processor or blender, or buy seeds already ground. Beat the egg yolks until thick, and while still beating gradually add the sugar. Stir in the mixed peel, allspice, and ground poppy seed. Beat the egg whites until stiff and fold carefully and thoroughly into the poppy seed mixture. Butter and lightly flour a spring-form cake tin, and pour in the batter. Put it into a pre-heated slow to moderate oven (325°F/170°C) and bake for about 50 minutes, or when a skewer looks dry after pressing into the cake's middle. Allow the cake to cool in the tin, then carefully remove the spring-form. Spread whipped cream, mascarpone, or fresh neufchâtel over the top of the cake and finish with a dusting of grated orange peel.

ELDERFLOWER SORBET

SERVES 4–6

2 1/2 cups water
6 oz (185 g) sugar
4 heads of fesh elderflowers
peeled rind and juice of 3 lemons
1 egg white, whipped

Put the water into a saucepan with the sugar. Heat until sugar is completely dissolved, stirring with a wooden spoon to prevent it catching to the bottom. Boil rapidly, uncovered, for about 5 to 8 minutes and add the whole elder-flowers. Turn off the heat and allow the flowers to infuse in the syrup for several minutes. Stir in the lemon rind and juice. Strain the syrup into a bowl, let it cool, then pour it into freezing trays and put into the freezer. When half frozen, turn it into a clean bowl and mix in the egg white, beating with a rotary beater to amalgamate the mixture. Put it back into the trays and freeze again. A sorbet becomes smoother with several beatings during the freezing process, although this is optional.

Serve this unusual and delicious ice either as a palate cleanser during a meal, or as a dessert.

MINTED HONEY SOUFFLÉ

SERVES 4

1/2 cup clear honey
1/2 teaspoon ground coriander seed
spray of spearmint (or 3/4 teaspoon dried mint)
crystallized mint leaves (page 209)
4 eggs, separated
1/2 cup milk
4 teaspoons gelatine, dissolved in hot water
1/2 cup cream, whipped

Place honey and coriander in the top half of a double saucepan over boiling water. Beat yolks and milk together, blend with the honey, using a wooden spoon. Add the sprig of mint, and continue stirring until custard coats the spoon.

Remove from heat, add melted gelatine. Cool custard by replacing hot water in the boiler with several changes of cold water, stirring constantly. When cooled, remove mint, and fold in the whipped cream and stiffly beaten egg whites. Turn into a serving bowl and chill in refrigerator. When set, spread whipped cream over the top and decorate with crystallized mint leaves.

MANGO CREAM WITH ANGELICA

SERVES 6–8

My mother's recipe for this fragrant, smooth dessert reminds me of school holidays spent long ago in Broome, about 1,200 miles (2,000 km) from Perth, in Western Australia, where my brother and I were at boarding school. We used to go home by ship once in every 12 months for the eight-week Christmas vacation, and Fred and I always invited a school friend so that they could experience a different Australia, and we could repay kindness shown to us during the year. A week's cruising in a small but immaculate Blue Funnel Line steamer with other youngsters going home to various stops along the desolate north-west coast, and to Java, Singapore, Malaya, and Hong Kong, was always fun, even though we sometimes struck frighteningly rough seas, and once the edge of a cyclone. The Captain put on full speed to race away from it, and while the ship pitched and rolled like a cork, we slithered, climbed, and ran down heaving decks.

At dinner in Broome, our Mango Cream was served in chilled glasses as we sat around the massive teak table, made by Father's Japanese carpenter (who also helped build his pearling luggers), under a whirring ceiling fan to stir the hot air, and to prevent platoons of moths and thin, jade-green grasshoppers from falling into the food. Outside, the sheet lightning flickered constantly, the vast colonies of cicadas who shrilled during the intense daytime heat gave occasional chirps, the warm breeze rustled the long pandanus leaves by the door, and the Aborigines in their camp nearby clicked ceremonial sticks, or danced their corroborees. Every noise was audible since we were surrounded by spacious verandas enclosed only by low, latticed wooden rails and huge, half-open, flat-iron "shutters" that were fastened down when violent "cock-eye-bobs," or fierce cyclones, struck. The iron roof was anchored securely to the ground by steel cables to stop the house from blowing away in a bad storm. Houses were built on top of high cement blocks for coolness, and to prevent white ants from eating the house down, as well as to deter snakes and scorpions from entering, which they did at times anyway. The stars there in the Tropic of Capricorn were closer and more plentiful, their incandescent brilliance lighting the sky to indigo; every night falling stars plunged blazing towards us, only to disappear into the galaxy again.

To make her Mango Cream, Mother had access to superb mangoes of several flavors, which Father and the Aborigine, Tommy, grew with pride, in between sorties for pearls at sea. Fresh cream was out of the question, the cow's milk, when available, was thin and poor because of lack of good feed in that red, arid soil: instead, nearly every family kept at least one goat for its nourishing milk. Our mother, a typical "English rose," had never been inside a kitchen before she went to Broome, but she gamely made the best of things and relied on canned cream and imported angelica. Of course there were no blenders in those days, so she used to laboriously squeeze all the juice from the flesh around the mango stones, after having sliced the rest of the flesh off and pulped it, and the canned cream was not whipped. Tora, the Japanese cook, our beloved childhood friend, was never allowed to make this dish, for it was Mother's speciality. Fresh cream is used in this adaptation.

2 tablespoons gelatine
4 tablespoons very hot water
4–6 fresh mangoes, peeled and cut away
from the seed, or 2 cans mango purée,
or sliced mango puréed in the blender

2 tablespoons sifted confectioners'
(icing) sugar (or icing sugar mixture)
2 tablespoons rum or liqueur
1¼ cups cream, whipped
extra whipped cream for decorating
candied angelica stalks, or crystallized
mint leaves

Dissolve the gelatine in the hot water and stir until clear. Put all the ingredients into a blender, except the whipped cream and angelica or crystallized mint. Turn to high until the mixture is amalgamated. (This may have to be done in batches, depending on the size of the blender.) Pour the mixture into a bowl and fold in the whipped cream. Spoon into individual glasses or silver goblets, or into one attractive bowl. Chill until set. Before serving, decorate with the extra whipped cream and sticks of candied angelica. If you do not have candied angelica or crystallized mint leaves, use fresh mint sprigs instead.

N.B. Puréed fresh guavas, or canned guavas puréed in a blender, may be used instead of the mangoes for a change.

MARMALADE
OF VIOLETS

8 oz (250 g) violet flowers
1½ lb (750 g) sugar
½ cup water

Take the violet flowers picked from their stalks and crush them in a mortar.

Boil the sugar and water to a syrup, and when boiling add the flowers. Allow it to come five or six times to the boil on a very slow fire. Stir it with a wooden spoon, and pour it while hot into little pots.

OPPOSITE: Gooseberry and balm sherbert (page 266).

ICE CREAM
OF ROSES

SERVES 4–5

2½ cups cream
2 handfuls fresh rose petals
yolks of 2 eggs
sugar

Boil the cream and put into it when it boils two handfuls of fresh rose petals, and leave them for two hours, well covered. Then pass this through a sieve, and mix with the cream the well-beaten yolks of two eggs, and sugar to taste. Add a little cochineal, and put it on the fire, stirring it all the time, but do not let it boil on any account. Put it on ice.

STRAWBERRY
CREAM

Several years in Kentish England spent with maternal grandparents during part of our childhood seemed like living in a heaven of vivid, yet gentle, greens; softly glowing flowers with pure, lingering fragrances; musical bird calls; different tastes of fruit and vegetables, and a life where all was ordered, calm, and gracious. (Such a contrast to Australia's semi-tropical Broome with its simmering heat, surreal landscapes, shrilling cicadas, raucous parrots, and the overpowering, sickly sweet scent of oleander flowers.) The secluded garden, with its velvet lawns, was large, beautiful, and very English — no Italianate influences here. Much of it was 200 years old and included a particularly venerable oak tree. The many walks and hidden places were a paradise for children to play in. There were the oak and horse chestnut trees to climb (and a warning not to clamber up ancient yew trees, which left black marks on clothes). At first we trod cautiously through the long grass in the orchard for fear of lurking snakes, which greatly amused our mother,

grandparents, uncles, and aunts. "Not here, darling," they would say to us.

An ivy-cloaked, brick-walled garden, intersected by a stone arched doorway, beckoned to another part of this fascinating Eden, where there was the kitchen garden with fruit and vegetables grown for the house. In late spring and summer there was an abundance of food — strawberries, redcurrants, blackcurrants, white currants, raspberries, gooseberries, asparagus, baby new potatoes, and other vegetables. Sun-warmed peaches and nectarines were plucked only by Grandfather from fruit trees espaliered against one side of the wall. In this sequestered garden, huge pink roses annually twined their way along ropes; and one dense, green, rose bush bore masses of small white blooms more exquisitely perfumed than any other flower. It was truly an enchanted garden and, sadly, no longer exists. Rows of new houses now take its place and the old trees have gone forever.

Sunday trifles were a treat; whipped cream was spread over this favorite pudding and it was strewn with candied violets and pink rose petals (see page 209 for how to crystallize flowers and leaves), silver cachous glistening among them. Strawberry cream garnish with crystallized mint leaves was another glorious flavor feast never forgotten. This is how it was made, at the peak of the strawberry season.

GRANDMOTHER'S STRAWBERRY CREAM

SERVES ABOUT 10, DEPENDING ON THE AMOUNT OF CREAM AND STRAWBERRIES USED

thickened cream
ripe strawberries, hulled
powdered (caster) sugar
crystallized mint leaves (page 209)

Chill a deep bowl and half fill it with cream. Whip the cream lightly, then put into it as many strawberries as possible, mashing them gently with a fork while doing so. (Cut large berries in half and put small ones in whole.) When the cream is saturated with strawberries, put the mixture into a serving bowl, smooth the top of the Strawberry Cream, and chill it for at least an hour in the refrigerator. Before serving, sift some powdered (caster) sugar over the top and decorate with crystallized mint leaves. (Blackberries, loganberries, raspberries, and boysenberries may be used instead of the strawberries.)

FRENCH CHOCOLATE MOUSSE GARNISHED WITH CRYSTALLIZED VIOLETS

SERVES 4

The quantities can be doubled to serve 8, or tripled to serve 12.

2 oz (60 g) dark cooking chocolate
1 1/2 oz (40 g) unsalted butter
3 eggs, separated
4 tablespoons powdered (caster) sugar
1 tablespoon rum
whipped cream for decorating, and crystallized violets, rose petals, or mint leaves

Melt the chocolate and butter in the top of a double saucepan, stirring occasionally, until very smooth. (Alternatively, stand a bowl — not a plastic one — in a saucepan of simmering water.)

Beat the eggs yolks and sugar together, then add to the chocolate, stirring until smooth.

Remove from the stove and whisk in the rum. Beat the egg whites until stiff and fold them into the chocolate mixture. Pour into individual dishes, or a serving bowl. Chill in the refrigerator until firm. Decorate with the whipped cream and the crystallized flowers or leaves.

OPPOSITE: Strawberries near a sunny window.

LEMON AND BALM SOUFFLÉ

SERVES 6

2 tablespoons gelatine
8 tablespoons very hot water
6 eggs, separated
12 oz (375 oz) powdered (caster) sugar
grated rind and strained juice of 4 lemons
1 tablespoon very finely chopped balm leaves
1¹/4 cups cream, whipped

Dissolve the gelatine in the hot water; stir with a spoon until clear. Beat the sugar thoroughly into the egg yolks and then gradually beat in the rind and juice of the lemons and add the balm leaves. Put the egg yolk mixture in a double saucepan and whisk over gentle heat until thick and creamy. Remove from the heat and beat a little longer. Whip the egg whites until they stand in peaks. Add the dissolved gelatine to the lemon mixture and fold in the whipped egg whites and cream. Spoon into a serving dish and set in the refrigerator.

PORT WINE AND BERGAMOT JELLY

3 rounded teaspoons gelatine
¹/2 cup hot water
2 tablespoons clear honey
2 tablespoons lemon juice
1 cup port wine
1 tablespoon finely chopped bergamot
(or spearmint)

Dissolve gelatine in hot water, stir in the rest of the ingredients in the order given. Pour into a tray and freeze. When ready to serve, roughly fork through the jelly to give it a frosty look, spoon into glasses and top with ice cream or cream. Decorate each serving with a sprig of bergamot, or the red, honeyed petals of bergamot flowers.

ANISEED SHORTBREAD COOKIES

MAKES ABOUT 18 MEDIUM-SIZED COOKIES

8 oz (250g) butter, or vegetable margarine
1 cup raw sugar
3 cups self-raising flour
2 teaspoons aniseed

Melt the butter in a saucepan, stir in the sugar and flour, then turn mixture into a shallow baking dish which has been rubbed with butter. Push the mixture into the corners and smooth the top with a wooden spoon, then sprinkle with aniseed. Bake in a moderate oven (350°F/180°C) for about 30 minutes. Cut the shortbread into squares and leave to cool in the dish.

GOOSEBERRY AND BALM SHERBET

SERVES 4

1 x 16 oz (155 g) can gooseberries
¹/3 pint (150 ml) cream
1 tablespoon boiling water
1 tablespoon gelatine
1 tablespoon chopped balm
4 balm sprigs

Place gooseberries and syrup in an electric blender with cream. Pour boiling water onto gelatine, stir until clear, and add to other ingredients in blender. Purée together until pulverized and pour into a mixing bowl; fold in the chopped balm. Chill in refrigerator until set. Or press gooseberries and syrup through a sieve, add dissolved gelatine and chopped balm, and chill. Serve in cold sherbet glasses with whipped cream, topped with a sprig of balm.

ANGELICA ICE CREAM

SERVES 3

2 tablespoons candied angelica, chopped
2 tablespoons confectioners' (icing) sugar
1 cup whipped cream
2 egg whites, stiffly beaten

Stir angelica and sugar into the cream, then fold in the egg whites. Turn into ice cream tray, and freeze. Serve with vanilla wafers.

LAVENDER ICE CREAM

SERVES 4–5

10 stalks of English or French lavender
3/4 cup sugar
1 1/4 cups milk
1 1/4 cups heavy cream
2 tablespoons rosewater
6 eggs, separated
several lavender buds with their leaves

Gently rub the lavender flowers from their stalks and, with the sugar, blend in a blender or food processor. Alternatively, after removing flowers from their stalks, chop finely, making about 2 tablespoons, then mix with the sugar. Heat milk but do not boil. Whisk egg yolks with 1/2 cup lavender sugar, reserving 1/4 cup until later. Add lavender sugar and egg yolk mixture to the milk in saucepan and stir over low heat until thickened. Remove from stove and continue to stir. If curdled, give it a whisk with a beater. Blend in rosewater. Whip cream, then whip egg whites until stiff and fold with the cream into the custard. Pour into a chilled container and freeze. Stir once or twice during freezing. When serving, scoop lavender ice cream into a glass, or other bowl and sprinkle the remaining 1/4 cup lavender sugar over the top. Place a few silver-leaved plump lavender buds around the ice cream.

HERB	SOUPS	SNACKS & SAVORIES	EGGS, BEEF, POULTRY, FISH	VEGETABLES & SALAD	DESSERTS
Basil	Tomato, pea or potato soup	Herb sandwiches, dips, tomato savories	Meat loaf, veal, spaghetti bolognaise, salmon or tuna	Salads, over tomatoes, in mashed potato, eggplant, marrow	
Bay Leaves	All soup and stock	Flavors paté, terrines	Steamed fish, oxtail stew, all casseroles	Vegetable casseroles, lentil stew	A leaf on baked rice pudding, baked custard
Bouquet Garni	All soups	Bechamel sauce	All stews and casseroles	Vegetarian casseroles	
Caraway Seed	Potato Soup	Cream cheese dips and spreads		Coleslaw, Cooked carrots, cabbage, onion	Stewed fruit, seedcake bread
Chives	Chilled soups, vichysoisse	Herb sandwiches, dips, spreads, garnish	Egg dishes, barbecued meat, cold chicken	In salads, Idaho potatoes, mashed potatoes	
Cinnamon	Sprinkle on fruit soups	Cinnamon toast, waffles; bark used to stir black coffee		A little sprinkled over glazed carrots, creamed spinach, baked sweet potato	Fruit pies, custard,
Coriander	Curry Soup	Ground in pickles	Ground in Seasoning, for veal, fish dishes, curries, oriental dishes	In oriental dishes	Fruit puddings, apple crumble, tea cake
Cumin	Curry Soup	Ground in pickles	Ground in dishes, seasoning, for veal, fish curries, oriental dishes	Ground in oriental cooking	Fruit puddings, apple crumble, tea cake
Dill (leaves and seed)	Leaves as soup garnish	Leaves in garlic bread, herb sandwiches; leaves and seed in sauce and dips	Leaves in fish, shellfish, egg and cheese dishes	Seeds in coleslaw, salad; leaves in vegetable stew, buttered vegetables	Seed in cakes and bread, seed tea aids digestion
Elder		Elderflower fritters; chutneys, relishes			Sorbets, jams, jellies

HERB	SOUPS	SNACKS & SAVORIES	EGGS, BEEF, POULTRY, FISH	VEGETABLES & SALAD	DESSERTS
Garlic Flakes Powder	All soups	Garlic bread; powder in sauces, dips	Steak Diane, grills, stews, casseroles	Salads and French Dressing	
Horehound					Candy
Hyssop	Leaves crumbled into soups		Stuffing for duck, pork or goose	Whole flowers used in salads	
Juniper			Stews and in casseroles; stuffing for poultry	Sauerkraut and coleslaw	
Lemongrass			Flavors fish, poultry	Used in Asian dishes	
Lemon Verbena					Flavors rice pudding and cakes
Marjoram	Beef Stock	Herb sandwiches, marjoram vinegar	Meat loaf, veal, steak	Potatoes, vegetable casseroles	Herb scones
Mint	Garnish on soup	Herb sandwiches	In egg dishes, mint sauce with lamb	With buttered peas, mashed potato	Mint ice, mint julep
Oregano	Tomato, pea soup	Pizza, in olive marinade, cheese savories, herb bread	Spaghetti bolognaise, Italian dishes, veal, egg dishes	In salads, potato salad; with cooked potato, artichokes	
Parsley	Vegetable, tomato, fish soups; as garnish	Herb in dips, sandwiches, herb bread; garnish on hot savories	Egg dishes, hamburgers, stuffings for meat and poultry; in tuna loaf	On Idaho potatoes, salad dressing, with potatoes, cauliflower	
Rosemary	Beef and mutton stock	Herb bread and scones, dumplings; liver paté	With baked lamb, lamb casseroles, stews, chicken	Herb dressing, with eggplant, tomatoes cabbage	
Sage	Minestrone, chicken soup	Meatballs,, cheese savories, herb bread, Welsh rarebit	Meat loaf, chicken stuffing, casseroles, omelets	Leek tart, vegetarian stews	
Tarragon	Fish soup	Tarragon vinegar, sauce tartare, chicken, livers, paté	Seafoods, chicken, egg dishes	In green salads	
Thyme	Beef broth, vegetable soup, chicken soup	Meat balls, cheese savories, paté	Meat loaf, braised rabbit, chicken, stuffing, egg dishes, liver	Tomatoes, broccoli, beans, lentil stew	
Yarrow				Adds tang	

Herb Teas & Beverages

A TEA OR "COFFEE" made from the leaves, flowers, bark, seeds, berries, or roots of certain herbs makes a pleasing, healthful drink for those who prefer a change from conventional tea and coffee. These beverages may be taken at any time of the day — first thing in the morning, at mid-morning, at lunch time, in the afternoon, after dinner, and before going to bed. They can be taken either hot or iced. Each one has different benefits and can assist in overcoming mild or chronic indispositions. As a preventive measure, taking specific herb teas over a period of time builds up a resistance to a number of illnesses. Herbs are potent in their own way, and their use should be balanced.

Herb teas are becoming increasingly popular and are being accepted by people in parts of the world other than the continental and Asian countries where they have always been popular. An improvement in health can often be noticed after having taken various kinds; it is also interesting to notice how clean one's palate feels after drinking a herb tea. Some teas are instantly enjoyed, most are pleasant to drink, others may take a little longer to gain favor and should be mixed with another well-liked herb, or a natural flavoring, to make them more palatable.

A herbal tea is an infusion of boiling water and herbs, either fresh or dried. The leaves are the most effective in some cases, and the seeds, berries, bark, flowers, or roots in others. Keep a separate teapot for these teas, and when using the dried leaves, powdered root, crushed seeds, or berries, put one teaspoon for each cup into the pot and pour boiling water onto them; allow to infuse for about three minutes, then strain into cups. If using fresh herb leaves for tea, use twice as much as the dried form, and infuse for several minutes longer. For flower teas, either fresh or dried, use the same amount as you would for the leaves. The traditional method for flower teas, to extract the most from them, is to bring a small saucepan (not aluminium) of measured water to a boil, add the flowers, put the lid on and simmer for one minute. Allow the tea to stand for a little longer, then strain into cups

A number of herb teas of various kinds are now available, either on their own or as a blend in teabags, and are gaining in esteem. The bags are infused in the usual way, by pouring freshly boiled water over them.

A tea worth mentioning is made from the valerian plant, *Valeriana officinalis*, the most beneficial part being the root, which is dried and ground. If growing your own, when the plant is mature dig out the root, wash it, cut into slices, and allow to dry until dehydrated. Grind to a powder, or into small granules, in the blender. The common dandelion, *Taraxacum officinale*, is another plant whose root makes a beneficial beverage. The fresh leaves are also of great value to eat. Dandelion root can be bought already ground, or granulated, and for some reason is not called dandelion tea, but "coffee" or "beverage." Root teas are made in the same way as leaf teas. A bark beverage that is extremely therapeutic is slippery elm bark tea, and is made quite differently from any teas we have mentioned (see page 277).

Two teas may be mixed, especially if the flowers are complementary and they do not both give the same benefits. In this way the value of the tea may be doubled. A quart (liter) may be made at the beginning of the day and stored in the refrigerator. No milk is added to herb teas. Honey, a squeeze of lemon, orange-flower water, or rosewater (the last two are usually available from continental or Greek delicatessens) can be stirred into the tea if you wish. In the summer, ice cubes, long stalks of fresh, leafy herbs, and a little mineral water or fresh fruit juice, all help to enhance the taste of these teas.

Many herbs teas, or infusions as they are often called, are excellent lotions for the skin, giving it a natural, soft bloom. The infusion must be cooled first, then lightly patted onto the face and neck with soaked balls of cotton wool.

Angelica leaf or root tea

All parts of angelica are health-giving. A tea made from the fresh or dried leaves is excellent for colds or influenza, and for soothing the nerves. The bruised root made into a tea relieves flatulence. The pleasant flavor of the leaves makes it suitable to mix with other herb teas which do not have such a pleasing taste. Pour angelica leaf tea into a hot bath for relaxation and fragrance.

Aniseed tea

This tea is made from the seeds, which should be crushed to release the medicinal oils. Allow this tea to draw for a little longer. It relieves indigestion and flatulence, is helpful in allaying colds, and brightens the eyes. It also freshens the palate and sweetens the breath. Small amounts of aniseed, ground to a powder, may be added to the food of young children to help their digestion. A warm milk and honey beverage with a little powdered aniseed added will help to soothe a fretful child. These simple home remedies should be given in moderation to very young children, and as they grow older the strength can be increased gradually. Moisten cotton wool pads in cooled aniseed tea and apply to the skin to lighten it.

Balm leaf tea

Lemon balm tea helps to reduce high temperatures as it induces perspiration. It also lessens the effects of exhaustion in hot weather. This tea assists the digestion and the appetite, helps to settle an upset stomach, and eases griping pains in the stomach. It is also an anti-depressant. Double strength balm tea in a hot bath cleanses and perfumes the skin.

Basil leaf tea

A tea of basil leaves is good for the lungs and diseases of the kidneys and bladder. Basil leaves infused in wine and patted onto the face helps to close enlarged pores. It combines well with borage leaf tea.

Bay leaf tea

A tea of bay leaves is excellent for the digestion and is somewhat astringent as well. A facial steam bath, for cleansing and clearing the skin, is made in the same way as the tea, with the addition of chamomile flowers, rosemary leaves, and rose petals (all either fresh or dried). This was a popular beauty treatment in days of old.

Bergamot leaf tea

A tea made from this herb was favored by the American pioneers as a remedy for sore throats and chest complaints; it was a cure they learned from the Indians. The tea poured into a hot bath is revitalizing and perfumes the water delightfully.

Borage leaf tea

A tea of borage is used as a heart tonic, as a stimulant for the adrenal glands, and as a purifier to the system. It was once said to engender courage and to give confidence to the timid. Mixed with basil it assists the kidneys and bladder, heart, and glands, as well as generally strengthening the system. Used as a facial steam, a tea made from the leaves and flowers of borage improves dry, sensitive skin.

Caraway seed tea

This tea is made in the same way as aniseed tea and it has many of the same benefits. Crush the seeds slightly before pouring on the boiling water. It is beneficial to the liver, gall bladder, and digestion and eases the discomfort of flatulence. It assists the activity of the glands and increases the action of the kidneys. Owing to caraway's digestive and cleansing properties, it is helpful in clearing the complexion.

Carob bean tea

Tea made from carob comes from the dried bean of the small carob tree, *Ceratonia siliqua*, native to the Mediterranean coastal regions. It is also known as St. John's Bread. It is being widely used by manufacturers of health foods as an excellent substitute for chocolate and cocoa. Carob "confectionery" is a good alternative to sugar-based products and will help to prevent decay in children's teeth, as well as being more nutritious. Carob powder is also a corrective in cases of diarrhea.

Chamomile flower tea

This is one of the best known herb teas. Make it in the way suggested for flower teas at the beginning of this chapter. Chamomile tea has long been used as a soothing beverage and is especially helpful when taken before going to bed.

Tea made from the flowers of German chamomile, an annual, is considered to have more potency than that made from perennial English chamomile; German chamomile also blooms more prolifically. For menstrual pain and nervous tension take a cup of chamomile tea. When the brain is overactive and tired, as when studying for exams, a cup of chamomile tea taken before going to bed, and after a hot bath with a few drops of lavender oil in it (lavender soothes the nerve endings of the body), will help to induce sound, natural sleep.

A *very weak* chamomile tea sweetened with honey is helpful for young children who are overtired, or who are teething. Chamomile tea, double strength, is excellent in a herbal bath and will reduce fatigue; it can be used together with lavender oil. An infusion of chamomile flowers, when cooled, makes a brightening hair rinse, and if one has normally blond highlights, the chamomile will make hair even fairer, especially if it is used over a long period.

Chervil leaf tea

Chervil has always been valued as a blood purifier and was considered an excellent tea to take in the spring. It helps the kidneys as well, and used to be taken to ease rheumatic conditions. Cloths soaked in the tea, wrung out, and applied to swellings and bruises, help to reduce them. Chervil is said to purify the system and to brighten dull eyes and clear the complexion.

Chicory root tea or coffee

Chicory beverage is from the roots, which are roasted and ground and, like dandelion, is called "coffee". It is excellent when recovering from a bilious attack and hepatitis, and is generally good for the liver and gall bladder. It also has laxative properties, as well as helping to rid the body of excess fluids. However, it is not recommended for people who are anemic. Sometimes chicory root is blended with real coffee.

Chive leaf tea

A tea made from chopped fresh chive leaves will stimulate the appetite, have a tonic effect on the kidneys, and is said to lower the blood pressure. As chives are a source of calcium, chive tea helps to strengthen nails and teeth.

Comfrey leaf tea

Comfrey tea has been a country remedy for countless ages and is used to heal internal injuries and broken bones, hence its common name of "knitbone." It contains a large amount of calcium and vitamin B12. Because of these properties it helps in the formation of strong teeth and bones. It also helps the circulation and cleanses the bloodstream. It is said to benefit those suffering from ulcers caused by varicose veins. Poultices soaked in strong comfrey tea can be applied to injured muscles and areas of bone weakness. The cooled tea patted on to the skin makes an excellent tonic for the complexion.

Coriander seed tea

Coriander, like other seed teas, is more powerful when the seeds are slightly crushed and the tea is left to infuse for longer than leaf teas. It too is excellent for the digestion, relieving griping pains, and flatulence, especially after eating carbohydrates. It is another herb tea which has been used traditionally for purifying the blood, thus clearing the complexion.

Cress leaf tea

All cresses are rich in vitamins and minerals, especially watercress, and contain sulfur, iron, iodine, and phosphorus. Cress tea is a natural blood purifier and is excellent for clearing the complexion and brightening the eyes. Apart from making one more robust, cress tea is said to help prevent hair from falling out. Parsley leaf tea combines well with cress leaf tea.

Dandelion coffee

This beverage is made from the roots of wild dandelions, *Taraxacum officinale*, as mentioned in the opening chapter of this section. It is sold by health food stores already packaged and ground to a powder, or in a granulated form. Some manufacturers use unnecessary additives, so try and make sure that the one you buy is made from pure dandelion root. Some brands, however, are blended with another *natural* product —which should be marked on the label — to make it more palatable because, on its own, dandelion coffee can be rather bitter for some tastes. This beverage acts as a tonic and stimulates the functions of the liver and urinary organs, which is why it helps to prevent rheumatism and similar complaints.

Delicious and beneficial orange cordial

"6 or 8 oranges, 2 lemons, 5 lb (2.5 kg) sugar, 3 pints (1.8 L) boiling water, 2 oz (60 g) tartaric acid, 1 oz (30 g) citric acid, 1 oz (30 g) Epsom salts. Pour boiling water over the juice and grated rinds and other ingredients. Stand until cold, then bottle. Keeps a long time." From the *C.W.A.'s Coronation Cookery Book.*

N.B. I have made this concentrated cordial many times, and it is an excellent substitute for supermarket drinks, especially during school holidays when children have a never-ending thirst. Put 1 tablespoon of the cordial in a glass, fill with iced water (or mineral water for grown-ups) and ice. For guests, garnish with a sprig of spearmint or leafy sticks of eau-de-Cologne mint or peppermint. We usually store the concentrated orange cordial in bottles in the refrigerator to help its keeping qualities, and for extra chill when drinking it.

Dill seed tea

Dill seed tea is made in the same way as other seed teas. It is especially good for soothing wind and colic in babies, and in days gone by chemists used to stock a stabilized version, which was called "dill water". Given in *very weak* proportions in boiled water, this is a time-honored remedy for young children. Dill tea helps the digestion and dispels flatulence. It is also reputed to strengthen the fingernails.

Elderflower tea

The most popular elder tree grown in gardens is usually *Sambucus aurea* which has decorative golden leaves and the same type of flat, creamy blossoms as the true elder, *S. nigra*, or black elder, so called because of the plain, dark green of the foliage. Flowers from the latter are considered more efficacious for health than those of the golden elder. A tea made from the fresh or dried blooms is an old remedy for influenza. It was also taken every morning during the spring as a medicine for purifying the blood.

Elderflowers also have many cosmetic uses (see pages 204–5) and they give a delicate flavor to foods, especially to a water ice (see page 260). If making tea or an infusion, follow the directions for flower teas on page 271.

Fennel seed tea

The most effective part of the fennel plant medicinally is the seeds, and the tea is made in exactly the same way as all the other seed teas. As well as relieving indigestion and helping to rid the body of uncomfortable gases, cooled fennel seed tea is excellent for bathing sore eyes. A strong infusion may be blended with honey and yogurt and spread on the face and neck. Leave for 15 minutes while you lie down with soaked cotton wool pads of the tea on your eyelids, then gently rinse off with tepid water. This treatment will leave the complexion smooth and clear and brighten the eyes.

Garlic

This is not recommended as a tea: its flavor is too pronounced, and there are other ways of using its remarkably effective qualities, as described on pages 14–15.

Horseradish

Like garlic, this is such a strongly flavored herb that a tea of it would be unpalatable. Once again, there are other ways of making use of its properties and these are described on page 64.

Lemongrass leaf tea

This is one of the most palatable of all herb teas and is recommended as an introduction to herbal beverages. Being rich in vitamin A, in a water-soluble form it has the effect of clearing the skin and refining its texture.

Lime flower tea or linden tea

The fresh or dried flowers from the large lime tree, *Tilia europaea*, are used and it is traditional in Europe to take this tea for calming the nerves and to soothe the mucous linings following a head cold. This delicately fragrant tea is an excellent general tonic, and it may be taken regularly. Make the tea in the way described for flower teas at the beginning of this chapter.

Lovage leaf tea

Lovage tea, made from the fresh or dried leaves, stimulates the digestive organs. The strained cooled tea is a soothing lotion for sore eyes. An infusion of the root is sometimes used for jaundice and bladder problems. A tea made from the seeds is recommended as a gargle for infections of the mouth and throat.

Marjoram and oregano leaf tea

Marjoram and oregano tea is helpful at the onset of a fever because it induces perspiration. It also relieves colds, cramps, digestive troubles, nervous headaches, and stomach pains. When mixed with chamomile flowers (which should be treated in the same way as the leaves) it acts as a tonic, as well as being soothing. A strong tea of the leaves, cooled and used as a final rinse, will help darken the hair of brunettes.

Mint leaf tea

Peppermint tea is possibly the best known of mint teas. Its medicinal value is in its purported ability to disperse congestion in the body, and to relieve indigestion, bronchitis, headaches, coughs, and colds. It is delicious and healthful when taken icy cold in the summer, and is refreshing and revitalizing on a hot day. Peppermint tea in double strength, cooled, and used as a hair rinse helps condition oily hair. Mint tea (made from spearmint leaves) is especially refreshing in very hot and humid weather. It is also good for the digestion and excellent for helping to dispel stomach gases; it cleanses the intestines, thus helping to overcome bad breath.

Mint julep

"Wash a large bunch of mint, then place it in a basin and cover with 1 cup of sugar and the strained juice of 5 lemons. Leave for 2 hours, then transfer the liquid to a glass jug. Add a large lump of ice, 2 bottles of ginger ale, and fresh sprigs of mint." From *The Coronation Cookery Book*.

Nettle leaf tea

The dried leaves of the common nettle weed, *Uritica dioica*, are widely used by natural therapists. Julius Caesar is reputed to have introduced it to Britain. The tea contains vitamin D, iron, calcium, and other important trace elements and is used as a spring tonic for the blood. It is taken in case of arterial degeneration, rheumatism, gout, and shortness of breath. The leaves, fresh or dried, make a delicious and nutritious soup.

Parsley leaf tea

Parsley is a very nutritious herb, containing vitamins A, B, and C, as well as organic iron, potassium, silicon, magnesium, and other trace elements. This tea assists the bladder, kidneys, and liver, and is excellent for people suffering from anemia. It is also helpful, together with other treatment, in overcoming chronic cystitis. It stimulates the appetite and is a tonic and cleansing tea. Parsley and watercress tea blend well with one another. One herbalist warns that pregnant women should avoid it. Cooled parsley tea may be rubbed into the hair before shampooing to make it shiny. Pads of cotton wool soaked in the cooled tea and patted on the skin close enlarged pores, freshen the skin, and reduce puffiness around the eyes.

Raspberry leaf tea

This tea is made from dried raspberry leaves and has traditionally been given to expectant mothers. It has the reputation of easing childbirth and the expulsion of the afterbirth, as well as assisting lactation and hastening convalescence. It is soothing, tones up the mucous membranes, allays nausea, and encourages good bowel action.

Rose-hip tea

This beverage is very popular as a preventative against colds, being an excellent source of vitamin C, as well as vitamins A, E, and B. The ripe fruits (hips) of wild roses are harvested, dried, and shredded. To make the tea, use one teaspoonful for each cup, pour boiling water over it, allow to infuse, then strain. It can be taken hot in the winter with a slice of lemon, a little honey, and pinch of spice, or iced in summer with sprigs of mint, or peppermint, honey, ice cubes, and lemon slices. Hibiscus flowers are often blended with rose-hip tea for "fragrant enjoyment."

Rosemary leaf tea

This tea is recommended for strengthening the memory and relieving headaches. It is a nerve tonic as well, and aids the digestion and kidneys. The cooled tea rubbed into the scalp is one of the best hair tonics, and used frequently will help the hair to become lustrous and dandruff-free. Make a stronger brew for this, as explained on page 205.

Sage leaf tea

Sage tea is one of the most venerable: the ancient Egyptians and Chinese were aware of this. It is recognized as promoting longevity, strengthening the memory, and restoring acuteness to the senses. It has a tonic effect on the liver, brain, and nerves. It is an excellent tea when blended with balm. The cooled tea makes a soothing mouth rinse for inflamed gums, and is helpful as a gargle for sore throats. A stronger brew, cooled, may also be rubbed into the hair to prevent it from going gray. As well, cotton wool soaked in the cooled tea and patted gently on to the skin will help close enlarged pores.

Sangria

This Spanish drink is most refreshing on a very hot day. An added flavor touch is given by steeping a few sprays of salad burnet in the jug after making the drink.

> *1 quart (1 L) red wine*
> *3 1/2 oz (100 g) sugar*
> *water to dissolve sugar*
> *1 pint (0.5 L) mineral water*
> *2 peaches*
> *1 banana*
> *1 pear*
> *1 slice melon*
> *2 pieces lemon*
> *2 oranges*
> *a pinch of cinnamon*
> *salad burnet sprays*

Chop the fruit and mix with the wine, sugar, and water. Add salad burnet sprays if desired. Serve cold with cubes of ice.

Savory leaf tea

Both winter and summer savory make pleasant-tasting teas; either the fresh or dried leaves may be used. The tea is used to treat colic, flatulence, giddiness, and respiratory troubles. Savory is an intestinal antiseptic and is also said to be an aphrodisiac!

Slippery elm bark tea

The highly nutritious bark comes from a small tree, *Ulmus fulva*, native to the United States and Canada. The only part used is the inner bark which is stripped and collected from the trunk and larger branches: it is dried and then powdered. When brewed into a beverage, or "gruel", it is very glutinous and can be difficult to become used to; however its powers of soothing the intestines, and its strengthening, healing, and very nutritious qualities make it worth persevering with. To make it, put a teaspoon of the powder into a cup, mix it with a pinch of cinnamon, and then add a little cold water to make a paste. Pour on very hot water, or milk, stirring vigorously, and add a teaspoon of clear honey. The mixture will be rather thick and smoothly gelatinous (if it goes lumpy push it through a fine sieve) and

this is the reason why it is so healing for the mucous membrane of the stomach and intestines. When taken before going to bed this draught will induce sleep. Although slippery elm is available in tablet form, we don't think it is quite as effective as the liquid.

Tarragon leaf tea

Herbalists recommend tarragon tea to ease indigestion and flatulence. By acting as a diuretic, it helps to rid the body of excess fluids.

Thyme leaf tea

Take this tea as an aid to digestion and to tone up the nervous system and respiratory organs; it is also an intestinal antiseptic, and has a delicious savory flavor. The cooled tea used as a mouth rinse freshens the breath. Cotton wool dipped into the cooled tea and patted onto the skin helps to freshen and clear the complexion.

Valerian root tea

This tea has remarkable sedative properties and soothes and calms the nerves, without being habit-forming. It also relieves migraine and heart palpitations and is derived from the plant *Valerian officinalis*. It should be taken just before going to bed. Some herbal therapists advise that this tea should not be taken by people suffering from liver complaints as it can cause nausea.

Valerian tea has the reputation of having an unpleasant smell, so either mix it with a very pleasant tea, for instance lemongrass, or lace it well with honey and fresh fruit juice.

There are many other medicinal herb teas which would take a whole book of their own to write about. Those we have selected are brewed from the culinary, wholesome herbs written about in this book, with the addition of a few that are used for teas or "coffees," and which are readily obtainable from most specialist shops.

Herb	Nerve Sedative	Digestion	Rheumatic Pain	Coughs & Colds	Poor Skin	Blood Tonic	Heart Tonic	Kidney Tonic	Liver Tonic
Aloe Vera	•	•			•	•		•	
Angelica	•	•		•	•	•			
Anise		•		•	•				
Balm	•	•		•	•		•	•	
Basil			•	•	•		•	•	
Bay	•	•	•	•	•				
Borage	•		•		•	•	•	•	
Caraway		•			•			•	
Chamomile	•	•		•	•				•
Chervil			•		•			•	•
Chicory		•			•				•
Chives		•				•		•	•
Comfrey		•		•	•	•			
Coriander		•			•	•			
Cress	•				•	•			
Dill	•	•		•		•			•
Elder			•	•	•	•			
Fennel		•			•				
Garlic	•	•	•	•	•	•			
Horehound				•	•			•	
Horseradish		•		•	•	•			
Hyssop		•	•	•					
Juniper		•	•	•		•		•	
Lavender	•	•	•		•				
Lemongrass					•			•	
Lemon Verbena	•	•							
Lovage		•		•	•	•		•	
Marjoram & Oregano	•	•	•	•		•			
Mugwort, Southernwood & Wormwood		•				•			
Parsley			•		•	•		•	
Peppermint	•	•		•		•			•
Rosemary	•	•					•	•	
Sage	•	•				•			•
Salad Burnet	•		•		•	•			
Savory		•			•	•			
Spearmint		•		•					•
Tarragon		•				•			
Thyme	•	•		•	•	•		•	
Valerian	•								
Yarrow						•		•	

A walk of pleached lime trees (Pilia cordata, also called linden trees) at Sissinghurst in England. Lime trees are used as decorative and sheltering hedges in some traditional herb gardens.

INDEX OF COMMON NAMES

GENERAL INDEX

DEDICATION
To Alexandra Coleman

Published 1997 by
STACKPOLE BOOKS
5067 Ritter Road
Mechanicsburg, PA 17055

Printed in Singapore by Kyodo Printing Co.

10   9   8   7   6   5   4   3   2   1

FIRST U.S. EDITION

Design by Kathie Baxter Smith

Library of Congress Cataloging-in-Publication Data

Hemphill, John
    What herb is that? : how to grow and use the culinary herbs. /
John & Rosemary Hemphill.—1st. U.S. ed.
        p.   cm.
    Includes index.
    ISBN 0-8117-1634-1
    1. Herbs 2. Herb gardening. 3. Herbs—Utilization. 4. Cookery (Herbs)
I. Hemphill, Rosemary. II. Title.
SB351.H5H346 1997   97-7947
635'.7—DC21   CIP

ACKNOWLEDGEMENTS

Special thanks to our daughter-in-law Elizabeth Hemphill for her contributions to this book.
Our sincere appreciation and thanks to the admirable team at Lansdowne Publishing
for their enthusiasm and caring interest in producing this book.
They are: Jane Curry, Managing Director; Steven Morris, Sales Manager;
Cheryl Hingley, Publishing Manager; Robert Coupe, Copy Editor;
Nicholas Szentkuti, Editor; Cynthia Blanche and Nick Sadlier, Proofreaders;
Kathie Baxter Smith, Book Designer.

Special thanks for her kindness and help on Mexican herbs to Maria Fernanda de Orduna
of the Mexican Consulate in Sydney, Australia. We would also like to thank Carol Selvarajah,
of Gourmet Asian Cuisine, Chef and Author, for her time and encouragement.
We would also like to thank Liane Colwell for enlightening us on her specialities: the
cuisines of North Africa, the Middle East, South America, Mexico, and the Caribbean.

Thanks to the management of the Fragrant Garden at Erina, NSW Australia and of the herb garden
at the Royal Botanic Gardens in Sydney, Australia, where we have taken a number of photographs. Thanks to
Mr and Mrs John Keep for permission to photograph their miniature herb garden at Killara, NSW (page 54).

Photographs: page 2, Essex Manor in England; pages 6–7, an English herb garden at Tintinhull House in Somerset: pages 8–9, Kennerton Green at Mittagong in New South Wales